PRICE AND PRODUCTIVITY MEASUREMENT

Volume 1 - Housing

Volume Editors
W. Erwin Diewert, Bert M. Balk, Dennis Fixler,
Kevin J. Fox, Alice O. Nakamura

Order this book online at www.trafford.com
or email orders@trafford.com

Most Trafford titles are also available at major online book retailers.

Printed in the United States of America.

ISBN: 978-1-4120-7984-6 (sc)

Trafford rev. 09/24/2011

www.trafford.com

North America & international
toll-free: 1 888 232 4444 (USA & Canada)
phone: 250 383 6864 ♦ fax: 812 355 4082

PRICE AND PRODUCTIVITY MEASUREMENT: Volume 1 -- Housing
W. Erwin Diewert, Bert M. Balk, Dennis Fixler, Kevin J. Fox and Alice O. Nakamura (editors)

W.E. Diewert, B.M. Balk, D. Fixler, K.J. Fox and A.O. Nakamura (2011),
PRICE AND PRODUCTIVITY MEASUREMENT: Volume 1 -- Housing. Trafford Press.

Chapter 1

INTRODUCTION TO PRICE AND PRODUCTIVITY MEASUREMENT FOR HOUSING

Bert M. Balk, W. Erwin Diewert and Alice O. Nakamura[1]

The winter of 2011 finds many nations still struggling with severe economic problems brought on by the burst of a bubble in residential housing prices. This situation incited urgent interest in whether the cost of owner occupied housing (OOH) services is being properly accounted for in the inflation statistics for nations. There would be interest in this topic anyway, of course, because shelter accounts for a large share of consumer expenditures. Moreover, there are important differences in how OOH services are accounted for in the official statistics of nations. The main approach in current use is rental equivalence. For example, in compiling the Consumer Price Index (CPI), the U.S. Bureau of Labor Statistics (BLS) uses rent data for rental units to form a rental equivalence measure for changes in the cost of OOH services.

The rental equivalence approach is often stated to be justified because it can be derived from the fundamental equation of capital theory: the same theoretical framework that also gives rise to the user cost approach to accounting for OOH services in measures of inflation for nations. The user cost approach is one of three other approaches in current use besides rental equivalency. In **chapter 2**, **W. Erwin Diewert** of the University of British Columbia and **Alice O. Nakamura** of the University of Alberta provide an overview of the main types of approaches in use. The authors go on to develop a new opportunity cost approach, first introduced in a paper presented by Diewert in 2006 that is published as chapter 6 of this volume. We take up this aspect of the Diewert-Nakamura chapter in the concluding section of this introduction, since that material builds on the other papers included in this volume.

This volume is more than the sum of its parts. The papers are sequenced so that a reader new to the topic area can pick up needed terminology in moving from one paper to the next. At the same time, the papers deal with some of the main unresolved issues of our time regarding the measurement of inflation for owner occupied housing. The authors of the papers in this volume include many of the key participants over the recent decades in the vast literature on this topic.

In **chapter 3**, **Arnold J. Katz** of the U.S. Bureau of Economic Analysis (BEA) explains that within the European Union, the standard method for evaluating owner occupied dwelling services in the national accounts has been a stratification variant of the rental equivalence approach. Katz explains, however, that the unsubsidized rental markets are too thin in many of the Eastern European countries to permit the use of rental equivalency. His paper discusses an

---

[1] Bert Balk is with the Rotterdam School of Management, Erasmus University Rotterdam and Statistics Netherlands, and can be reached at email bbalk@rsm.nl. Erwin Diewert is with the Department of Economics at the University of British Columbia. He can be reached at diewert@econ.ubc.ca. Alice Nakamura is with the University of Alberta School of Business and can be reached at alice.nakamura@ualberta.ca.

Balk, B.M. W.E. Diewert and A.O Nakamura (2011),
"Introduction to Price and Productivity Measurement for Housing," chapter 1, pp. 1-6 in
W.E. Diewert, B.M. Balk, D. Fixler, K.J. Fox and A.O. Nakamura (2011),
PRICE AND PRODUCTIVITY MEASUREMENT: Volume 1 -- Housing. Trafford Press.

alternative method for evaluating dwelling services based on a simplified user cost measure. Katz notes that the standard user cost measure is derived under the principle that, in equilibrium, the purchase price of a durable good will equal the discounted present value of its expected net income (or benefits); i.e., it will equal the discounted present value of its expected future services less the discounted present value of its expected future operating costs.

In **chapter 4**, **Theodore M. Crone** and **Leonard I. Nakamura** of the Federal Reserve Bank of Philadelphia and **Richard P. Voith** of Econsult argue that hedonic methods can be used to estimate the capitalization rate for owner occupied housing. The authors specify a model for the value for house i in time period t, V_{it},

$$(1) \qquad \ln V_{it} = \beta_t X_{it} + e_{it}, \qquad\qquad i = 1,\ldots,I,$$

where X_i is a K element row vector of house traits, and β_t is a vector of the estimated percentage contributions to the house value of the housing traits. The stream of OOH services that implicitly is equal to the rent, R_{it}, is hypothesized to depend on the value of the dwelling and a capitalization rate, C_t. If $R_{it} = C_t V_{it}$, then equation (1) can be rewritten as $\ln(R_{it}/C_t) = \beta_t X_{it} + e_{it}$, or as

$$(2) \qquad \ln(R_{it}) = \beta_t X_{it} + \ln(C_t) + e_{it}, \qquad\qquad i = 1,\ldots,I.$$

A corresponding hedonic regression for the rent for rental units is given by:

$$(3) \qquad \ln(R_{jt}) = \gamma_t X_{jt} + u_{jt}, \qquad\qquad j = 1,\ldots,J.$$

In this equation, unlike the case of owner occupied units, the capitalization rate does not appear because the price of the service flow is observed directly for rentals.

The authors show that the capitalization rate affects the measured inflation index of owner occupied housing. They also argue that if owners and renters value housing traits similarly, then $\beta_t = \gamma_t$ and the owner and renter hedonic equations, (2) and (3) respectively, will differ only by the constant, $\ln(C_t)$. In this case, they argue that the pooled owner and rental data can be used to estimate the capitalization rate as well as the housing characteristics prices. Making use of the capitalization rates and trait prices estimated using data from the bi-annual American Housing Survey (AHS), the authors calculate Fisher price indexes and inflation rates for both rented and owner occupied housing services.

In **chapter 5**, **Claudia Kurz** and **Johannes Hoffmann** of the Deutsche Bundesbank explain that, while the importance of owner occupied housing in Germany is less than in most other industrialised countries, nevertheless a little over 40 percent of households live in their own homes. For the German CPI, the price component for owner occupied dwellings is imputed using a rental equivalence approach, much as in the United States. To assess the appropriateness of the official German imputation method for owner occupied housing service costs, Kurz and Hoffmann use data from the German Socio Economic Panel (GSOEP). The GSOEP reports major physical and locational characteristics of dwellings, rents actually paid by renters, and what owners say their dwellings could be rented for (i.e., the owner reported *rent equivalents*). Kurz and Hoffmann restrict their analysis to West Germany and the period of 1985 through 1997.

The authors adopt a hedonic regression approach, building on their own prior research. In this new study, they use the same functional form for the equations for both owner reported rent equivalents and for the rents of renters. Kurz and Hoffmann investigate the differences in the movements of their hedonic index versus the official CPI index for Germany. They find that until 1988, the measures are quite close. However, starting in 1989, the rates of increase for the hedonic indexes are higher than for the CPI rent subindex. The authors point out that 1989 is when migration from East Germany started to put pressure on the German housing market.

The papers by Katz, by Crone, L.I. Nakamura and Voith, and by Kurz and Hoffmann all start from the premise that, because both the rental equivalence and the user cost approaches can be derived from the fundamental equation of capital theory, it is therefore a matter of data availability and empirical convenience which of these approaches is used to account for shelter in measures of inflation. This premise is questioned in **chapter 7**. More specifically, **Alan Heston** of the University of Pennsylvania and **Alice O. Nakamura** of the University of Alberta question the presumption that housing cost information for *either* renters or owner occupiers can be used for assessing movements over time and space in the cost of housing for *both* renters and owners. They take a step in the direction of empirically exploring the questions they raise.

The empirical work reported by Heston and Nakamura is based on a survey of federal government employees conducted as part of a Safe Harbor process regarding a U.S. government Cost of Living Allowance (COLA) program. This program pays an allowance above the federal salary schedule in three geographic areas (Alaska, the Caribbean and the Pacific) based on prices in these areas relative to the Washington D.C. area. The COLA survey data include a large number of dwelling characteristics, and both renters and owner occupiers were asked the Consumer Expenditure Survey (designated as both CES and CE in the literature) question about what they believe their dwellings would rent for. Using this data, the Heston and Nakamura show that, in moving from relatively low to relatively high value homes, rent-to-value ratios fall. The authors argue that this result raises questions about the validity of using housing cost data collected *just from renters* to estimate price movements for owner occupies too.

In **chapter 8**, **Thesia I. Garner** and **Randal Verbrugge** of the U.S. Bureau of Labor Statistics (BLS) provide empirical evidence for the United States that rents and *ex ante* user costs diverge markedly, and for extended periods of time. This temporal divergence is found not only for the United States as a whole, but also for selected major metropolitan areas. This paper constructs, for the five largest cities in the United States, user costs and rents *for the same structure, in levels* (i.e., measured in dollars). These measures are constructed using Consumer Expenditure Survey data from 1982 to 2002, along with house price appreciation forecasts from Verbrugge (2008). The data are used to construct both a price/rent ratio and a user cost estimate for a hypothetical median-valued structure over time for each of the five metropolitan areas.

The overall picture that emerges bolsters the findings of Verbrugge (2008): the estimated user costs and rents diverge. According to Garner and Verbrugge, this divergence reflects out-of-scope financial asset movements and the costs associated with buying and selling homes. They conclude that, given the state of current-generation user cost measures, statistical agencies should use, if possible, use rental equivalence to measure homeowner user costs, rather than attempting to directly assess user costs. They acknowledge, however, that in some countries the use rental equivalence may not be practicable. To price the service flow from an owned dwelling in those situations, they recommend the user cost approach.

Chapter 6 is a reprint of a paper that W. Erwin Diewert presented at a November 6-7, 2006 OECD-IMF Workshop on Real Estate Price Indexes which was held in Paris. Diewert comments on the choice of appropriate target indexes for real estate prices. He argues that if the SNA is expanded to exhibit the service flows that are associated with the household and production sectors' purchases of durable goods, then the resulting Durables Augmented System of National Accounts (DASNA) provides a natural framework for a family of real estate price indexes. He explains that in this proposed augmented system of national accounts, household wealth and consumption will be measured in real and nominal terms. This will entail measures of the household sector's stock of residential wealth and it will be of interest to decompose this value measure into price and quantity (or volume) components.

Diewert next takes up the treatment of depreciation and renovations in the construction of constant quality real estate price indexes. He discusses stratification methods and methods that make use of periodic appraisals of real estate property that are carried out for taxation purposes. He also takes up the decomposition of real estate values into land and structure components. Diewert then turns his attention to a paper by Verbrugge: the paper that has now been published in revised form as Verbrugge (2008).

Diewert feels that for the opportunity costs of owning a house, from the viewpoint of an owner occupier, the relevant time horizon for an annualized average rate of expected price appreciation is at least 6 to 12 years. He notes that once we use annualized forecasts of expected price inflation over longer time horizons, the volatility in the ex ante user cost formula will be much diminished. Diewert also calls attention to Verbrugge's point that high real estate transactions costs presumably are what prevent the exploitation of arbitrage opportunities between owning and renting a property; user costs can thus differ considerably from the corresponding rental equivalence measures over the lifetime of a property cycle.

Diewert concludes this paper with a proposal for a new theoretical basis for accounting for the cost of owner occupied housing in measures of inflation:

> "[P]erhaps the "correct" opportunity cost of housing for an owner occupier is not his or her internal user cost but the maximum of the internal user cost and what the property could rent for on the rental market. After all, the concept of opportunity cost is supposed to represent the maximum sacrifice that one makes in order to consume or use some object and so the above point would seem to follow. If this point of view is accepted, then at certain points in the property cycle, user costs would replace market rents as the "correct" pricing concept for owner occupied housing, which would dramatically affect Consumer Price Indexes and the conduct of monetary policy."

Building on the Diewert proposal for an opportunity cost approach to accounting for owner occupied housing in measures of inflation, in **chapter 2**, **W. Erwin Diewert** and **Alice O. Nakamura** of the University of Alberta argue that the time has come to accept the accumulated evidence of Verbrugge and others that user costs and rents do not reliably move together. They then turn their attention to the task of further developing Diewert's opportunity cost approach.

The term "opportunity cost" refers to the cost of the best alternative that must be forgone in taking the option chosen. They thus seek to compare implications for homeowner wealth of selling at the beginning of period t with the alternatives of planning to own a home for m more years and of either renting out or occupying the home for the coming year. This comparison is assumed to be carried out at the beginning of period t based on the information available then about the market value of the home and interest rates and the forecasted average increase per year in home market value if the home is held for another m years. Refinancing can be viewed as a way of a homeowner selling or buying back a fraction of a home.

Diewert and Nakamura define the OOH opportunity cost (OOHOC) index as follows:

For each household living in owner occupied housing (OOH), the *owner occupied housing opportunity cost* (OOHOC) is the maximum of what it would cost to rent an equivalent dwelling (the rental opportunity cost, ROC) and the financial opportunity costs (FOC).

The OOHOC index for a nation is defined as an expenditure share weighted sum of a rental equivalency index and a financial opportunity cost index, with the expenditure share weights depending on the estimated proportion of owner occupied homes for which FOC exceeds ROC.

The authors explain the new OOHOC index in steps. First, they focus on the ROC and the FOC components of the index for an individual homeowner. Then, they address the issue of how to move from OOHOC values for individual homeowners to an OOHOC index for a nation and review key features of the proposed OOHOC index.

Acceptance of the opportunity cost approach to the pricing of the services of owner occupied dwellings would affect the CPI of countries. In addition, implementing the OOHOC approach would probably increase the measured per capita income gaps between rich and poor households within a nation like the United States and between rich and poor countries. The material in chapter 7 by Heston and Nakamura indicates that rent to asset value ratios for expensive homes in the United States are about half the corresponding values for entry level homes. It seems likely that this same sort of finding applies to other rich countries. Financial opportunity costs of owner occupied homes are roughly proportional to asset values, so the finding in Heston and Nakamura implies that for high end homes, financial opportunity costs may be twice or more the size of the corresponding rental equivalence opportunity costs. Thus the opportunity cost approach to pricing owner occupied housing services (which takes the *maximum* of the rental and financial opportunity costs) presumably will give a much higher estimate of the value of OOH services than is given by the rental equivalence approach.

In **chapter 9**, **Rósmundur Guðnason** and **Guðrún R. Jónsdóttir** of Statistics Iceland explain that the house price component of the Icelandic CPI is based on market prices for houses obtained from sales contracts collected by the Land Registry. Sales contracts are standardized throughout the country. Every sales contract contains information on the property, its owners and the sale price. A sales contract also contains details for how payment is arranged, and this information can be used for calculating the present value of a property.

In Iceland, the service flow from owner occupied housing is measured using what Statistics Iceland refers to as a *simple user cost*. The housing price index is computed using information on changes in the present value of real estate as declared in sales contracts. This index is calculated as a superlative index (Fisher) using the values for 2002-2005 as the weights for the Laspeyres part and the values for 2003-2006 to calculate the Paasche part of the Fisher index. The weights are updated monthly. The owner occupied housing depreciation rate used in the Statistics Iceland user cost calculation is mainly based on the age of the housing stock.

Finally, **Andrew Baldwin** of Statistics Canada, **Alice O. Nakamura** of the University of Alberta and **Marc Prud'homme** of Statistics Canada in **chapter 10** present six alternative homeownership series based on four main concepts. These are the six types of series defined and updated periodically for the Statistics Canada analytical series program. All-items level indexes embedding the various alternative owner occupied housing price series are also presented so that the effects of the different owner occupied housing concepts on the overall CPI can be observed. The estimates of comparative shelter costs are for houses in Ottawa for 1996 to 2005.

References

Verbrugge, R. (2008), "The Puzzling Divergence of Rents and User Costs, 1980-2004," *Review of Income and Wealth* 54 (4), 671-699.

Full Citations for the Chapters in this Volume:

Baldwin, A., A.O. Nakamura and M. Prud'homme (2011), "Owner Occupied Housing in the CPI: The Statistics Canada Analytical Series," chapter 10, pp. 151-160 in Diewert, W.E., B.M. Balk, D. Fixler, K.J. Fox and A.O. Nakamura (2011), *PRICE AND PRODUCTIVITY MEASUREMENT: Volume 1 -- Housing*. Trafford Press.

Crone, T.M., L.I. Nakamura and R.P. Voith (2011), "Hedonic Estimates of the Cost of Housing Services: Rental and Owner Occupied Units," chapter 4, pp. 51-68 in Diewert, W.E., B.M. Balk, D. Fixler, K.J. Fox and A.O. Nakamura (2011), *PRICE AND PRODUCTIVITY MEASUREMENT: Volume 1 -- Housing*. Trafford Press.

Diewert, W.E. (2011), "The Paris OECD-IMF Workshop on Real Estate Price Indexes: Conclusions and Future Directions," chapter 6, pp. 87-116 in Diewert, W.E., B.M. Balk, D. Fixler, K.J. Fox and A.O. Nakamura (2011), *PRICE AND PRODUCTIVITY MEASUREMENT: Volume 1 -- Housing*. Trafford Press.

Diewert, W.E. and Alice O. Nakamura (2011), "Accounting for Housing in a CPI," chapter 2, pp. 7-32 in Diewert, W.E., B.M. Balk, D. Fixler, K.J. Fox and A.O. Nakamura (2011), *PRICE AND PRODUCTIVITY MEASUREMENT: Volume 1 -- Housing*. Trafford Press.

Garner, T.I. and R. Verbrugge (2011), "The Puzzling Divergence of Rents and User Costs, 1980-2004: Summary and Extensions," chapter 8, pp. 125-146 in Diewert, W.E., B.M. Balk, D. Fixler, K.J. Fox and A.O. Nakamura (2011), *PRICE AND PRODUCTIVITY MEASUREMENT: Volume 1 -- Housing*. Trafford Press.

Guðnason, R. and G.R. Jónsdóttir (2011), "Owner Occupied Housing in the Icelandic CPI," chapter 9, pp. 147-150 in Diewert, W.E., B.M. Balk, D. Fixler, K.J. Fox and A.O. Nakamura (2011), *PRICE AND PRODUCTIVITY MEASUREMENT: Volume 1 -- Housing*. Trafford Press.

Heston, A. and A.O. Nakamura (2011), "Reported Prices and Rents of Housing: Reflections of Costs, Amenities or Both?" chapter 7, pp. 117-124 in Diewert, W.E., B.M. Balk, D. Fixler, K.J. Fox and A.O. Nakamura (2011), *PRICE AND PRODUCTIVITY MEASUREMENT: Volume 1 -- Housing*. Trafford Press.

Katz, A.J. (2011), "Estimating Dwelling Services in the Candidate Countries: Theoretical and Practical Considerations in Developing Methodologies Based on a User Cost of Capital Measure," chapter 3, pp. 33-50 in Diewert, W.E., B.M. Balk, D. Fixler, K.J. Fox and A.O. Nakamura (2011), *PRICE AND PRODUCTIVITY MEASUREMENT: Volume 1 -- Housing*. Trafford Press.

Kurz, C. and J. Hoffmann (2011), "A Rental Equivalence Index for Owner Occupied Housing in West Germany," chapter 5, pp. 69-86 in Diewert, W.E., B.M. Balk, D. Fixler, K.J. Fox and A.O. Nakamura (2011), *PRICE AND PRODUCTIVITY MEASUREMENT: Volume 1 -- Housing*. Trafford Press.

Chapter 2

ACCOUNTING FOR HOUSING IN A CPI

W. Erwin Diewert and Alice O. Nakamura[1]

1.   Introduction

Stephen Cecchetti (2007), a former Executive Vice President and Director of Research at the New York Federal Reserve Bank, writes that: "Price stability is about helping people make their long-term plans." The Consumer Price Index (CPI) produced by the U.S. Bureau of Labor Statistics (the BLS), is the most widely used measure of inflation. The Federal Reserve uses the CPI in various forms, along with various forms of the Personal Consumption Expenditures (PCE) price index,[2] in its efforts to achieve price stability. As Cecchetti also explains, the large expenditure share for owner occupied housing (OOH) means that the way OOH is accounted for in a price index makes a great deal of difference.[3] We note too that the large share for housing in consumer expenditure means that inflation in the cost of housing services greatly affects people's living costs and longer term plans.

The rental equivalency approach is used to account for the cost of OOH services in the CPI and in the PCE price index, including core and trimmed variants of these inflation measures. Poole, Ptacek and Verbrugge (2005) of the BLS explain that for renters, "rental equivalence" is easily measured as the amount of rent paid. For owners living in their owned homes --- i.e., for owner occupiers -- this cost is unobserved because owner occupiers, in effect, rent to themselves.

---

[1] Erwin Diewert is with the Department of Economics at the University of British Columbia (diewert@econ.ubc.ca). Alice Nakamura is with the University of Alberta School of Business (alice.nakamura@ualberta.ca). Financial assistance from the OECD, the Australian Research Council, and the Canadian SSHRC is gratefully acknowledged, as is the hospitality of the Centre for Applied Economic Research at the University of New South Wales. The authors also thank Stephan Arthur, Dennis Capozza, Dennis Fixler, Johannes Hoffmann, Arnold Katz, Anne Laferrère, Emi Nakamura, David Roberts, Mick Silver, and Paul Schreyer for comments that greatly improved the paper, as well as Richard Dion and Pierre Duguay and their colleagues at the Bank of Canada, Marc Prud'homme and Andy Baldwin and their colleagues at Statistics Canada, and Leonard Nakamura and his colleagues for input during Alice Nakamura's 2008-2011 visits to the Bank of Canada and to the Philadelphia Federal Reserve Bank. However, we remain solely responsible for any errors and all opinions.

[2] Mishkin (2007a) explains that the Federal Reserve also pays attention to the rate of growth of the core PCE price index, which excludes food and energy prices. Rich and Steindel (2007) evaluate four measures of core inflation. The authors find no compelling evidence for preferring any one of these to the others. Bernanke (2008) notes the continuing efforts of researchers to develop improved inflation measures and to better use these measures.

[3] McCully (2006) explains that the PCE price index re-weights and supplements price data the BLS uses to compile the CPI so as to better fit the scope, concepts, and methods used for the U.S. National Income and Product Accounts (the NIPAs) that are, in turn, used to produce measures of output and productivity for the national economy.

Diewert, W. Erwin and Alice O. Nakamura (2011), "Accounting for Housing in a CPI," chapter 2, pp. 7-32 in W.E. Diewert, B.M. Balk, D. Fixler, K.J. Fox and A.O. Nakamura (2011),
***PRICE AND PRODUCTIVITY MEASUREMENT: Volume 1 -- Housing.* Trafford Press.**

Thus the BLS uses the rents of rental units in the same localities as the sampled owner occupied homes to compute the rental equivalence for owner occupied housing (OOH) services. This paper raises questions about, and suggests an alternative to, sole reliance on the rental equivalence approach for accounting for OOH in a CPI.

Bauer, Haltom, and Peterman (2004) with the Federal Reserve Bank of Atlanta argue that some of the observed post-2002 increases in rental vacancy rates were causally attributable to *increases* in the demand for owned homes. The belief is that rapid and sustained increases in the prices for housing in many localities led some renters who had planned on purchasing homes later to enter the housing market earlier for fear of being permanently priced out of the market if they did not do this. Behaviour of this sort would have helped sustain the increases in house prices while contributing to a softening in rental markets. Concerns as to how the treatment of owner occupied housing was affecting the movements of the CPI spilled over into the financial press. For example, in Market Watch, Robb (2006) wrote that:

> "The way the government computes the CPI has created a distortion that made inflation look tame when home prices were soaring, but is now making inflation look worse as price gains moderate. It's all because the government measures everyone's housing costs -- renters and homeowners by looking at rents, not at the cost of owning."

As Cecchetti explains, criticisms like those above led to arguments that OOH services should be priced more directly. Cecchetti (2007) notes that:

> "There is an argument that, rather than including observed rents, the existing price of a home should be in the consumer price index....

> Making this change in the consumer price index would make an enormous difference. To see how big, start with the fact that since 2000, the U.S. headline CPI has risen at an average annual rate of 2.75%, while the traditional core CPI has gone up 2.20% per year on average. If government statisticians had been using the price of homes sold rather than rents, consumer price inflation would have registered an annual increase of something like 4% per year – roughly one and one-quarter percentage points higher. And core CPI inflation would have been something like 3.8%; that's more than one and one-half percentage points above the official reading. Had these been the inflation readings, it's hard to imagine the Fed keeping their federal funds rate target below 2% for three years."

Direct inclusion of home prices in the CPI has been resisted by the BLS on the grounds that it is the dwelling services of OOH that the BLS is trying to price; not investment services. Nevertheless, there is no way of living in a home without investing in housing. Also, a homeowner with a mortgage cannot continue living in their home and cannot rent it out without keeping their mortgage payments up to date. Nor can they sell the home without discharging their mortgage. Thus concern has grown that the rental equivalency approach is not properly measuring inflation for OOH services. Verbrugge (2008) notes that:

> "Between 1995 and 2004, the owners-equivalent-rent (OER) subindex of the CPI rose by about 30%, but the Office of Federal Housing Enterprise Oversight (OFHEO) house price index rose by over 61%, a divergence which many commentators viewed as 'perverse' and unacceptable."

We argue that the shelter services provided by otherwise equivalent owned and rented accommodations are different products, just as owned and rented cars and fine art and party dresses and suits are different products. Moreover, since so many more households have opted to live in owned rather than rented accommodations in the United States, we argue that there is no way of effectively monitoring inflation as experienced by households in a period like the post 2002 years without more directly accounting for the cost of OOH services.

In section 2, we take stock of how statistical agencies in different nations are currently accounting for housing in their CPIs. Of the four measures currently in use, the rental equivalence and user cost ones have been the favourites of economists. Both these approaches can be derived from the fundamental equation of capital theory, as outlined in section 3. This theoretical basis is not the only way of justifying these approaches, but it is the basis usually noted in the official statistics literature. However, because of the assumptions involved, the use of the fundamental equation of capital theory is on less firm ground in applications to housing than to financial asset markets. Also, there is empirical evidence for housing markets that conflicts with implications of the fundamental equation of capital theory. Concerns about these approaches are taken up in section 4.

In section 5, we argue that an *opportunity cost* approach is the correct theoretical framework for accounting for OOH in a CPI. This approach, first mentioned in Diewert (2006), is developed more fully here.[4] We explore the relationship of this new approach to the usual rental equivalency approach and to the way in which the user cost approach is implemented by Verbrugge (2008). The new approach leads to an Owner Occupied Housing Opportunity Cost (OOHOC) index that is a weighted average of the rental and the financial opportunity costs. In section 6, we outline some of the broader reasons for favouring the proposed new approach.

2. Different Concepts of the Cost of Owner Occupied Housing (OOH)

Here we briefly review the four main existing approaches for accounting of housing in official statistics: the rental equivalence, user cost, acquisitions and payments approaches.[5]

2.1 The Rental Equivalence Approach

The rental equivalence approach values the services yielded by a dwelling using the observed market rent for the same sort of dwelling for the same period of time (if such a rental value exists). Here we outline the implementation of this approach by the BLS for accounting for OOH in the CPI.[6] We then also examine the treatment of OOH services in the Personal Consumption Expenditure component of the National Income and Product Accounts (NIPAs) compiled by the Bureau of Economic Analysis (BEA) using data inputs from the Census Bureau.

The U.S. shelter index component of the CPI is the household expenditure weighted average of several components. The two main shelter index components are the Rent of Primary Residence Index, hereafter referred to as the *rent index*, and the Owners' Equivalent Rent of Primary Residence Index (hereafter referred to as the *rental equivalence index*). Both price observations and expenditure weights are needed for compiling the rent index and the rental equivalence index. Johnson (2006) of the BLS explains that the expenditure share weights are

---

[4] Diewert (2006) is published in this volume as Diewert (2011).

[5] See the ILO et al. (2004) CPI manual, Christensen, Dupont and Schreyer (2005) and Eiglsperger (2006).

[6] This section draws on the U.S. Bureau of Labor Statistics (BLS) (2007).

computed using Consumer Expenditure Survey (CES) data. Sampled census <u>renters</u> are asked the following about the dwellings they occupy:

> "What is the rental charge to your ... unit including any extra charges for garage & parking facilities? Do not include direct payments by local, state or federal agencies. What period of time does this cover?"

And <u>owner occupiers</u> are asked:

> "If someone were to rent your home today, how much do you think it would rent for monthly, unfurnished, and without utilities?"

The CES information is used only for the CPI expenditure share weights and this is the only data used that is collected from owner occupiers as well as renters. In contrast, the price information for housing services is only collected from renters.

To determine housing price changes, the BLS first produces a sample of local area block groups. It is assumed that changes in owners' equivalent rent in small geographic areas (3-4 city blocks per block group) will be similar to the changes in actual rents for renters in those localities. Hence, each rental unit that is priced does double duty: it represents the renters within the block group, and it represents owner occupiers. Adjustments are made for landlord provided utilities and for the different effects of aging on owned versus rented housing.[7]

The main focus of this chapter is on the CPI. However, here we also some pay attention to the treatment of OOH in the U.S. National Income and Product Accounts (NIPAs). That treatment is what often is being referred to when mention is made that the U.S. uses the rental equivalence approach, but the details of how rental equivalence is implemented differ from the CPI case. Of course, if incorrect estimates of inflation are used in compiling the NIPAs, this can result in incorrect estimates of output and productivity growth. Many nations benchmark their productivity against the U.S. case, which makes the possibility that the U.S. productivity numbers are biased due to the U.S. price treatment of OOH a serious concern for many other nations as well. Also, the data sets used in accounting for OOH in the NIPAs are potentially useful as well for the new opportunity cost approach we suggest in section 5.

Housing services are a component of Personal Consumption Expenditures (PCE), and consequently are also part of the Gross Domestic Product (GDP) in the NIPAs. The rental value of tenant occupied housing and the imputed rental value of OOH are both included in the PCE housing services component. Mayerhauser and Reinsdorf (2007) explain that treating owner occupiers as renting from themselves is viewed as necessary in order for GDP to be invariant when housing units shift between tenant occupancy and owner occupancy.

Garner at the BLS and Short at the U.S. Census Bureau explain in detail how the gross rental value of owner occupied units is operationally imputed for the NIPAs and the PCE price index and how this process differs from the BLS methods for the CPI program. Garner and Short (2008) write that, first, rent-to-value ratios are computed from data collected in the decennial Residential Finance Survey (RFS).[8] The most recent Residential Finance Survey is the 2001 one.

---

[7] For historical specifics on the treatment of rental housing in the CPI see Crone, L.I. Nakamura, and Voith (2008).

[8] The Census Bureau has conducted the Residential Finance Survey (RFS) as part of every decennial census since 1950. The survey collects and produces data about the financing of nonfarm, privately-owned residential properties. More information can be found at http://www.census.gov/hhes/www/rfs/rfscollect.html.

For the 2001 RFS, a sample of about 50,000 addresses was drawn from the address file for the Census 2000.[9] Then questionnaires were mailed to a sample of property owners and to lenders who held mortgages on the sampled properties. The RFS provides a comprehensive view of mortgage finance in the United States, including information about loans and also demographic information about the property owners. Responding to the RFS is mandatory for those sampled. This is an important consideration for collecting information from mortgage lenders. The RFS is exempt from statutes prohibiting release of financial records by financial institutions.

The RFS based rent-to-value ratios are applied to the mid-point market values of the owner occupied units within corresponding value classes, as reported in the American Housing Survey (AHS). The AHS collects data on the nation's rental and owner occupied housing, including apartments, single-family homes, mobile homes, and vacant housing units. National AHS data are collected biannually for about 55,000 homes. The survey is conducted by the Census Bureau for the Department of Housing and Urban Development.[10]

Total rental services are the product of the RFS-based value ratios in a benchmark year times the number of sample units in each value class as determined from the AHS. The average OOH equivalent value over all value classes provides an average rent estimate in a benchmark year. Between benchmark years, this estimate must be updated taking into account inflation as well as improvements in the quality of owned dwellings and any inflation in rents for dwellings of a given quality. The inflation factors are based on the OOH rent component of the CPI, while the quality change adjustment is based on estimated BEA adjustment factors.

2.2   The User Cost Approach

It is often stated that the user cost for owner occupied housing can be thought of as the cost to a household of purchasing a home at the beginning of a unit time period, living in it during the period, and re-selling it at the end of the period. Like the rental equivalence approach, the user cost approach is routinely used for a variety of assets other than housing. For example, the approach is used in the capital asset pricing literature, in production function studies, in the measurement of total factor productivity growth, and in the analysis of tax depreciation rules.

The *full ex ante user cost* consists of *normal maintenance expenditures* plus *property taxes* plus *depreciation expenses* (loss of value of the dwelling unit due to the effects of aging and wear and tear that is not offset by normal maintenance expenditures)[11] plus *waiting costs* (the costs of forgone interest due to the funds tied up in an owned dwelling) and *anticipated capital gains* or losses due to housing market specific inflation over the given time period. The

---

[9] These addresses were limited to counties and independent cities in the 394 sampling areas used for the Census Bureau's American Housing Survey National Sample.

[10] The BEA then uses the component measures compiled by the Census Bureau in producing the PCE component of the NIPAs. The Census Bureau also implements a different approximation of net rental income based on a return to equity approach presented in Smeeding et al. (1993). In that methodology, homeowners were assumed to have sold their homes and captured the equity from the sales, and are then assumed to have invested the equity and to have earned a given rate of return. This approach is referred to as the capital market approach.

[11] If the dwelling unit is remodeled or extensive maintenance expenditures have been undertaken, then there has been new investment added to the unit and the proper accounting treatment is more complex.

full ex post user cost is defined the same way except that ex post (i.e., actual) capital gains or losses are used in place of ex ante anticipated gains or losses.

Official statistics agencies that have adopted user cost approaches have so far adopted simplifications rather than the full user cost approach. Here we report on two nations that use simplified variants of the user cost approach.

2.2.1 The Canadian case[12]

Statistics Canada states that they use a modified user cost for OOH services. The Statistics Canada OOH measure is very different from the user cost as defined above, or in recent international manuals. The Statistics Canada measure includes the loss of value due to physical depreciation plus the following sorts of household operating costs: (a) the cost of ongoing maintenance and repairs and upkeep; (b) the cost of homeowners' insurance and property taxes; and (c) mortgage interest cost. This treatment of OOH *omits both* the waiting cost of foregone interest on funds tied up in an owned dwelling and also financial appreciation or depreciation. If the physical depreciation term were dropped from the Canadian treatment, this would be a variant of the payments approach (see section 2.4).

Baldwin, Nakamura and Prud'homme (2006, 2011) explain that the mortgage interest component of the official concept is intended to estimate price induced changes in the amount of mortgage interest owed by the target population on outstanding mortgages. The Statistics Canada practice is to hold the volume of mortgage loans, by age of mortgage, constant so that interest owed depends only on house prices and interest rates; not on the changes in lump sum payments or changes in the loan-to-value ratios or the amortization periods of the outstanding loans.[13]

Erdur and Prud'Homme (2007) note that data on house prices enter into five parts of the OOH component of the Canadian CPI: mortgage interest cost, replacement cost (without land), insurance, realtor commissions, and legal fees. Because of this, it is unfortunate that Statistics Canada has only been able to afford to collect *new* house price information. It is known that new house prices often move differently from prices for pre-owned homes. At least, however, the Statistics Canada treatment does use some direct evidence about house price movements.

2.2.2 The Icelandic case

Statistics Iceland labels the OOH component of their CPI as an "owner equivalent rent" index, but describes this as a simplified user cost, as Diewert (2003) defines this term.[14] Copies of all sales deeds for residential housing are filed with the Icelandic Land Registry. The deeds state the purchase prices of the properties together with the buyer liabilities and details of the interest and scheduling of payments on the debt. The Land Registry evaluates all these details and computes the present discounted value for the sale. The Icelandic owner equivalent rent is intended to reflect changes in market prices of housing and also financing costs and depreciation.

---

[12] The information in this section is mostly from Statistics Canada (2007) and Statistics Canada (1995). For more on the treatment of OOH in the Canadian CPI, see also Baldwin, Nakamura and Prud'homme (2006, 2011).

[13] See Statistics Canada (1995, pp. 113-117).

[14] Material in this section is based on Guðnason (2005a, 2005b), as well as Guðnason and Jónsdóttir (2011).

2.3 The Acquisitions Approach

For both durable and nondurable goods, the acquisitions approach charges the entire price of a purchase to the period of the purchase. The approach can potentially be applied to OOH. This approach is the one used by all official statistics agencies for all goods and services covered by a CPI (other than OOH services in the case of the nations like the United States that use other approaches for accounting for the cost of OOH). With this approach, the objective is to measure the average change in prices of the products acquired by households each period, irrespective of whether they were wholly or even partially paid for (e.g., credit purchases) or used in that period.

Only goods that the household sector purchases from *other* sectors are in scope with the acquisitions approach. For most products, the direct sales by households to other households are negligible. Thus, limiting coverage to purchases from other sectors makes little difference. However, when the acquisitions approach is used for OOH, the housing related expenditures that enter the CPI are mostly expenditures on new dwellings excluding land. This is because most second hand dwellings, and even most of the land used for new home construction, are excluded. The acquisitions approach is used by Australia and New Zealand (Statistics New Zealand 2006). This approach has also been tentatively chosen for the European Union's Harmonized Indices of Consumer Prices (HICPs), which is the euro area measure of consumer price inflation.[15]

2.4 The Payments Approach

The payments approach only measures actual cash outflows associated with OOH. Thus the consumption of OOH services gets very little weight from fully owned dwellings. When there is moderate or high general inflation, mortgage payments swell, but there is no offsetting benefit to the homeowner since the appreciation in the housing asset is ignored. The payments approach produces high values in periods of inflation: erroneously high values in our view.

The Central Statistics Office of Ireland (2003) uses the payments approach. For owner occupiers, the Irish CPI covers the costs for repairs and decorations and other home maintenance services; house insurance; local authority charges, and mortgage interest. Mortgage interest payments are measured using a fixed basket of mortgages up to twenty years in duration.

3. The Theory of Household User Costs

As noted above, no nation uses the full user cost approach. However, reports on the treatment of OOH in official statistics make ubiquitous reference to the shared theoretical underpinnings for the user cost and the rental equivalency approaches, and it is the full user cost that is relevant in that context. Hence here we consider the *full* user cost approach in fuller detail.

---

[15] As of now, however, OOH is still omitted from the HICPs. See the European Communities (2004). According to Eiglsperger (2006): "The Harmonised Index of Consumer Prices (HICP) plays a prominent role in the monetary policy strategy of the European Central Bank (ECB).... [M]ost of the expenditure of owner-occupiers on housing (OOH)... are not included in the HICP at present. This can be traced back to the different practices of treating OOH in national consumer price indices (CPIs)...."

Diewert (1974, p. 504) sets out the following user cost principles for consumer durables:

> "To form the rental price (or user cost) for the services of one unit of the nth good during period t, we imagine that the consumer purchases the good during period t and then sells it during the following period (possibly to himself). Then the discounted expected rental price for the nth consumer good during period t is given by the discounted cost of the purchase of the nth good during period t minus the discounted resale value of the depreciated good during period t + 1."

The "resale value of the depreciated good during period $t+1$" referred to in the above quotation includes not only the loss of value due to physical depreciation but also the waiting costs (i.e., the costs of forgone interest) and financial capital gains or losses.[16] Dougherty and van Order (1982) helped adapt and establish the user cost as a conceptual framework in the real estate literature. Bajari, Benkard, and Krainer (2003, p. 3) observe that:

> "Dougherty and Van Order (1982) were among the first to recognize that the user cost ... should be equal to the rental price of a single unit of housing services charged by a profit-maximizing landlord. Thus, the inherently difficult task of measuring an unobservable marginal rate of substitution is replaced by the much easier task of measuring rents."

Attention to timing matters. Realized prices are determined at points in time. Rates of interest are regarded as fixed at points in time. But rates of inflation are defined for time intervals. If there is inflation, money is less valuable when received at the end versus the beginning of a period. An end of period t value can be converted to its equivalent at the beginning of that same (*not* the next) period by discounting by $1+r^t$, where r^t is the period t nominal interest rate.

Katz (2011) reviews the theoretical framework that can be used to derive both user cost and rental equivalence measures from the fundamental equation of capital theory:

> "The 'user cost of capital' measure is based on the fundamental equation of capital theory. This equation, which applies equally to both financial and non-financial assets ... states that in equilibrium, the price of an asset will equal the present discounted value of the future net income that is expected to be derived from owning it."

The end of period t user cost for a durable that had already been used for v periods as of the start of period t is denoted by u_v^t. In box 1, the derivation of the user cost measure by Katz (2011, appendix A) is shown, recast using the notation for our paper.[17] We denote the value of a home that is v years old *at the start* of period t by V_v^t. Given only the information available at the start of period t, the *expected* price a home could be sold for *at the end* of period t, which is the start of period $t+1$, is denoted by V_{v+1}^{t+1}. And O_v^t denotes the *anticipated* operating costs, largely consisting of normal maintenance plus property taxes, that are treated as being paid at the end of the period. Katz explains that the traditional user cost measure is derived by assuming that

---

[16] Diewert (1974, 1980) followed Fisher (1897) and Hicks (1939) in deriving the user cost using a discrete time approach rather than the continuous time approaches used by Jorgenson (1963, 1967), Griliches (1963), Jorgenson and Griliches (1967, 1972) and Christensen and Jorgenson (1969, 1973). Recent related contributions include Hulten and Wykoff (1981a, 1981b, 1996), T.P. Hill (1999, 2000, 2005), Diewert and Lawrence (2000), R.J. Hill and T.P. Hill (2003), Corrado, Hulten and Sichel (2005), Diewert (2003, 2005a, 2005b) and Diewert and Wykoff (2011).

[17] Diewert (2005b) also carefully distinguishes between beginning and end of period user costs and recommends the use of end of period user costs since they are more consistent with financial accounting conventions.

flow transactions within a period actually occur at the end of the period. Thus he derives the following <u>end of period user cost</u>, shown in box 1 as equation (3-4):[18]

$$u_v^t \equiv r^t V_v^t + O_v^t - (V_{v+1}^{t+1} - V_v^t).$$

Box 1. Derivation of the User Cost Measure from Katz (2011, Appendix A)

The user cost of capital measure provides an estimate of the market rental price based on costs of owners. It is directly derived from the assumption that, in equilibrium, the purchase price of a durable good will equal the discounted present value of its expected net benefits; i.e., it will equal the discounted present value of its expected future services less the discounted present value of its expected future operating costs. To see this, let V_v^t denote the purchase <u>price of a v year old durable at the beginning of year t</u>; let V_{v+1}^{t+1} denote the expected purchase price of the durable at the beginning of year t+1 when the durable is one year older; let u_v^t denote the expected end of period value of the period t services of this durable; let O_v^t denote the expected period t operating expenses to be paid at the end of period t for the v year old durable; and let r^t denote the expected nominal discount rate (i.e., the rate of return on the best alternative investment) in year t. Expected variables are measured as of the beginning of year t.

Assume the entire value of the durable's services in a year will be received at the year's end, and that the durable is expected to have a <u>service life of m years</u>. From the definition of the discounted present value, we have

$$(3\text{-}1) \quad V_v^t = \frac{u_v^t}{1+r^t} + \frac{u_{v+1}^{t+1}}{(1+r^t)(1+r^{t+1})} + \ldots + \frac{u_{m-1}^{t+m-v-1}}{\Pi_{i=t}^{t+m-v-1}(1+r^i)} - \frac{O_v^t}{1+r^t} - \frac{O_{v+1}^{t+1}}{(1+r^t)(1+r^{t+1})} - \ldots - \frac{O_{m-1}^{t+m-v-1}}{\Pi_{i=t}^{t+m-v-1}(1+r^i)}.$$

When the durable is one year older, the expected price of the durable at the beginning of year t+1 is:

$$(3\text{-}2) \quad V_{v+1}^{t+1} = \frac{u_{v+1}^{t+1}}{1+r^{t+1}} + \frac{u_{v+2}^{t+2}}{(1+r^{t+1})(1+r^{t+2})} + \ldots + \frac{u_{m-1}^{t+m-v-1}}{\Pi_{i=t+1}^{t+m-v-1}(1+r^i)} - \frac{O_{v+1}^{t+1}}{1+r^{t+1}} - \ldots - \frac{O_{m-1}^{t+m-v-1}}{\Pi_{i=t+1}^{t+m-v-1}(1+r^i)}$$

Dividing both sides of (3-2) by $(1+r^t)$ and subtracting the result from equation (3-1) yields

$$(3\text{-}3) \quad V_v^t - \frac{V_{v+1}^{t+1}}{1+r^{t+1}} = \frac{u_v^t}{1+r^t} - \frac{O_v^t}{1+r^t}.$$

Multiplying through equation (3-3) by $(1+r^t)$ and combining terms, one obtains the <u>end of period t user cost</u>:

$$(3\text{-}4) \quad u_v^t = r^t V_v^t + O_v^t - (V_{v+1}^{t+1} - V_v^t).$$

Note that m in box 1 (above expression (3-1)) denotes the remaining service life of the durable measured in years. The estimated market value of a home a year later (V_{v+1}^{t+1}) is computed in the context that the home has a remaining service life for the homeowner of m years.

---

[18] So, unlike the home value variable where we need to refer to both the beginning and the end of period values, we only need to refer to the end of period values for the other anticipated variables and denote them simply using t as the superscript, as Katz does. And, unlike Katz, we also forego using a special designation for expected values.

4.   Rental Equivalence, User Cost History, and the Verbrugge Variant (VV) User Cost

We begin in this section by briefly taking stock of efforts at the BLS and BEA to assess the user cost approach as a possible alternative to rental equivalence. A group of careful studies that have been specially influential on these topics have been conducted by Thesia Garner and Randall Verbrugge (2011), and by Verbrugge in his own work and with various other collaborators.[19] The second part of this section is devoted to the Verbrugge (2008) variant of the user cost approach.

4.1   Long Standing Interest at the BLS and BEA

Both the BEA and BLS have experimented over the years with the user cost as well as the rental equivalence approach. Already by 1980, the BEA had published a de facto satellite account for the services of consumer durables that is detailed in Katz and Peskin (1980). Also at the BEA, Katz explored the sensitivity of user cost estimates to alternative assumptions about expected rates of inflation and patterns of depreciation in a 1982 paper, and examined related theoretical and empirical issues in a 1983 paper. And prior to 1983, for the CPI, the BLS built up estimates of homeowner expenses by estimating individual user cost components. That approach, which Greenlees (2003) of the BLS terms an "ad-hoc user cost" approach, made use of data on home purchase prices, mortgage interest, maintenance, taxes and insurance. Gillingham (1980) describes the BLS' failed attempt to construct a user cost measure of housing services for the CPI. He became discouraged at being able to construct a usable measure and wrote that his results "…provide empirical support for the contention that it is impossible to construct a valid user cost measure which is consistent with the information provided by rent markets without either direct or, through direct measurement of the opportunity cost of equity capital, indirect use of that information."

Carson (2006) also explains that, in the early 1980s, there were serious problems with the quality of the available house price and mortgage interest data. These data were only available then for houses with FHA-insured mortgages: a small and shrinking share of the market for owner occupied housing. Also, the influential Stigler Report (Stigler 1961, p. 53) had come out two decades earlier strongly in favour of rental equivalency.[20] These factors led the BLS to switch in 1983 to the rental equivalence approach.[21]

When first introduced by the BLS, the rental equivalence index was produced by reweighting the rent sample to better represent the distribution of owner occupied units. Revised procedures for calculating a rental equivalence index were adopted in 1987 and used through 1997. For that period, BLS drew a housing sample that had both owner and renter occupied

---

[19] See also Crone, L. Nakamura, and Voith (2011).

[20] The Stigler Report (Stigler 1961, p. 53) states that: "The welfare of consumers depends on the flow of services from houses and not upon the stocks acquired in any given period." The report concluded that (p. 48): "If a satisfactory rent index for units comparable to those that are owner-occupied can be developed, this committee recommends its substitution in the CPI for the present series for the prices of new houses and related expenses."

[21] See Gillingham and Lane (1982). The rental equivalence approach was implemented for the CPI-U in January 1983 and for the CPI for Urban Wage Earners and Clerical Workers (CPI-W) in January 1985.

housing units. However, due to technical problems with the 1987 changes, in 1998 the BLS reinstated the 1983 variant of the rental equivalence approach that used price data only on rents to calculate both the rent index for renters and the rental equivalence index for OOH services.

Already in their 2005 paper, Poole, Ptacek and Verbrugge acknowledge that the rapid rise in housing prices over the preceding few years coupled with slow increases in the OOH component of the CPI had led to concern among many economic analysts about the treatment of OOH services in the CPI. In their 2005 paper, they also state that the user cost approach is the only serious alternative to rental equivalency. Poole, Ptacek and Verbrugge go on to identify problems with the user cost approach, a key one being that, as they implement the approach, it would not have mirrored the post 2002 increases in home prices, and hence would not have relieved concerns that the OOH component of the CPI had failed to reflect any positive impacts on the costs of OOH services during the post 2002 run-up of prices for owner occupied housing.

Mayerhauser and Reinsdorf (2007) offer a defence of the OOH component of the CPI that can easily be understood in the context of a user cost formulation like the Katz one summarized in box 1 or the user cost formulation of Poole, Ptacek and Verbrugge (2005). They point out that a current period rise in home values raises the wealth of homeowners and thus can be viewed as reducing the net cost of ownership. They argue that, because capital gains on residences were extraordinarily high in the post 2002 years and interest rates were low, the net cost of occupying an owned residence was truly low in those years for most homeowners. In other words, Mayerhauser and Reinsdorf argue that the rental equivalence results for OOH services in the post 2002 period mirror reality. The incongruity of this conclusion considered in the context of the reported rising financial stress for increasing numbers of homeowners over the post 2002 years caused us to look more closely at the specifics of the formulations that have been applied for the user cost of OOH.

4.2 The Verbrugge Variant (VV) of the User Cost Approach

The specification of the user cost implemented in Poole, Ptacek and Verbrugge (2005) is based on derivations presented in Verbrugge (2008), where alternative ways of handling the home value appreciation term are also investigated more fully. Here, we label the formulation of the user cost presented as equation (1) in Verbrugge (2008) as the Verbrugge variant, hereafter referred to for short as the <u>VV user cost</u>.

The VV user cost is derived by treating homeowners as though they costlessly sell and buy back their homes each year.[22] Stated using our notation, where V^t is the beginning of period value of the home ignoring, as Verbrugge does, the age of the home; r^t is a nominal interest rate; γ_H^t is a term which collects the rates of depreciation, maintenance, and property taxes; and $E[\pi]$ is an estimate of the rate of expected house price appreciation, the VV user cost formula is:

---

[22] This user cost variant follows naturally from application of the statement of the user cost approach given by Diewert (1974) in the opening quotation for section 3 about how a consumer is imagined to be buying their home and then selling it back each period -- "(possibly to himself)." We note that in section 6 of his paper, Verbrugge (2008) relaxes the assumption that there are no costs of buying and selling a house and he uses this fact to try to help explain the divergence between the rental price of a home and its user cost.

(4-1)
$$u^t = r^t V^t + \gamma_H^t V^t - E[\pi] V^t$$
$$= \text{forgone interest} + \text{operating costs} - \text{expected t to } (t+1) \text{ change in home value.}$$

This is essentially formula (3-4) in box 1 of this paper.

Verbrugge experiments with a number of alternative ways of measuring the final term of (4-1) for the expected change in home value from the beginning to the end of year t, but his preferred forecasting equation includes a forecast of the home price change based on 4 quarters of prior home price information. With this setup, *changes* in home prices have an immediate within-year impact on the user cost. When home prices are rising, the final term of (4-1) serves to offset the contribution of the first term, $r^t V^t$.

4.3 Accepting the Verbrugge Verdict that User Costs and Rents Often Diverge

In the official statistics literature, the user cost and the rental equivalence approaches are usually positioned as arising from the same body of theory, as briefly outlined in section 3. That underlying theory yields some empirically testable predictions.

Capozza and Seguin (1995/1996) point out that under the assumptions usually made in deriving both the user cost and rental equivalency approaches from the fundamental equation of capital theory, we should observe gross and net rental yields that are invariant across and within rental housing markets. This is the same basic implication that follows from the theoretical framework Diewert (1974) provides for durable goods in general, and that Gillingham (1980) and also Dougherty and Van Order (1982) specialize for real estate markets.

Thus, the theory implies that, except as justified by departures from the maintained assumptions for the theory, rents should track user costs for observationally equivalent dwellings, and rent-to-value ratios should be constant over time and space. However, empirical efforts to confirm these theoretical implications have yielded mostly negative results. Verbrugge (2008) is very clear about the negative findings of his empirical investigations:

> "This paper demonstrates that, in the context of U.S. housing data, rents and ex ante user costs diverge markedly – both in growth rates and in levels – for extended periods of time, a seeming failure of arbitrage and a puzzle from the perspective of standard capital theory.... The divergence holds not only at the aggregate level, but at the metropolitan-market level as well, and is robust across different house price and rent measures."

Verbrugge shows empirically that, since 1998, his preferred VV user cost tracks neither rent nor house price movements. He takes this as evidence that the user cost approach should not be used.

Verbrugge's (2008) empirical exploration of the VV user cost caused us to notice something missing from the formulation that has thus far gone unnoticed, to which we turn our attention in section 5.

A number of others have also found results at odds with the stated theoretical predictions. For example, using another large U.S. dataset, Heston and Nakamura (2011) show that rent-to-value ratios differ by location and by the value of the property. Controlling for location, Heston and Nakamura find that the rent-to-value ratios fall dramatically in moving from relatively low to relatively high value homes.

Many factors have been suggested in the literature for why user costs might differ from rents in some places and times. One suggestion is that landlords change rents infrequently. Rental rate stickiness has been shown empirically to be particularly important for tenants continuing on from the previous year, which is the case for the majority of tenants.[23] A second factor that could cause rents and user costs to diverge in some situations is that owners and renters are subject to differing sorts of uncertainty regarding changes over time in household operating expenses. Sinai and Souleles (2003) note that, although owners face the risk of capital losses when they sell, the longer the holding periods, the more these future risks will be discounted. Moreover, owners often have some margin of control over the timing of when to sell.

A third factor is the thinness of the rental market for luxury homes. Most people have an apparent preference for living in owned housing. Higher income people are mostly in a position to indulge this preference even when they need to own and maintain multiple *de facto* "primary residences" in order to live under their own roof most of the time. Luxury homes tend to be offered for rent mostly under conditions that limit the options of a renter. Many of these rental arrangements involve house sitting responsibilities, or are very temporary. Moreover, to find renters, the owners of luxury homes must compete on price for tenants most of whom normally rent lower quality housing units and cannot afford to pay much more than what they normally would pay.[24]

Tax program rules that treat owner occupiers differently from landlords are a fourth factor that could cause user costs and rents to diverge. Wood, Watson and Yates (1998) find that differences in loan-to-value ratios are positively related to gross rent-value differentials, and argue that this outcome arises because federal government tax provisions make rental investments more attractive for highly leveraged investors at lower tax rates than would otherwise be the case. They also find that brokerage costs on the sale of rental properties are directly related to the size of gross rent-value differentials. Jud and Winkler (2005) point out that most past studies fail to incorporate refinancing options for homeowners. They suggest that during periods of falling interest rates, the ability to refinance is likely to generate substantial equity gains for homeowners. In their analysis, they explicitly consider refinancing options that homeowners exercise. In the following section, we build on these insights of Jud and Winkler.

We argue, moreover, that the fact that owner occupied and rental accommodation services are qualitatively different products is confirmed by the fact that owner occupiers and renters face different risks, the fact that rental markets become thinner for higher value homes, and the special tax provisions that have been enacted in the United States for owner occupiers. We believe that qualitative differences between otherwise similar owner occupied and rental accommodations are the main reason why most of the transitions between rented and owned accommodations is in the renter-to-owner direction.[25]

---

[23] See Gordon and van Goethem (2004) and Genesove (2003). Also, Hoffmann and Kurz-Kim (2006, p. 5) report the following: "In our sample, prices last on average more than two years... but then change by nearly 10 %." And, Hoffmann and Kurz-Kim (2006) find German rents are changed only once every four years on average.

[24] It also seems likely to us that, moving up the value scale, an increasing percentage of homes offered for rent are, in fact, offered with the terms of payment including house sitting duties along with the monetary rent obligations. Situations like this should, of course, be caught by the questions asked as part of the collection of the rent data, but it seems likely that not all the cases like this are properly identified.

[25] See the Harvard University Joint Center for Housing Studies (2008).

5.   Diewert's OOH Opportunity Cost Approach

The time has come, we feel, to accept the evidence of Verbrugge and others that user costs and rents do not reliably move together! This verdict implies we must rethink the approach for accounting for OOH in the price statistics of nations. We argue in the rest of this paper for a shift to the new opportunity cost approach for accounting for the cost of housing.

The term "opportunity cost" refers to the cost of the best alternative that must be forgone in taking the option chosen. Thus, we seek to compare implications for homeowner wealth of selling at the beginning of period t with the alternatives of planning to own a home for m more years and of either renting out or occupying the home for the coming year. This comparison is assumed to be carried out at the beginning of period t based on the information available then about the market value of the home and interest rates and the forecasted average increase per year in home market value if the home is held for another m years.

Refinancing can be viewed as a way of a homeowner selling or buying back a fraction of an owned home. In contrast to selling and buying titles to properties, financing and refinancing costs for mortgages and other loans secured by liens on property titles are quite low, in the United States at least. We imagine that a homeowner mentally notes at the start of each year the market price and the forecast for the annual average growth in value for a home that the owner expects to hold for m more years. The homeowner is presumed to use this information as input to decisions made at the start of the year on whether to adjust their debt for the coming year, whether to sell at the start of the year or to plan on continuing to own their home for m more years, and whether to rent out or occupy the home for the coming year if they continue to own it.

Owner occupiers in period t continue to own their homes with the chosen levels of debt, and to occupy rather than renting their homes out. Thus in choosing to own and occupy, they pass up the opportunity of selling at the start of the period, and also the opportunity of renting out their home that year. At the level of an individual homeowner, the opportunity cost approach amounts to treating the cost to the owner occupant of their housing choice as the greater of the foregone benefit they would have received by selling at the start of period t or renting out the owned home and collecting the rent payments.

The owner occupied housing opportunity cost index can now be defined as follows:

For each household living in owner occupied housing (OOH), the *owner occupied housing opportunity cost* (OOHOC) is the maximum of what it would cost to rent an equivalent dwelling (the rental opportunity cost, ROC) and the financial opportunity costs (FOC).

The OOHOC index for a nation is defined as an expenditure share weighted sum of a rental equivalency index and a financial opportunity cost index, with the expenditure share weights depending on the estimated proportion of owner occupied homes for which FOC exceeds ROC.

In sections 5.1 and 5.2, respectively, we focus on the ROC and then the FOC components of the index for an individual homeowner. Then in section 5.3, we address the issue of how to move from OOHOC values for individual homeowners to an OOHOC index for a nation. Finally, section 5.4 reviews key features of the proposed OOHOC index.

5.1 The Rental Opportunity Cost Component

The rental opportunity cost component is operationally equivalent to the usual rental equivalency measure introduced in section 2, but the justification for this component here does not rest on an appeal to the fundamental equation of capital theory and is not tied to the potential sale value for the home in the current or subsequent periods. In the present context, the ROC component is simply the rent for period t on an owned dwelling that the owner forgoes by living there that period. That is, it is the rent the owner could have collected by renting the place out rather than living there.[26]

We next turn our attention to the financial opportunity cost of the money tied up in an owned dwelling. A home, once purchased, can yield owner occupied housing services over many years. The user cost framework provides guidance on how to infer the period by period financial costs of OOH services using the observable home purchase data. We can use the user cost framework this way even in situations when the capital theory assumptions under which the user cost equals the expected rent are not satisfied.

5.2 The Financial Opportunity Cost Component

The user cost formulation we recommend for the FOC component of the opportunity cost is referred to here as the Diewert variant, or DV, user cost. For this specification, we let r^t denote the rate of return a homeowner could have received by investing funds that are tied up in the owned home. In addition, we take account of the fact that many homeowners have debt that is secured against their homes and must make regular specified payments on that debt to continue to be in a position to occupy or to rent out their homes.

Research has shown that owner occupied homes, on the whole, exhibit little physical depreciation over time given modern standards for home maintenance.[27] (This is in contrast to the situation for rental housing units that have been shown to lose significant value, on average, with increasing age.) Hence, since we are focusing on owner occupied housing here, we drop the dwelling age subscript v from this point on, as we did in introducing the Verbrugge variant (VV) user cost in equation (4-1).

We also take account of the fact that the vast majority of homeowners own their homes for many years. Indeed, if we take account as well of the phenomenon of serial home ownership, with owner occupiers rolling forward the equity accumulated from one owned home to the next, then the time horizon (given by m in box 1) should arguably be the entire number of years a homeowner plans to continue to live in owned housing. Many people move into their own owned

---

[26] Notice that, in computing the ROC component, we do not subtract the cost the owner would need to incur to live somewhere else if they rented the home out. The opportunity cost of living in an owned home, which is the maximum of the ROC and FOC components, is what the person would presumably compare with the costs of alternative housing arrangements in making their choice about where to live for period t. It does, however, make sense to think of the ROC value for an individual homeowner as a lower bound on the value they place on living in the home in light of the fact that most people, in the United States at least, seem to have a strong preference for living in owned accommodations.

[27] Here "normal maintenance" for owned homes is essentially being defined to include the amount of maintenance and renovation expenditures required to just maintain the overall "quality" of the home at a constant level.

homes as soon as they can afford to after reaching adulthood and die still owning their own homes. The expected remaining years, m, until a homeowner expects to withdraw all the equity they have in their home is an important parameter for determining the FOC component. However, if homeowner-specific information about m is lacking, perhaps m could be set at a value no lower than the median years that homeowners report having been in their present homes.

Having stated the above choices and views, we are now ready to specify the FOC component for an individual homeowner. Here we ignore the case of homeowners who have negative home equity: a more complex and obviously important case in the present circumstances which we are considering now in separate research with Leonard Nakamura. We also abstract from transactions costs and taxes: further complications that we are also considering in our new research with Leonard Nakamura.

As of the start of period t, a homeowner with nonnegative equity could sell, paying off any debt (D^t) in the process, and could collect the (non negative) sum of $V^t - D^t$. Or the homeowner could choose to continue owning the dwelling, in which case they must make payments on any debt they have, and must pay the normal home operating costs; they must do this whether they choose to live in their home or rent it out for the coming year. If they continue to own the dwelling -- either living in it or renting it out -- they will forego the interest they could have earned on the equity tied up in their home and will incur maintenance costs and carrying costs on any debt, but they will also enjoy any capital gains or incur any capital losses that materialize.

The financial user cost for owning the home in period t and living in it, discounted to the start of period t, is:

$$(5\text{-}2a) \qquad \frac{u^t}{1+r^t} \equiv [V^t - D^t] - \left[\frac{-r_D^t D^t - O^t + (\overline{V^{t+1}} - D^t)}{1+r^t}\right],$$

where $\overline{V^{t+1}}$ is the value of the home at the beginning of period t plus the expected *average* appreciation of the home value over the number of years before the homeowner plans to sell. Thus, the second term in square brackets is the forecasted expected value of the home as of the end of period t which is the beginning of period t+1 ($\overline{V^{t+1}}$) minus the period t debt service costs ($r_D^t D^t$) and operating costs (O^t) that must be paid in order to either occupy or rent out the dwelling for period t. If we multiply expression (5-2a) through by the discount factor, $1+r^t$, we now obtain an expression for the ex ante end of period user cost:

$$(5\text{-}2b) \qquad u^t \equiv r_D^t D^t + r^t(V^t - D^t) + O^t - (\overline{V^{t+1}} - V^t).$$

The importance of the debt related terms in (5-2a) and (5-2b) can be better appreciated by considering some specific types of homeowners. Consider a type A homeowner who owns their home free and clear. For them, the end of period user cost for period t, discounted to the start of the period, is:

(5-3a)
$$\frac{u^t}{1+r^t}\bigg|_{typeA} \equiv [V^t] - \left[\frac{-O^t + \overline{V^{t+1}}}{1+r^t}\right] = \frac{O^t + r^t V^t - (\overline{V^{t+1}} - V^t)}{1+r^t}.$$

The user cost considered as of the end of the period is found by multiplying (5-3a) through by $1+r^t$, yielding:

(5-3b)
$$u^t\big|_{typeA} \equiv r^t V^t + O^t - (\overline{V^{t+1}} - V^t).$$

Notice that this is essentially the customary user cost expression, as derived by Katz (2011) and others; e.g., see equation (3-4) in box 1 above. This is the same basic formulation used as well by Verbrugge; e.g., see (4-1) above.

Type B homeowners do not fully own their homes, but have positive home equity: the most prevalent case for U.S. homeowners. If the homeowner were to sell at the beginning of period t, the realized proceeds of the sale (after repaying the debt) would be $V^t - D^t$. The end of period user cost for period t for these homeowners, discounted to the start of period t, is:

(5-4a)
$$\frac{u^t}{1+r^t}\bigg|_{typeB} \equiv [V^t - D^t] - \left[\frac{-r_D^t D^t - O^t + (\overline{V^{t+1}} - D^t)}{1+r^t}\right]$$
$$= \frac{r_D^t D^t + O^t + r^t(V^t - D^t) - (\overline{V^{t+1}} - V^t)}{1+r^t}.$$

The user cost, as of the end of the period, is found by multiplying (5-4a) through by $1+r^t$:

(5-4b)
$$u^t\big|_{typeB} \equiv r_D^t D^t + r^t(V^t - D^t) + O^t - (\overline{V^{t+1}} - V^t).$$

Type C homeowners have zero home equity. In this case, if the homeowner sells at the start of period t, we assume simply that they get nothing from the sale. And if they continue to own and live in the home, they do so without having any equity tied up by this choice and hence are not foregoing any earnings on funds tied up in their home. The end of period user cost for period t, considered as of the start of period t, is:

(5-5a)
$$\frac{u^t}{1+r^t}\bigg|_{typeC} \equiv -\left[\frac{-r_D^t D^t - O^t + (\overline{V^{t+1}} - D^t)}{1+r^t}\right].$$

The user cost considered as of the end of the period is:[28]

(5-5b)
$$u^t\big|_{typeC} \equiv r_D^t D^r + O^t - (\overline{V^{t+1}} - V^t).$$

---

[28] Note that in this zero equity case, it seems like the payments approach is justified at first glance. However, the payments approach neglects the expected capital gains term and during periods of high or moderate inflation, this term must be taken into account.

We next consider the extreme case in which the interest rate for borrowing equals the returns on investments (i.e., $r_D^t = r^t$). Now, (5-4a) and (5-4b) reduce to (5-3a) and (5-3b). That is, the expressions for the homeowners who have debt but still have positive equity in their homes reduce to the expressions for the user cost for the homeowners who own their dwellings free and clear. We see, therefore, that the traditional user cost expression, as derived by Katz, and the VV user cost implicitly assume that homeowners who have mortgages or other home equity loans are charged an interest rate on this debt that equals the rate of return on their financial investments.

Most well off households have mostly low cost debt whereas many poor households have mostly have high cost debt. The importance of this fact can be demonstrated using the end of period user cost for a type B homeowner. For a homeowner who has positive home equity and only low cost debt with $r_D^t < r^t$, expression (5-4b) can be written as:

$$
\begin{aligned}
u^t\big|_{\text{typeB}} &\equiv r_D^t D^t + r^t(V^t - D^t) + O^t - (\overline{V^{t+1}} - V^t) \\
&= r_D^t V^t - (r^t - r_D^t)D^t + O^t - (\overline{V^{t+1}} - V^t),
\end{aligned}
$$

(5-6)

where the term $(r^t - r_D^t)$ is positive. Hence, for these homeowners, *higher debt reduces the financial cost of OOH services*. Indeed, this is a potential motivation for a Type B homeowner to increase their low cost borrowing to the greatest extent possible. The only rational constraint on doing this, from an economic perspective, is that higher debt can also bring a greater risk of home foreclosure or personal bankruptcy in the event of a downturn in the economy or personal problems such as job loss or illness.

The case of a homeowner with only high cost debt (i.e., with $r_D^t > r^t$) is different. Now (5-4b) reduces to:

$$
\begin{aligned}
u^t\big|_{\text{typeB}} &\equiv r_D^t D^t + r^t(V^t - D^t) + O^t - (\overline{V^{t+1}} - V^t) \\
&= r^t V^t + (r_D^t - r^t)D^t + O^t - (\overline{V^{t+1}} - V^t),
\end{aligned}
$$

(5-8)

where $(r_D^t - r^t)$ is positive. So *now, higher debt means a higher financial cost of OOH services.* Most subprime loans are high cost, with interest rates at least three interest rate points above Treasures of comparable maturities.

We come now to the question of how the DV user cost would behave over a housing bubble. In this portion of our analysis, we use the general (5-2b) expression for the end of period user cost. Moreover, we will define $r_{H(m)}^t$ as the expected rate of home price change under the assumption a home will be held for m more years. Now, (5-2b) can be rewritten as

$$
\begin{aligned}
u^t &\equiv r_D^t D^t + r^t(V^t - D^t) - r_{H(m)}^t V^t + O^t \\
&= (r_D^t - r^t)D^t + (r^t - r_{H(m)}^t)V^t + O^t,
\end{aligned}
$$

(5-9)

where $r_{H(m)}^t V^t = \overline{V^{t+1}} - V^t$. Hence the FOC for a household can be negative when, for example, the borrowing rate is less than the expected rate of return on financial assets, and the expected rate of return on financial assets is less than the expected annual rate of return on housing assets. However, the OOHOC for a household will never be zero or negative because it is defined as the maximum of the ROC and the FOC, with the rental opportunity cost necessarily being positive.

Notice also that the FOC component will rise as home prices rise, and first and foremost, when the expected rate of return on financial investments (r^t) is greater than the expected rate of return on the housing asset ($r^t_{H(m)}$). Going into a bubble, the first term, $(r^t_D - r^t)D^t$, will be hard to forecast even in terms of sign, but we would expect the changes in this term to be small compared to the changes in the second term, $(r^t - r^t_{H(m)})V^t$. During the expansion phase of a bubble, home values, and hence V^t, will grow rapidly, but the longer run return on housing assets should not change as much and hence the financial user cost of OOH, given by equation (9), should increase. This result underlines the importance of incorporating longer run expectations into the user cost formula. Of course, when the bubble bursts, the financial user cost will rapidly decline, although the decline will be offset somewhat by the possible decline as well in $r^t_{H(m)}$.[29]

5.3   Moving to the National Level

To estimate the FOC and the corresponding rental opportunity cost (ROC) values, values are needed for the following financial variables: R^t and V^t for each sampled home, the rental value and the market value if the home were sold then; r^t, which is the average rate of return on household financial investments; and the amounts of low cost and of high cost household debt, by which we mean the amounts of debt at interest rates that are less than r^t and the amounts that are at interest rates that are greater than r^t.

In the United States, the needed information for compiling the FOC and ROC measures of the proposed new opportunity cost measures might be obtained by adding a small number of questions to the Consumer Expenditure Survey (CES). The Residential Finance Survey (RFS), and the American Housing Survey (AHS) might be used as well.

For each home of each type, the FOC and ROC values must be compared, and the OOH opportunity cost for the home must be set equal to the maximum of these values. The results of these comparisons would feed into the determination of the expenditure share weights needed for combining the FOC and ROC components of the OOHOC index. Our analysis suggests that the new OOHOC index will always be positive and will be only modestly more volatile than a conventional rental equivalency index.

---

[29] Locked in aspects of the financing arrangements of home buyers may also matter in this regard. We are exploring this issue now in a follow-up study.

5.4   Noteworthy Features of the OOHOC Index

We close this section on the new opportunity cost approach by noting some of its desirable features:

- In the post 2002 period, the Diewert variant (DV) user cost, which is one of the two components of the new opportunity cost approach for accounting for OOH in a consumer price index, would have risen in response to rising home prices, due to the prominent role played by the debt homeowners incurred to buy homes in the context of the steep run-up of home prices over the 2002-2005 time period.

- The DV user cost would not always track rents over periods like the post 2002 years when other evidence suggests that rents and the financial cost of OOH services were moving in opposite directions. More generally, there are strong reasons why the home rental and owner occupied housing services markets can, and often have, displayed quite different price behaviour. Under some conditions, formula (5-9) would also apply to the owner of a rental property who is thinking about what rent to set. In real life circumstances, however, we would expect that landlords will tend to treat sunk costs and year-to-year supply and demand conditions differently than owner occupiers. A landlord who builds or buys a rental property will want to set rents at least equal to the user cost. However, once the property is built or bought, the cost is sunk and supply and demand factors for rental properties may cause the market rents to diverge from the expected user costs. Evidence of this factor at work includes, in our view, cycles in the construction of rental units; when the user costs of landlords exceed market rents, new rental property construction slumps, and vice versa when the user costs of landlords are below current market rents.

- The problem of negative user costs would be eliminated, since the rental equivalent is the minimum value the new opportunity cost measure could take on for any given home.

- The new opportunity cost index would be far less volatile than the user cost measure investigated by Verbrugge (2008) and by Garner and Verbrugge (2011). One reason for the lower volatility is the use of the rental equivalent as a minimum for the opportunity cost for any one home. A second reason is the use of appreciation rates averaged over the expected number of future years the owner occupier will own and live in a home. And a third reason is the way in which debt is brought into the new measure.

6.   Concluding Remarks

Our first main objective in this paper is to call attention to the need for more direct measures of inflation for owner occupied housing services. Our second main objective is to suggest a new approach -- the opportunity cost approach -- for accounting for OOH services in consumer price indexes.

In their paper, "Can Measurement Error Explain the Productivity Paradox?" Diewert and Fox (1999) write:

"We believe that economic mismeasurement in general can help to explain the post-1973 productivity growth decline in OECD countries." (p. 3)

We believe that time and research will eventually prove that the above Diewert-Fox diagnosis of the post-1973 productivity growth decline applies, with different specifics, to the post housing bubble period. We believe that, in the context of strong and poorly measured inflation in the market for owner occupied housing, households, financial institutions, pension and other fund managers of many types, and regulators all were prone to making erroneous predictions that, in many cases, led to serious losses of economic value.

Farlow (2005) ventures the observation that house price booms, just like government budget deficits, are popular with older consumers and governments, both of which may benefit from 'borrowing' from future generations. In other words, Farlow suggests that some of those charged with management of the economy and some businesses and consumers stood to gain from, and hence may have welcomed, the price signal confusion caused by poor official statistics measures of OOH inflation.

However, it is clear by now that many people were greatly harmed by the steep rise and then collapse of housing prices in the post 2002 period. In addition to all the foreclosures, many of those having to switch from owned to rental housing following the burst of the bubble suffered, or will suffer, large losses. According to the Harvard Center for Housing Studies (2008), the owner occupiers who switch to renting mostly do so as part of coping with marriage breakdowns, job losses, and health problems (including age related disability conditions). Homeowners in the bottom income quartile were found to be three times more likely than those in the top income quartile to switch from owning to renting.[30]

Mishkin (2007b) argues that central banks with supervisory authority can reduce the likelihood of bubbles forming through prudential supervision of the financial system. But Girouard, Kennedy, van den Noord and André (2006) suggest that the reaction of central bankers to housing price inflation will necessarily usually depend on the treatment of housing costs in the inflation measures being used by central banks. Among other reasons, the official mandates of central banks typically focus on managing *measured* inflation.

In the past, house price bubbles tended to be mostly local. However, the central bank task of controlling housing market inflation has taken on international importance by now. Though there is little international trade in housing services, housing is part of household wealth which also comprises internationally traded assets. The IMF (2004, chapter 2) concludes that house prices became relatively more synchronized beginning in the 1990s. Estrella (2002) points out that a higher level of securitization linked the mortgage market more closely to broader capital markets. Shiller (2007) writes that, "While home price booms have been known for centuries, the recent boom is unique in its pervasiveness." If separate CPI components for rental and owner occupied housing were monitored on an ongoing basis, this would help identify aberrant housing market conditions.

Barack Obama and Joe Biden (2008, p. 13) have pledged to give the Federal Reserve greater oversight over a broader array of financial institutions. They write that the nature of such oversight should be commensurate with the degree and extent of taxpayer exposure and should

---

[30] See also Wolff and Zacharias (2008) regarding damage to lower income households with loans secured against their homes.

include liquidity and capital requirements. We believe that an important addition to this pledge should be to give the BLS, BEA and Census Bureau the funds and the mandate to aggressively develop proper measures of inflation for owner occupied housing services.

Central banks and national governments, in fact, already have many policy instruments at their disposal that they could use, in the future, to control inflation in housing markets. What they lack are appropriate *measures* of inflation in the market for owner occupied housing services. The proposed new opportunity cost measure builds on the achievements of the U.S. official statistics system in producing a high quality rental equivalence measure. Augmenting this measure as proposed for the new opportunity cost approach for accounting for OOH in a CPI will not be simple or cheap. However, the current financial crisis makes it clear that the costs of *not* having an adequate measure for inflation in the cost of owner occupied housing services can be far greater.

References

Bajari, P., C.L. Benkard and J. Krainer (2003), "House Prices and Consumer Welfare," NBER Working Paper No. W9783. http://ssrn.com/abstract=418285

Baldwin, A., A.O. Nakamura and M. Prud'homme (2006/2011), "Different Concepts for Measuring Owner Occupied Housing Costs in a CPI: Statistics Canada's Analytical Series," presented at an OECD-IMF Workshop in London England. Published now as chapter 10, pp. 151-160 in Diewert, W.E., B.M. Balk, D. Fixler, K.J. Fox and A.O. Nakamura (2011), *PRICE AND PRODUCTIVITY MEASUREMENT: Volume 1 -- Housing*. Trafford Press.

Bauer, A., N. Haltom, and W. Peterman (2004), "Examining Contributions to Core Consumer Inflation Measures," working paper 2004-7, Federal Reserve Bank of Atlanta. http://www.frbatlanta.org/filelegacydocs/wp0407.pdf

Bernanke, B.S. (2008), "Outstanding Issues in the Analysis of Inflation," presented June 9, 2008 at the Federal Reserve Bank of Boston's 53rd Annual Economic Conference, Chatham, Massachusetts.

Bureau of Labor Statistics (BLS). See U.S. Bureau of Labor Statistics.

Capozza, D. and P. Seguin (1995/1996), Expectations, Efficiency and Euphoria in the Housing Market, Working Paper No.5179, NBER Working Paper Series, Cambridge, Mass.: National Bureau of Economic Research. Published in *Regional Science and Urban Economics* 26, 369-385.

Carson, J.G. (2006), "Is It Time to Change the Method?" published in *Business Economics* as part of a symposium of papers by J. Carson, D. Johnson and C. Steindel that were originally presented at the September 2005 annual meeting of the National Association for Business Economics in a session on the treatment of owner-occupied housing in the Consumer Price Index. http://www.springerlink.com/content/485n68uv9711077m/

Cecchetti, S. (2007), "Housing in Inflation Measurement," http://www.voxeu.org/index.php?q=node/248

Central Statistics Office Ireland (2003), "House Prices and the Consumer Price Index: Explanatory Note," http://www.cso.ie/surveysandmethodologies/surveys/prices/documents/houseprices&cpi.pdf

Christensen, A.-K., J. Dupont and P. Schreyer (2005), "International Comparability of the Consumer Price Index: Owner-Occupied Housing," presented at the OECD Seminar, "Inflation Measures: Too High -- Too Low -- Internationally Comparable? Paris 21-22, June.

Christensen, L.R. and D.W. Jorgenson (1969), "The Measurement of U.S. Real Capital Input, 1929-1967," *Review of Income and Wealth* 15, 293-320.

Christensen, L.R. and D.W. Jorgenson (1973), "Measuring the Performance of the Private Sector of the U.S. Economy, 1929-1969," in M. Moss (ed.), *Measuring Economic and Social Performance*, Columbia University Press, 233-351.

Corrado, C., C. Hulten and D Sichel (2005), "Measuring Capital and Technology: An Expanded Framework," in C. Corrado, J. Haltiwanger and D. Sichel (eds.), *Measuring Capital in the New Economy*, University of Chicago Press, 11-45.

Crone, T.M., L.I. Nakamura, and R.P. Voith (2008), "Rents Have Been Rising, Not Falling, in the Postwar Period," *Review of Economics and Statistics*, forthcoming.

Crone, T.M., L.I. Nakamura and R.P. Voith (2011), "Hedonic Estimates of the Cost of Housing Services: Rental and Owner Occupied Units," chapter 4, pp. 51-68 in Diewert, W.E., B.M. Balk, D. Fixler, K.J. Fox and A.O. Nakamura (2011), *PRICE AND PRODUCTIVITY MEASUREMENT: Volume 1 -- Housing*. Trafford Press.

Diewert, W.E. (1974), "Intertemporal Consumer Theory and the Demand for Durables," *Econometrica* 42, 497-516.

Diewert, W.E. (1980), "Aggregation Problems in the Measurement of Capital", in D. Usher (ed.), *The Measurement of Capital*, University of Chicago Press, 433-528.

Diewert, W.E. (2002), "Harmonized Indexes of Consumer Prices: Their Conceptual Foundations," *Swiss Journal of Economics and Statistics* 138, 547-637. http://www.econ.ubc.ca/diewert/harindex.pdf

Diewert, W.E. (2003), "The Treatment of Owner Occupied Housing and Other Durables in a Consumer Price Index," Discussion Paper 03-08, Department of Economics, University of British Columbia. http://www.econ.ubc.ca/discpapers/dp0308.pdf. Forthcoming in W.E. Diewert, J. Greenless and C. Hulten (eds.), *Price Index Concepts and Measurement,* NBER Studies in Income and Wealth, University of Chicago Press.

Diewert, W.E. (2005a), "The Measurement of Business Capital, Income and Performance," a tutorial presented at the University Autonoma of Barcelona, Spain, September 21-22, 2005. http://www.econ.ubc.ca/diewert/barcelona.htm

Diewert, W.E. (2005b), "Issues in the Measurement of Capital Services, Depreciation, Asset Price Changes and Interest Rates", pp. 479-542 in *Measuring Capital in the New Economy*, C. Corrado, J. Haltiwanger and D. Sichel (eds.), Chicago: University of Chicago Press.

Diewert, W.E., (2006/2011), The Paris OECD-IMF Workshop on Real Estate Price Indexes: Conclusions and future Directions. Paper presented at the OECD-IMF Workshop on Real Estate Price Indexes held in Paris, 6-7 November 2006. http://www.econ.ubc.ca/diewert/dp0701.pdf Published as Diewert, W.E. (2011), "The Paris OECD-IMF Workshop on Real Estate Price Indexes: Conclusions and Future Directions," chapter 6, pp. 87-116 in Diewert, W.E., B.M. Balk, D. Fixler, K.J. Fox and A.O. Nakamura (2011), *PRICE AND PRODUCTIVITY MEASUREMENT: Volume 1 -- Housing*. Trafford Press.

Diewert, W.E. and K.J. Fox (1999), "Can Measurement Error Explain the Productivity Paradox?" Canadian Journal of Economics 32, 251-280, 1999. http://www.econ.ubc.ca/diewert/dfcje.pdf

Diewert, W.E. and D.A. Lawrence (2000), "Progress in Measuring the Price and Quantity of Capital," in L. J. Lau (ed.), *Econometrics Volume 2: Econometrics and the cost of Capital: Essays in Honor of Dale W. Jorgenson*, MIT Press, 273-326.

Diewert, W.E. and F.C. Wykoff (2011), "Depreciation, Deterioration and Obsolescence when there is Embodied or Disembodied Technical Change," forthcoming in Diewert, W.E., B.M. Balk, D. Fixler, K.J. Fox and A.O. Nakamura (2011), *PRICE AND PRODUCTIVITY MEASUREMENT: Volume 8 -- Capital and Income*, Trafford Press. Also available at http://www.econ.ubc.ca/diewert/dp0602.pdf

Dougherty, A. and R. Van Order (1982), "Inflation, housing cost and the consumer price index," American Economic Review, 72, 154-165.

Eiglsperger, M. (2006), "The Treatment of Owner-Occupied Housing in the Harmonised Index of Consumer Prices," presented at the workshop on "CPI Measurement: Central Banks Views and Concerns," Bank for International Settlements in Basel, Switzerland.

Erdur, S. and M. Prud'Homme (2007), "Current Research and Practices for Estimating House Price Indices at Statistics Canada: A Note," presented at the Ottawa Group 2007 meetings held October 10-12 in Ottawa, Canada.

Estrella, A. (2002), "Securitization and the Efficacy of Monetary Policy," Federal Reserve Bank of New York, *Economic Policy Review* 9 (May), 243-255.

European Communities (2004), *HARMONIZED INDICES OF CONSUMER PRICES (HICPs): A SHORT GUIDE.* http://epp.eurostat.ec.europa.eu/portal/page?_pageid=2714,1,2714_61582099&_dad=portal&_schema=PORTAL#GUIDE

Farlow, A. (2005), "UK House Prices, Consumption and GDP, in A Global Context," working paper, Department of Economics and Oriel College, University of Oxford. http://www.econ.ox.ac.uk/members/andrew.farlow/Farlow%20Housing%20and%20Consumption.pdf

Fisher, I. (1897), "The Role of Capital in Economic Theory," *Economic Journal* 7, 341-367.

Garner, T.I. and K.S. Short (2008), "Micro and Macro Estimates of Owner-Occupied Dwelling Services in the U.S.: Can They Be Reconciled?" presented in Plenary Session 5, 30th General Conference of the International Association for Research in Income and Wealth, Portoroz, Slovenia, August 24-30, 2008.

Garner, T.I. and R. Verbrugge (2011), "The Puzzling Divergence of Rents and User Costs, 1980-2004: Summary and Extensions," chapter 8, pp. 125-146 in Diewert, W.E., B.M. Balk, D. Fixler, K.J. Fox and A.O. Nakamura (2011), *PRICE AND PRODUCTIVITY MEASUREMENT: Volume 1 -- Housing*. Trafford Press.

Genesove, D. (2003), "The Nominal Rigidity of Apartment Rents," *Review of Economics and Statistics* 85 (November), 844-853

Gillingham, R. (1980), "Estimating the User Cost of Owner-occupied Housing," *Monthly Labor Review* 103 (February), 31-35.

Gillingham, R. and W. Lane (1982), "Changing the Treatment of Shelter Costs for Homeowners in the CPI," *Monthly Labor Review* 105 (June 1982), 9-14.

Gordon, R.J. and T. van Goethem (2004), "A Century of Downward Bias in the Most Important Component of the CPI: The Case of Rental Shelter, 1914-2003," forthcoming in E.R. Berndt and C.R. Hulten (eds.), *Hard-to-Measure Goods and Services: Essays in Memory of Zvi Griliches*, Studies in Income and Wealth No. 67, University of Chicago Press. http://faculty-web.at.northwestern.edu/economics/gordon/p360_forpub_040729.pdf

Girouard, N., M. Kennedy, P. van den Noord and C. André (2006), "Recent House Price Developments: The Role of Fundamentals", paper presented at the OECD-IMF Workshop on Real Estate Price Indexes, Paris, November 6-7. http://www.oecd.org/dataoecd/3/6/37583208.pdf

Greenlees, J.S. (2003). "U. S. Consumer Price Index: Changes in the Cost of Shelter," presentation at Brookings Workshop on Economic Measurement, May 23, 2003. http://www.brookings.edu/es/research/projects/productivity/workshops/20030523_summary.pdf

Griliches, Z. (1963), "Capital Stock in Investment Functions: Some Problems of Concept and Measurement", pp. 115-137 in *Measurement in Economics*, Stanford California: Stanford University Press; reprinted as pp. 123-143 in *Technology, Education and Productivity*, Z. Griliches (ed.), (1988), Oxford: Basil Blackwell.

Guðnason, R. (2005a), "How Do We Measure Inflation?" Statistics Iceland, http://www.statice.is/lisalib/getfile.aspx?itemid=4377

Guðnason, R. (2005b), "Market Prices and User Cost," presented at the OECD Seminar, "Inflation Measures: Too High -- Too Low -- Internationally Comparable? Paris 21-22 June 2005. http://www.oecd.org/dataoecd/54/39/35013825.pdf

Guðnason, R. and G. Jónsdóttir (2011), "The Icelandic CPI House Price Index," chapter 9, pp. 147-150 in Diewert, W.E., B.M. Balk, D. Fixler, K.J. Fox and A.O. Nakamura (2011), *PRICE AND PRODUCTIVITY MEASUREMENT: Volume 1 -- Housing*. Trafford Press.

Harvard University Joint Center for Housing Studies (2008), *The State of the Nation's Housing 2008*. http://www.jchs.harvard.edu/publications/markets/son2008/son2008.pdf

Heston, A. and A.O. Nakamura (2011), "Questions About the Treatment of Owner Occupied Housing in Spatial and Temporal Price Indexes and in National Accounts," chapter 7, pp. 117-124 in Diewert, W.E., B.M. Balk, D. Fixler, K.J. Fox and A.O. Nakamura (2011), *PRICE AND PRODUCTIVITY MEASUREMENT: Volume 1 -- Housing*. Trafford Press.

Hicks, J.R. (1939), *Value and Capital*, Clarendon Press (2nd edition 1946).

Hill, R.J. and T.P. Hill (2003), "Expectations, Capital Gains and Income," *Economic Inquiry* 41, 607-619.

Hill, T.P. (1999), "Capital Stocks, Capital Services and Depreciation," paper presented at the third meeting of the Canberra Group on Capital Stock Statistics, Washington, D.C..

Hill, T.P. (2000), "Economic Depreciation and the SNA"; paper presented at the 26th Conference of the International Association for Research on Income and Wealth, Cracow, Poland.

Hill, T.P. (2005), "Depreciation in National Accounts", Canberra II Group on Capital Measurement paper, March.

Hoffmann, J. and J.-R. Kurz-Kim (2006), "Consumer Price Adjustment under the Microscope: Germany in a Period of Low Inflation," Discussion Paper Series 1, Economic Studies, No 16/2006, Deutsche Bundesbank, Wilhelm-Epstein-Strasse 14, 60431, Postfach 10 06 02, 60006, Frankfurt am Main.

Hulten, C.R. and F.C. Wykoff (1981a), "The Estimation of Economic Depreciation Using Vintage Asset Prices", *Journal of Econometrics* 15, 367-396.

Hulten, C.R. and F.C. Wykoff (1981b), "The Measurement of Economic Depreciation", in C.R. Hulten (ed.), *Depreciation, Inflation and the Taxation of Income from Capital*, Urban Institute Press, 81-125.

Hulten, C.R. and F.C. Wykoff (1996), "Issues in the Measurement of Economic Depreciation: Introductory Remarks," *Economic Inquiry* 34, 10-23.

ILO, IMF, OECD, UNECE, Eurostat and the World Bank (2004), "Consumer Price Index Manual: Theory and Practice," Geneva. http://www.ilo.org/public/english/bureau/stat/guides/cpi/index.htm

IMF (2004), *World Economic Outlook The Global Demographic Transition* September 2004. http://www.imf.org/external/pubs/ft/weo/2004/02/

Johnson, D.S. (2006), "Is It Time to Change the Method?" published in *Business Economics* as part of a symposium of papers by J. Carson, D. Johnson and C. Steindel that were originally presented at the September 2005 annual meeting of the National Association for Business Economics in a session on the treatment of owner-occupied housing in the Consumer Price Index. http://www.springerlink.com/content/485n68uv9711077m/

Jorgenson, D.W. (1963), "Capital Theory and Investment Behavior," *American Economic Review* 53 (2) May, 247-259.

Jorgenson, D.W. (1967), "The Theory of Investment Behaviour," in R. Ferber (ed.), *Determinants of Investment Behaviour*, National Bureau of Economic Research, 129-155.

Jorgenson, D.W. and Z. Griliches (1967), "The Explanation of Productivity Change," *Review of Economic Studies* 34, 249-283.

Jorgenson, D.W. and Z. Griliches (1972), "Issues in Growth Accounting: A Reply to Edward F. Denison," *Survey of Current Business* 52 (4), Part II (May), 65-94.

Jud, G.D. and D.T. Winkler (2005), "Returns to Single-Family Owner-Occupied Housing," *Journal of Real Estate Practice and Education* 8 (1), 25-44.

Katz, A.J. (1982), "The Value of Services Provided by the Stock of Consumer Durables, 1947-79: Alternative User Cost Measures," in BEA Working Paper No. 2: *Measuring Nonmarket Economic Activity*, National Technical Information Service, December, Accession No. PB 83-167-395.

Katz, A.J. (1983), "Valuing the Services of Consumer Durables," *Review of Income and Wealth*, Series 29, December, 405-427.

Katz, A.J. (2011), "Estimating Dwelling Services in the Candidate Countries: Theoretical and Practical Considerations in Developing Methodologies Based on a User Cost of Capital Measure," chapter 3, pp. 33-50 in Diewert, W.E., B.M. Balk, D. Fixler, K.J. Fox and A.O. Nakamura (2011), *PRICE AND PRODUCTIVITY MEASUREMENT: Volume 1 -- Housing*. Trafford Press.

Katz, A.J. and J. Peskin (1980), "The Value of Services Provided by the Stock of Consumer Durables, 1947-77: An Opportunity Cost Measure," *Survey of Current Business* 60, July, 22-31.

Martin, F.D., J.S. Landefeld, and J. Peskin (1984), "The Value of Services Provided by the Stock of Government-Owned Fixed Capital in the United States, 1948-79," *Review of Income and Wealth, Series 30*, September, 331-349.

Mayer, C.J. and G.V. Engelhardt (1996): "Gifts, Down Payments, and Housing Affordability," *Journal of Housing Research* 7 (1), 59-77.

Mayerhauser, N. and M. Reinsdorf (2007), "Housing Services in the National Economic Accounts," http://www.bea.gov/papers/pdf/RIPfactsheet.pdf

McCully, C. (2006), "The PCE Price Index: Core Issues," BEA Advisory Committee Meeting, November 3, 2006. http://www.bea.gov/about/pdf/1106_ACM_PCE.pdf

Mian, A. and A. Sufi (2008), "The Consequences of Mortgage Credit Expansion: Evidence from the 2007 Mortgage Default Crisis," working paper, Chicago Graduate School of Business.

Mishkin, F.S. (2007a) "Headline versus Core Inflation in the Conduct of Monetary Policy," delivered on October 20, 2007 at the *Business Cycles, International Transmission and Macroeconomic Policies Conference*, HEC Montreal, Montreal, Canada.

Mishkin, F.S. (2007b), "Housing and the Monetary Transmission Mechanism." Prepared for Federal Reserve Bank of Kansas City's 2007 Jackson Hole Symposium, Jackson Hole, Wyoming.

Obama, B. and J. Biden (2008), *BLUEPRINT FOR CHANGE: Obama and Biden's Plan for America*. http://www.scribd.com/doc/7732794/Obama-Blueprint-for-Change

OECD (2001a), *Measuring Productivity: Measurement of Aggregate and Industry-Level Productivity Growth*, OECD.

OECD (2001b), *Measuring Capital: Measurement of Capital Stocks, Consumption of Fixed Capital and Capital Services*, OECD.

Ptacek. F. and R. Baskin (1996), "Revision of The CPI Housing Sample and Estimators." *Monthly Labor Review*. December, 31-39.

Poole, R., F. Ptacek and R. Verbrugge (2005), "Treatment of Owner-Occupied Housing in the CPI," presented to the Federal Economic Statistics Advisory Committee (FESAC) on December 9, 2005. http://www.bls.gov/bls/fesacp1120905.pdf

Rich, R.W., and C. Steindel (2007), "A Comparison of Measures of Core Inflation," Federal Reserve Bank of New York, *Economic Policy Review* 13 (December).

Robb, G. (2006), "Housing Slowdown Behind Rise in Inflation," *MarketWatch* May. http://www.marketwatch.com/news/story/higher-rents-driving-rise-core/story.aspx?guid=%7B06FC27E0-AFD4-4555-86A6-B74788186F41%7D

Smeeding, T., P. Saunders, J. Coder, S. Jenkins, J. Fritzell, A.J.M. Haganaars, R. Hauser, and M. Wolfson (1993), "Poverty , Inequality, and Family Living Standards Impacts across Seven Nations: The Effect of Non-cash Subsidies for Health, Education, and Housing," The Review of Income and Wealth, 39(3), 229-256.

Shiller, R.J. (2007), "Understanding Recent Trends in House Prices and Home Ownership," presented at "Housing, Housing Finance, and Monetary Policy," based on a presentation at a symposium sponsored by the Federal Reserve Bank of Kansas City in Jackson Hole, Wyoming, August 30-September 1, 2007. http://www.macromarkets.com/about_us/publications/real_estate/shiller_jacksonhole.pdf

Sinai, T.M. and N.S. Souleles (2003), "Owner-Occupied Housing as a Hedge Against Rent Risk," *FRB Philadelphia Working Paper No. 05-10*.

Statistics Canada (1995), "The Consumer Price Index Reference Paper: Update based on 1992 expenditures," Catalogue 62-553 Occasional. http://www.statcan.ca/english/sdds/document/2301_D4_T9_V1_B.pdf

Statistics Canada (2007), Consumer Price Index (CPI): Detailed information for May 2007, http://www.statcan.ca/cgi-bin/imdb/p2SV.pl?Function=getSurvey&SDDS=2301&lang=en&db=IMDB&dbg=f&adm=8&dis=2

Statistics New Zealand (2006), "Consumers Price Index Review" September 2006 (revised), http://www2.stats.govt.nz/domino/external/pasfull/pasfull.nsf/4c2567ef00247c6a4c2567be0008d2f8/4c2567ef00247c6acc257203001390a4?OpenDocument

Stigler, G.J. (1961), *The Price Statistics of the Federal Government*, National Bureau of Economic Research.

U.S. Bureau of Labor Statistics (BLS), U.S. Department of Labor (1983), *Trends in Multifactor Productivity, 1948-81,* Bulletin 2178, September.

U.S. Bureau of Labor Statistics (BLS) (2007), "Consumer Price Indexes for Rent and Rental Equivalence," http://www.bls.gov/cpi/cpifact6.htm.

Verbrugge, R. (2008), "The Puzzling Divergence of Rents and User Costs, 1980-2004," *Review of Income and Wealth* 54 (4), 671-699.

Wolff, E.N. and A. Zacharias (2008), "Accounting for Wealth in the Measurement of Household Income," forthcoming in Diewert, W.E., B.M. Balk, D. Fixler, K.J. Fox and A.O. Nakamura (2011), *PRICE AND PRODUCTIVITY MEASUREMENT: Volume 3 -- Services*, Trafford Press.

Wood, G.A., R. Watson and J. Yates (1998), "Transaction Costs, Taxation and Gross Rental Yields in Private Rental Housing," Working Paper No. 172, Economics Department, Murdoch University.

Chapter 3

ESTIMATING DWELLING SERVICES IN THE CANDIDATE COUNTRIES: THEORETICAL AND PRACTICAL CONSIDERATIONS IN DEVELOPING METHODOLOGIES BASED ON A USER COST OF CAPITAL MEASURE

Arnold J. Katz[1]

1.   Introduction

Within the European Union, the standard method for evaluating owner-occupied dwelling services in the national accounts has been the stratification variant of the rental equivalence approach. Unfortunately, this method could not be satisfactorily implemented by many of the candidate countries from Eastern Europe that were acceding to membership in the European Union in the late 1990s. Their implementation problems are rooted in the reality that some of these countries had, and still have, small private rental sectors that are not representative of the overall housing market. This paper discusses an alternative method for evaluating these dwelling services based on the user cost of capital measure that was developed by a Eurostat task force.

The paper is organized as follows. First, the background to the task force is given. Next, the theory behind the user cost method is described. Then, a short history of the method used by U.S. statistical agencies is given. Initial considerations and empirical recommendations for evaluating dwelling services are presented in sections 3-9. Section 10 offers lessons learned and modifications to the initial recommendations. In the concluding section of the paper, the author shares his views on the project taken up by the task force. A mathematical appendix is also provided that shows the formal derivation of the user cost measure.

2.   Background

Because official measures of GDP and other aggregates are used in formulating economic policy and to determine transfers for member countries within the European Union (EU), the European Commission (EC) tries to ensure that the national accounts of Member States (MS) are

---

[1] The author is with the U.S. Bureau of Economic Analysis (BE-54) and can be reached at arnold.katz@bea.gov. The views expressed are solely the author's and do not necessarily reflect those of the Bureau of Economic Analysis or the U.S. Department of Commerce.

Katz, A.J. (2011), "Estimating Dwelling Services in the Candidate Countries: Theoretical and Practical Considerations in Developing Methodologies Based on a User Cost of Capital Measure," chapter 3, pp. 33-50 in W.E. Diewert, B.M. Balk, D. Fixler, K.J. Fox and A.O. Nakamura (2011), *PRICE AND PRODUCTIVITY MEASUREMENT: Volume 1 -- Housing.* Trafford Press.

estimated using comparable methodologies. To this end, in 1995, the EC issued a detailed statement on how dwelling services in all Member States are to be measured using the so-called "stratification method."[2] This method essentially involves dividing the stock of dwellings of a country into various strata, sampling the actual rents paid for dwellings currently being rented to estimate the average rent paid in each stratum per rented dwelling, and valuing the dwelling services of all units in a given stratum (including owner-occupied dwellings) by the product of the number of dwelling units in the stratum and its estimated average rent per unit. A similar methodology is used in the United States. There, rents are imputed to owner-occupied dwellings by dividing the stock of dwellings into strata based on dwelling value, determining the average rent to value ratio for comparable units (in the same value class) that are actually rented out and multiplying these ratios by the total value of the owner-occupied units in the stratum.

In 1998, there were thirteen countries that were candidates to join the European Union. These candidate countries (CCs) consisted of: Bulgaria, Cyprus, the Czeck Republic, Estonia, Hungary, Latvia, Lithuania, Malta, Poland, Romania, the Slovak Republic, Slovenia, and Turkey. CCs are required to comply with all EU legislation including the Commission Decision on Dwelling Services (CD). Eurostat organized two projects to assist the CCs with their estimates. The first was the A8 Dwelling Services Project (A8 hereafter), which existed between October 1998 and May 2000. Its initial goal was to provide technical assistance to national statistical offices for implementing the stratification method. This goal was later abandoned because it became clear that there were a number of fundamental reasons why CCs are not able to comply. Having abandoned the goal of stratification, the project gave an overview of the estimation methods and data sources that are currently in use in the CCs, considered various methodological problems, and recommended improvements for some of the CCs.

The work that A8 started was carried forward by the Dwelling Services Task Force, which operated between June 2000 and September 2000. This task force sought to find alternative approaches to the stratification method.[3]

The first task was to determine when the stratification method would be inappropriate for a country. The recommendation was that: "In the case of privately rented dwellings constituting less than 10% of the total dwelling stock by number *and* where there is a large disparity between private and other paid rents (say, by a factor of three), as an alternative objective assessment, the user-cost method may be applied," (European Commission 2001, p. 68).

The task force examined the two recognized alternatives to the stratification method: self-assessment and user cost. Self-assessment was ruled out as too subjective. This left user cost as the only viable measure. Hence the task force put most of its effort into specifying a user cost measure that is consistent with the requirements of the CD.

---

[2] See the Commission Decision of 18 July 1995 specifying the principles for estimating dwelling services for the purpose of implementing Article 1 of Council Directive 89/130/EEC, Euratom on the harmonization of the compilation of gross national product at market prices (95/309/EC, Euratom), OJ No L 186, 5.8 1995, p. 59 (http://europa.eu.int/eur-lex/en/lif/dat/1995/en_395D0309.html).

[3] The Dwelling Services Task Force was an initiative of Eurostat Units B1 and B2 and reported to the National Accounts Working Party. Eurostat Unit B3 was also interested in the issue because dwelling services have been a problem for the work on the Harmonized Index of Consumer Prices and Purchasing Power Parities. Rather than set up its own separate task force, Eurostat B3 joined the one reporting to the National Accounts Working Party. Thus this Dwelling Service Task Force sought to provide solutions that would accommodate the combined needs of the interested Eurostat units that had been instrumental in its creation. For related technical issues, see Diewert (2002).

The task force noted that the user cost approach reverses the normal accounting procedure and builds up output from its components. Thus, gross rentals equal the sum of intermediate consumption, consumption of fixed capital (CFC), compensation of employees (which is zero for owner occupiers), other (net) taxes on production, and the net operating surplus. The task force recommended that as many of the cost elements as possible should be valued by direct measurement. Where there are imputations rather than measurements, these should be based on standardized assumptions to ensure comparability of results. To better estimate CFC, as soon as possible, the CCs should establish perpetual inventory models (see footnote 9 of this chapter) for estimating CFC for dwellings and these should be partitioned into the owner-occupied and public and privately paid rental sectors. The net operating surplus should not be set to zero. Instead, the task force recommended that this should be:

> "… calculated as a rate of return applied to a market valuation of the owner-occupied dwelling stock based on the adjusted current replacement cost method. The rate of return should be based on as much empirical evidence as possible and ideally should represent an average rate typically obtained from the application of similar productive assets in the most similar activities,"
>
> (European Commission 2001, p. 73).

The "Task force on estimation methods for dwelling services in the Candidate Countries," was also formed to define a user cost approach and to consider practical options for its implementation by the CCs. It functioned from November 2001 through July 2002. [4]

After an initial meeting of the experts, a questionnaire was sent to the central statistical offices of the participating CCs to determine what data they had available that could be used to implement a user cost measure. Taking account of the data realities, several methodologies were developed that could be used to estimate user cost measures of the rental value of owner-occupied housing. One of the major constraints on the task force's work was that it was necessary for every participating country to be able to implement at least one of the proposed methodologies. Draft templates for the proposed methodologies were developed that gave detailed step-by-step instructions for making the empirical calculations. The suitability of the draft templates was discussed and agreed to by the participating countries at the first meeting of the task force. The participating countries then produced experimental estimates for the period 1997-2000 using the templates. Estimates were also made using several different assumptions about the rate of return and the rate of depreciation of dwellings so that a sensitivity analysis could be conducted. These estimates were presented at the second meeting of the task force. At that meeting, some problems were identified (particularly with the estimation of the net operating surplus) and solutions were recommended. The templates were revised to reflect the solutions and participating countries used the revised templates to make new experimental calculations.

---

[4] It was an initiative of Eurostat Units B1 and B2 and reported to the National Accounts Working Party. The aim was to develop practical methods and have participating CCs carry out experimental calculations. The Czech Republic, Hungary, Poland, Slovak Republic and Slovenia were involved. The task force was led by Roger Akers. After its final meeting, he was replaced by Mojca Skrlec Sinkovec. Arnold J. Katz prepared the templates that formed the basis of the empirical work and served as the principal expert. Mr. Norbert Hartmann, Mr. Seppo Varjonen, Ms. Silke Stapel, and experts from the participating CCs also made important contributions. A final report, Eurostat B1 (2002), was presented at the Regional Coordinator's Workshop of the International Comparison Program 2003-2005 held in Luxembourg, March 24-28, as were the template and associated notes and a paper by Katz (2003a, 2003b) on the theory and application of the user cost measure. This paper draws on this material.

3.   The User Cost Measure in Theory

The "user cost of capital" measure is based on the fundamental equation of capital theory. This equation, which applies equally to both financial and non-financial assets, has been known since at least the middle of the 19th century. It states that in equilibrium, the price of an asset will equal the present discounted value of the future net income that is expected to be derived from owning it. For non-financial assets, the relevant "net income" consists of the net rental income that would be obtained from renting out the durable. When durables are used by their owners rather than rented out, the value of their services represents costs that are implicitly incurred by their owner users, i.e., this value represents the opportunity costs of forgoing the receipt of the rental income. As shown in the appendix to this paper, the fundamental equation can be easily manipulated to obtain the traditional user cost of capital measure, which expresses the implicit rental value of a durable good as the sum of depreciation, a real net operating surplus, and various operating costs.

There are three relevant theoretical points that are the source of some controversy.

Point 1 arises because, as shown in the appendix, the traditional version of the user cost formula is derived by assuming that all of a durable's services are received on the last day of the income period (generally a year). Elsewhere I have argued that to make the user cost measure more consistent with the principles used in national economic accounting, one should assume that equal quantities of a durable's services are received in every fraction of the year. When this is done, the user cost measure is approximately equal to the traditional expression (given in equation (A4) of the appendix) divided by the square root of one plus the nominal rate of return, which is the value obtained by assuming that all services are received on the mid-day of the year. Thus, it yields estimates that are smaller than those obtained using equation (A4).

Although Diewert (2003) recently discussed some related questions, there does not appear to have been any further discussion on this point.[5] Thus, given that the expression in equation (A4) has become standard in the literature, the task force decided to avoid this controversy and carried out all practical work with the traditional version of the user cost measure that assumes that all of a durable's services are received at the end of the income period.

Point 2 also has to do with the proper measure of depreciation (or consumption of fixed capital as it is now termed in most of the literature on national economic accounting). The change in the market value of a durable from the beginning of the income period to the end of the period can be partitioned into depreciation and capital gains components. The depreciation component measures the difference in price between the given durable and an identical one that is one year older, both prices being measured at the same point in time.[6] Recently, Hill (1999) coined the term "cross section depreciation" to denote this measure of depreciation and the term "time series depreciation" to denote the entire change in the durable's market value over the course of the income period. Thus, the user cost measure in equation (A4) can be described as

---

[5] See Katz (1982, p. 47) and (1983, p. 408). See also Diewert and Nakamura (2011).

[6] Economists have differed over whether the prices of the durables should be measured as of the beginning of the income period, the end of the period, or at some other time, see Katz (1983, p. 418). Because the annual measure of depreciation that appears in the NIPAs is equal to the sum of the four quarterly estimates, it is effectively measured using prices as of the middle of the year.

being equal to the sum of the real net operating surplus (the nominal net operating surplus less the expected capital gain on the durable) plus cross section depreciation. Equivalently, it can also be described as consisting of the nominal net operating surplus plus time series depreciation. The question of whether economic depreciation should be measured by the time series or the cross section measure was debated extensively in the 1930s and 1940s. For the past 50 years, most national accountants have appeared to accept the cross section measure, which is essentially depreciation at current replacement cost, as the appropriate measure for national accounting. However, recently some have challenged that and advocated the use of the time series measure.[7]

While not really a source of controversy with respect to estimating dwelling costs, a third theoretical point needs to be stressed as well. User costs include such operating costs as expenditures on maintenance and repair. These expenditures have been part of mathematical models of user costs since at least the time of Hotelling (1925) and their interaction with other factors that affect depreciation is stressed by Faucett (1980). Their inclusion in estimates of dwelling costs is obvious to most national income accountants because, when dwellings are actually rented out, the residual entrepreneurial income is estimated after these expenditures are subtracted out. In short, maintenance and repair expenditures are often a substitute for purchases of new capital goods. Estimates of capital input and output should be largely independent of whether such expenditures are capitalized or not. However, it appears that these expenditures are often omitted from estimates of capital input and not treated as an input at all in various estimates of aggregate production functions.

The method for estimating constant-price values with the user cost measure is now standard in the literature. In a paper written for the U.S. Bureau of Economic Analysis (BEA) of the U.S. Department of Commerce, Wykoff (1980) pointed out that the Jorgensonian user cost measure of capital services can be described as the product of a quantity of capital services and a (unit) price of capital services. The latter consists of the product of the price of the capital good and an expression equal to the nominal rate of return plus the rate of depreciation less the expected rate of capital gain in the durable's price. Thus, rates of return are treated like prices and the standard way to express the measure in constant prices is to use the service price in the base year and the quantities for each given year.

4.   Historical Application of the User Cost Measure by U.S. Statistical Agencies

In conjunction with a number of collaborators, Jorgenson has shown how the user cost measure could be employed to develop a set of capital accounts for each vintage of asset. The most complete exposition of how such accounts could be integrated into a national accounting framework is found in Christensen and Jorgenson (1973). The Bureau of Labor Statistics (BLS) of the U.S. Department of Labor adopted a variant of the user cost measure of capital services in its work on measuring multifactor productivity (see BLS 1983). Here capital services are measured in constant prices. This finesses the problem of having to develop a theoretically correct current-price measure of these services that does not suffer from excessive volatility.

---

[7] Diewert (2005a, 2005b) cites Hill (1999, 2000) on the use of times series depreciation for national accounting.

In the mid 1970's, the BLS attempted to develop a measure of dwelling services based on the user cost measure for use in its consumer price index. This attempt was unsuccessful. The large changes in the real own rate of return for dwellings in the 1970's undoubtedly played a major role in the inability to obtain a current-price measure that was not excessively volatile.[8]

5. Initial Considerations and Recommendations for Measuring Dwelling Services

When dwelling services are estimated with the user cost measure, exactly what costs should be counted? The answer to this basic question is straightforward. The user cost computation is actually the reverse of the usual imputation for dwelling services based on the "stratification" method. With that method, the value of dwelling services is measured by the rents charged for comparable dwellings that are actually rented out. Various associated dwelling costs are then subtracted from this rent to obtain a net operating surplus. With the user cost measure, this calculation is reversed. The net operating surplus is imputed using the opportunity cost principle; i.e., the net operating surplus is imputed on the basis of what owner occupiers could have earned on alternative investments. Then, the dwelling costs that are subtracted in the stratification method are added to the imputed net operating surplus to obtain the imputed rent. These costs include: consumption of fixed capital (CFC) for dwellings, expenditures on ordinary maintenance and repair of dwellings, net premiums on insurance for dwellings, and taxes paid less subsidies received on dwellings and their associated land.

6. Consumption of Fixed Capital

CFC is one of the most important components of the user cost measure. Because it is extremely desirable for the user cost estimates to be consistent with the rest of the national accounts, the task force recommended that if a CC already had an estimate of CFC for owner-occupied dwellings for another part of the accounts, that estimate should be used here. It was recommended that if estimates of CFC on dwellings are not already available, then they should be estimated using the perpetual inventory method (PIM).[9] There are two basic reasons for using

---

[8] BEA also explored the possibility of employing a user cost measure in evaluating the services of consumer durables. Katz (1983) examined the theoretical and empirical issues involved in developing an appropriate measure. Katz (1982) examined how sensitive user cost estimates of the services of consumer durables were to alternative assumptions about expected rates of inflation and patterns of depreciation. Earlier, BEA published a de facto satellite account for the services of consumer durables in Katz and Peskin (1980) that used a crude version of the user cost measure termed an "opportunity cost measure." A similar opportunity cost measure was used at BEA by Martin, Landefeld, and Peskin (1984) in their de facto satellite account for the services of government capital.

[9] For those unfamiliar with the PIM, it can be summarized as follows. Constant-price CFC is estimated by taking the product of the beginning-of-year net stock at constant prices and the depreciation rate and summing it with one-half of the product of constant-price investment in dwellings (of a constant quality) and the depreciation rate. The end-of-year net stock at constant prices is estimated by taking its beginning-of-year value, adding constant-price investment in dwellings, and subtracting constant-price CFC on dwellings. Thus, both CFC and the net stock are essentially weighted averages of past investment. Current-price CFC is estimated by multiplying the constant-price value of CFC by the average value of the appropriate price index for the given year. Current-price net stocks are similarly estimated by multiplying the constant-price value of the net stocks by the end-of-year price index.

the PIM. First, variants on it can be easily constructed so that all CCs can implement it. Second, the nations of Western Europe generally estimate CFC using the PIM and it is desirable to use similar methodologies. Schedules of straight-line declines in prices (equal values of constant-price CFC in each year of an asset's life) were recommended as the preferred variant of the PIM because that appears to be the most prevalent method in Western European countries.

In moving from estimating CFC for a single dwelling to that for the entire stock of dwellings, it is also necessary to take account of three complicating factors. One is that dwellings that enter the stock during the year due to new investment undergo some depreciation during this year. A second is that some goods that are in the stock at the beginning of the year undergo depreciation and are discarded from the stock before the end of the year. And a third is that depreciation takes place continuously during the year rather than on one specific date. It is because of attempts to deal with these factors that CFC in U.S. national accounting is calculated by assuming that new investment depreciates by only half the amount that it would if it had taken place entirely on the first day of the year and CFC is calculated using year-average prices (i.e., average prices during the year).[10] It was recommended that this half-year convention be integrated into the CCs' estimates.

Yet another complicating factor is that the straight-line method is not the easiest method to implement because depreciation rates are different for assets of different ages and all assets are eventually fully depreciated and, consequently, discarded. The straight-line method requires keeping track of accumulated depreciation for each vintage of assets. However, there is little reason for requiring its use given that a simpler alternative exists that can produce results that closely approximate those obtained using it. Specifically, simulations were conducted that showed that total estimates of user costs produced using straight-line depreciation and an approximately normal distribution of service lives around the mean life could be closely approximated by geometric depreciation with a declining-balance rate of 1.6. With this method, the rate of depreciation is held constant over the asset's life; in the first year of an asset's life, it is 1.6 times what it would have been with the straight-line method. Because depreciation rates are made independent of an asset's age, depreciation does not have to be estimated separately for each vintage of assets, which substantially simplifies the calculations.

As noted above, because the data requirements for a PIM using geometric depreciation are so meager and the equations so simple, it was anticipated that all of the CCs would be able to implement the method. All that is required is an initial value of the (net) capital stock in constant prices and series of fixed capital formation for subsequent years in both current and constant prices. The latter series are required to estimate GDP; hence all nations that produce GDP estimates have these. There is still the problem, however, of obtaining the estimate of the initial value of the capital stock.

Because of the general lack of available price data in the CCs, it was necessary to provide specific guidance regarding the proper price indexes for the CFC calculations. In the final instructions, Katz (2003b) pointed out that the appropriate price index is the deflator for gross fixed capital formation (GFCF) for owner-occupied dwellings, i.e., the one used to convert current-price estimates of GFCF to constant-price ones. If this index does not exist, a similar one is to be substituted. The instructions recommend that, in order of their usefulness, possible

---

[10] See OECD (2002, p.96).

alternatives include the deflator for GFCF for all dwellings, the deflator for GFCF for all structures, and an index of relevant construction costs. (For these deflators, the appropriate value is the average annual value.) Note that in the United States, all of the deflators for investment in structures are derived from at most a half dozen unique indexes of construction costs.

It was left up to the individual countries to determine the appropriate average service life for dwellings, which when divided into the assumed rate of declining-balance (1.6) yields the depreciation rate. It was pointed out that some Western European countries use a life of 50 years, which would yield a depreciation rate of 3.2 percent. In contrast, the United States uses a 0.91-declining balance rate for residential structures, which corresponds to a geometric depreciation rate of 1.14 percent for 1-4-unit (new) dwellings and a rate of 1.4 percent for 5-or-more-unit dwellings. The United States uses rates that are more than double these geometric depreciation rates for major replacements and for additions and alterations to dwellings. Perhaps analyses of past censuses would give some indication of what service life assumptions are reasonable.[11]

7.   Net Stock of Dwellings and Associated Land

To estimate the user cost of capital measure, it is necessary to have an estimate of the value of the net stock of owner-occupied dwellings at constant prices for the beginning of the period in which the user cost estimates are to be made. Because it appeared that many of the CCs did not have such estimates and some CCs lacked the data required for the preferred method for estimating net stocks, several alternative methods for obtaining these estimates were recommended. First, if a long time series on fixed capital formation for dwellings in constant prices is available, the stock estimate can be obtained using the PIM and geometric depreciation. This method incorporates the effects of improvements to existing dwellings because these are included in fixed capital formation. It also has the advantage of being consistent with the PIM that is used to estimate CFC, which would ordinarily make this the preferred method. However, the method has disadvantages. In order to be useful in estimating the net stock, the time series on CFC must be very long, i.e., it must cover at least forty years. (Note that the shorter the time series, the more important are errors caused by inaccurate estimates of the initial or seed value of the capital stock.) Given significant war damage or sales or transfers of dwellings between sectors, the series on CFC must be adjusted for these factors. Such adjustments are not easy.

The initial value of the stock of dwellings can also be estimated using the physical inventory method. This method requires physical data on dwellings usually obtained in a census. Fortunately, most CCs appear to have this data. Basically, the method involves placing a value on all dwellings reported in a recent census. The number of existing dwelling units is converted into the number of equivalent new units by adjusting existing units for their age (depreciation) and differences in quality. All units are valued at current prices using a price index for fixed capital formation in dwellings, or if this is unavailable, an index of relevant construction costs.

---

[11] For example, based on the U.S. experience, if one examined census data, one would ordinarily not expect to see significant rates of discard from the cohort of dwellings constructed in a given year until those dwellings had reached about 70 to 80 percent of the appropriate average service life.

The chief difficulty in implementing the physical inventory method is in making proper adjustments for the effects of depreciation. To make such adjustments, two variants of the basic physical inventory method were recommended.

Variant 1 requires data from only the single recent census. However, it also requires that the data on dwelling units be stratified by their year of construction (or age). The requirement will be met if, for example, separate data are available on all dwelling units in the stock that are 0-10 years old, 11-20 years old, etc.

Variant 2 does not require age-stratified data. However, it does require data from a second census conducted at least several decades before the recent one. By assuming constant growth rates for some of the major determinants of the stock, such as the quality and number of units, it is possible to convert the number of units in the recent census from the actual (physical) numbers of units into equivalent numbers of new units. Because this method essentially substitutes assumptions for the actual data used in the first variant, it is less preferred than that method. Both of these variants of the physical inventory method do not have the same problems of dealing with war damage as the PIM estimates do. However, as noted earlier, the stock estimates derived from the PIM reflect the effects of improvements to dwellings while, when the variants of the physical inventory method discussed above are used, these effects would have to be allowed for by explicit quality adjustments to the data.

For both variants of the physical inventory method, it was recommended that adjustments for the effects of age on the value of the stock be made using the same 1.6-declining-balance rate of depreciation that is recommended when the PIM is used. By using the same depreciation rate to value the stock and CFC, the two estimates are made more consistent and estimates of total user costs are less sensitive to alternative assumptions about the service life of dwellings.

It was recommended that wherever possible, the estimates of fixed capital formation that are used in the PIM or the estimates of equivalent numbers of new units that are estimated with the physical inventory method should be adjusted for quality change.

In addition to valuing the stock of dwellings, it is also necessary to value their associated land, i.e., the land that the dwellings sit on and which would be included in their selling price, if they were being sold. (Land can be thought of as a fixed capital good that differs from other fixed capital goods in that it does not suffer any depreciation.) Valuing land, however, is extremely problematical. Even in Western Europe, prices per unit of land in a central city can easily exceed those in rural areas by more than a thousand fold. Where land is taxed, it may be possible to infer the assessed value of the land. Otherwise, rough rules of thumb may have to be used such as assuming that land is a fixed percentage of the value of the dwelling located on it.

8. Other Operating Expenses

All expenses incurred on dwellings should be reflected in the user cost measure of dwelling services. Expenses that are capitalized and included in gross fixed capital formation, such as expenditures on improvements, will be reflected in the estimates of the value of the stock of dwellings and, therefore, in the estimates of the net operating surplus. They will also be reflected in the estimates of CFC. All expenses that are not capitalized need to be treated as other operating expenses and explicitly added to the other components of the user cost measure. These expenses include expenditures on intermediate goods, such as those for ordinary maintenance and repair, net insurance premiums, and taxes less subsidies. Note that if the expenditures on maintenance and repair are of the kind that a tenant would make, they should not be included in the housing imputation but should be measured elsewhere in the accounts together with other expenditures that are not for dwellings. The task force anticipated that there would be little trouble in obtaining data on other operating expenses because this information is generally required to estimate the various accounts according to SNA93 and its European version, ESA95.

Net insurance premiums on dwellings are an important operating expense. This expense does not include insurance on the contents of the dwelling; such insurance is of a kind that a tenant would have and is measured elsewhere in the accounts. Insurance premiums are measured net of any payments received for incurred losses. Strictly speaking, the losses should be measured when they are incurred rather than when they are paid and premiums are measured when they are earned; the losses reflect the relevant insurance company's views about the liability it has incurred as a result of the loss (not the views of the insured about the magnitude of the loss). According to SNA93, the measure should also include premium supplements, which are the expected investment income on technical reserves other than on own assets (of the insurance company); this income should exclude capital gains.[12] Initial indications were that the data required to refine the estimates of insurance may be lacking in the CCs.

The final component of other operating expenses is taxes less subsidies paid. Many countries levy taxes on the value of dwellings and the land they are situated on. These are often referred to as property taxes. Because such taxes are costs that would not be borne by an investor in a financial asset, they represent opportunity costs that need to be included in the user cost measure. Some countries levy taxes on housing services. These taxes would also be added here. Conversely, any subsidies that owner occupiers receive need to be subtracted.

9.   Net Operating Surplus

The most important and problematic component of the user cost of capital measure is the imputed real net operating surplus.[13] This surplus is estimated as the difference between the nominal net surplus received from an investment in an alternative asset and the expected capital gains on the durable itself. It is clear from the derivation of the user cost measure itself that the latter gains are those arising from changes in the price of the durable (when new) and not those from general inflation.

Computationally, the nominal net operating surplus is estimated as the product of an assumed nominal rate of return and the value of the net stock of dwellings and their land. It was recommended that the stock's value be measured as the average of the beginning- and end-of-

---

[12] This measure was introduced in SNA93 (Commission of the European Communities et al. 1993, p. 575).

[13] For those who are unfamiliar with the concept of an operating surplus, an explanation is in order. In the United States, it has been customary to measure the rental income of persons as a profit-type residual income after the subtraction from space (gross) rent of all associated dwelling costs including the payment of mortgage interest. In the SNA, the operating surplus is the residual income accruing to capital before payments are made to debt (e.g. dividends and interest). Thus the operating surplus includes the return to both the debt and equity portions of capital.

year values of the net stock. This incorporates the effects on the stock's value of gross investment during the year, depreciation, and changes in the price level for (new) dwellings.

The determination of the appropriate real rate of return is contentious. In theory, on the basis of the opportunity cost principle, the nominal rate of return is measured as the rate on the best alternative investment. In practice, different rates have been used in empirical work. The rates are almost always those obtained from investment in financial assets, including rates paid on loans as well as those earned on bonds and other assets. The most important practical problem in empirically implementing the user cost measure is the year-to-year volatility of the real own rate of return. This is only a problem for current-price measures. Constant-price measures utilize prices, rates of inflation, and rates of return of the base (reference) year. Therefore, the real own rate of return for a given type of asset is a constant and there is no volatility.

The different rates of return used in practice reflect differences in analyst thoughts with respect to some basic questions. These questions include: whether a before- or after-tax rate should be used, whether the same rate should be applied to the debt and equity portions of the stock, whether a borrowing or lending rate should be used, and whether the rate should reflect differences in risk.[14] In the present context, a definitive answer can be given to the first question. The objective is to approximate the rental value for dwellings obtained with the stratification method and this value is measured before taxes. Thus, we can definitely state that a before-tax rate should be used in the imputation. The last question reflects the concern that the risk on the alternative financial asset should be comparable to that of the durable in question. In the present context, this means that because investments in dwellings and land are generally made on a long term basis and may be less risky than investments in other types of goods, there is a case for using returns on long-term assets that are less risky, such as long-term government bonds.

The solutions to the remaining questions center around three possible methods: (1) applying a lending rate to both the debt and equity portions of the stock, (2) applying a borrowing rate to both the debt and equity portions of the stock, and (3) applying a lending rate to the equity portion of the stock and a borrowing rate to the debt portion. In general, the rates at which money is borrowed (on loans) are higher than those at which it is lent (by consumers to financial institutions in the form of saving accounts, bonds, or similar financial instruments). The opportunity cost principle of using the highest rate points to using a borrowing rate. Also, it can be argued that when owner occupants have taken out loans on dwellings, the expected benefits must be greater than the expected costs including any interest paid. In many instances, borrowers have the option to pay off some or all of their loans early and thereby "earn" the interest rates charged on the loans. The foregoing arguments point to using the rate actually paid on mortgage loans on at least the debt portion of the stock. Consequently, if data are available on the amount of the stock financed by debt, the return on the debt portion of the stock should be estimated by the amount of interest actually paid on the debt.

This leaves the question of what rate of return should be applied to the equity portion of the stock if data to support the calculation of method 3 are available or what rate should be applied to the entire stock if these data are not available. The principle of using the highest rate suggests the use of a borrowing rate. However, it can be argued that the relatively high rates "earned" by borrowers do not represent true alternatives to owner occupiers who have no debt.

---

[14] For a discussion of these issues, see Katz (1983).

Thus, the theoretical arguments are inconclusive and either borrowing or lending rates are permissible.

Another theoretical point is whether the real rates of return in effect when a durable is purchased should be used to estimate the durable's services throughout its lifetime, or whether the rate to be used to value services in any given year should be the real rate in effect for comparable purchases of a new durable in the given year. Some economists have favored the former "vintage" approach to measuring rates of return.[15] However, most economists have favored the latter approach of using a single rate for all durables. In particular, some have argued that the vintage approach seems to deny that old durables can be perfect substitutes for newer durables that are identical, except for their ages. Such a denial would appear to erode the theoretical foundations on which the entire user cost of capital derivation is based. One of the implications of this approach is that if a borrowing rate is used to make the estimates, the rate should be the one on newly issued loans rather than the average rate on all loans outstanding.

Having decided on the general parameters of how, in theory, the real rate of return should be measured, we turn to the thorny question of how it should be estimated in practice. Initially, the task force decided against assuming what the rate of return was and attempted to see if reasonable estimates of it could be made from data available in the CCs. While it was recognized that estimated rates could be very volatile, there were some strong reasons for seeking to estimate them. Specifically, it was felt that real rates of return to housing could vary significantly over time in any single county (they varied tremendously in the United States between 1979 and 1984), real rates of return might vary significantly among countries, and rates of inflation in housing and land prices might differ significantly from each other.

These considerations led to a recommendation that real rates of return be initially estimated by taking an appropriate nominal interest rate on long-term loans and subtracting from it an estimate of the rate of inflation. Different rates of inflation would be used for the rates applicable to land and those to the dwellings themselves. Specifically, the rate of inflation in dwelling prices should be based on the same price index that is used to estimate consumption of fixed capital, i.e., the deflator for fixed capital formation in owner-occupied dwellings, or when that is unavailable, an index of relevant construction costs. Theoretically, the rate for land prices should be based on actual selling prices for land. Such price indexes are not available in many countries. When that is the case, a measure of general price inflation should be used instead. The rates of change of the consumer price index and the implicit deflator for GDP are two measures of price inflation that were recommended as appropriate.

Regardless of how the real rate of return was estimated for a given year, it was recommended that the rate be smoothed by taking a moving average of past rates. There are several reasons for such smoothing. In the past, the volatility of interest rate series has been the biggest obstacle to employing the user cost measure. Smoothing should mitigate this problem. Moreover, the theoretically relevant rate is an expected rate and many have argued that the best method of estimating an expected rate is by making it a function of actual past rates.

---

[15] For example, see Mohr (1984).

10. Lessons Learned and Modifications to the Initial Recommendations

Sample calculations made by representatives of statistical offices of some of the CCs exhibited many of the problems that have turned up in past attempts to implement user cost measures. As expected, most of these centered on attempts to estimate appropriate real rates of return on dwellings. In the estimates made by some countries, there was extreme year-to-year volatility. Attempts to smooth these by taking weighted averages of past rates did little to mitigate the problem. The variation in estimated rates among countries was unreasonably large, and some countries had rates of return that were unacceptably high. They produced imputed values for housing services that were a much higher percentage of GDP than in other European countries. Other countries had estimates of real rates of return that were unreasonably low. Some even had negative rates for several years in a row. The task force felt that such results could not be theoretically justified and had little worth for practical work.

The failure to obtain reasonable estimates of real rates of return appears to be largely due to the lack of fully developed markets for financial funds. Many of the CCs appeared to lack large scale markets for mortgage loans. In some countries, the only statistics on long-term debt were for government bonds. These were often closely administered by government authorities and set at rates that were lower than the rate of increase in the consumer price index, which resulted in estimated negative real rates of return.

Many of the past practical studies employing user cost measures have resolved problems in estimating real rates of return by assuming that it is a constant over time. This was essentially the approach taken by the task force. The members of the task force agreed that the best way to resolve the practical problems was to determine a real rate of return for dwellings and associated land that would be used by all countries. This rate would be used in all estimates made during the next five years. The rate would then be reviewed to determine if it should be modified.

The remaining question was what value of the real rate of return is appropriate? Evidence was presented to the task force that suggested that, at least in Western European countries, the appropriate real rate of return for owner-occupied dwellings was lower than that for other durables, perhaps in the 2.5 to 3.0 percent range.[16] It was the consensus of the task force that given the actual situation in the CCs, real rates of return on both dwellings and land should be assumed to be 2.5 percent. In the subsequent sample calculations performed by the participating CCs, this rate resulted in estimates of dwelling services that ranged between 7 and 9 percent of each country's GDP. This was judged as being reasonable because dwelling services generally averaged about 8 percent of GDP in the countries of Western Europe.

Obtaining estimates of land values turned out to be extremely problematical. There appeared to be very little data, if any, on what values of land were implied in any tax assessments. This left us with only the hope that there might be some agreement as to what might be a reasonable rule of thumb. It was pointed out that in the United States, when there is new construction, the value of land generally accounts for about a quarter of the total sales price.

---

[16] This included calculations by Hartmann (2003) using data from the German national accounts, which showed that if land associated with dwellings were included in the net stock of dwellings, a real rate of return of 2.5 percent would be realistic based on rents obtained from the German stratification model.

Some of the experts on the task force noted that the value of land was relatively higher in Western Europe; it was generally more than one third and sometimes more than one half of the total sales price. However, some experts from the CCs insisted that the value of land in their countries was worth less than five percent of the value of the dwellings that were built on it. This appeared to be contradicted by the fact that in some CCs even newly constructed high value dwellings outside of central cities are built on relatively small plots. If land were so cheap, one would expect the plots for such dwellings to be larger. The task force concluded that the valuation of land is largely based on variables that are specific to a given locality and that rules of thumb that work in one country cannot be assumed to apply to other countries. Consequently, there seemed to be no alternative to allowing countries to estimate the value of their land independently of each other without imposing any specific guidelines.

It appeared that a number of the CCs would not have the data required to estimate the premium supplements that are part of net insurance premiums. To promote comparability in the estimates, the task force recommended that all CCs forgo estimating such supplements. Similarly, few countries had separate data on insurance losses for dwellings and their contents. It was recommended that such losses be split in proportion to the relative values of the stock of dwellings and their estimated contents.

Table 1 presents estimates from the final report of the project (see Eurostat B1, 2002). The estimates show how the various components of the output of owner-occupied dwellings differed between the participating CCs and some member states when estimates for the former were derived by the user cost method with an assumed real rate of return of 2.5 percent. U.S. data have been added to this table. These data are based on estimates that were recently published in the U.S. national income and product accounts. The estimates for the CCs and the member states are very similar. There are, however, major differences between the estimates for these two sets of countries and those for the United States. Consumption of fixed capital and expenditures on maintenance and repair account for much smaller shares of the output of dwellings in the United States while taxes on production account for a much larger share. Some of these differences may be due to differences between the statistical methodologies used in the United States and Europe. Major replacements to dwellings, such as the replacement of roofs and water heaters, are treated as capital formation in the United States but as current maintenance and repair in Europe. Conversely, costs of acquisition are included in capital formation in Europe but a large part of it is treated as current intermediate expenditure in the United States. The rate of depreciation for dwellings used in the United States is much lower than comparable rates used in Europe. How much this impacts the relative estimates of consumption of fixed capital is not clear. Nevertheless, the difference in taxes is a real one and it does not seem likely that statistical differences account for most of the other differences.

The percentage of the output of owner-occupied dwellings accounted for by the net operating surplus is relatively large in the United States. Assuming that the value of residential land is equal to one third of the value of the net stock of dwellings, the real rate of return on dwellings and land in the United States was about 3.7 percent in 1998, which is much higher than it is in Europe. To put this another way, the value of residential land would have to be about equal to the value of dwellings in order for the real rate of return on dwellings and associated land to be 2.5 percent. Moreover, the composition of the operating surplus is clearly different in the United States and Europe. In the United States it is largely a return on debt (i.e., it is largely used to pay mortgage interest) while in much of Europe it is largely a return on equity.

Table 1. Components of Output of Owner-Occupied Dwellings in Participating Candidate Countries, Some Member States, and the U.S., in percent, 1998.

	Czech Rep.	Hungary	Poland	Slovak Rep.	Slovenia	Germany	Nether-lands	Finland	U.S.
Output of owner-occupied dwellings	100.0	100.0	100.0	100.0	100.0	100.0	100.0	100.0	100.0
Intermediate consumption	25.1	16.2	17.9	11.5	19.5	12.1	20.0	22.9	17.3
Current maintenance and repairs	25.2	15.2	17.6	11.4	19.2	---	---	17.1	3.9
Insurance services	-0.1	1.0	0.2	0.1	0.3	--	---	5.8	1.4
Other Intermediate consumption	0.0	0.0	0.0	0.0	0.0	---	---	0.0	12.0
Value added	74.9	83.8	82.1	88.5	80.5	87.9	80.0	77.1	82.8
Consumption of fixed capital	29.1	34.7	27.3	48.7	34.0	32.5	41.0	41.4	16.0
Other taxes on production	0.8	0.0	1.1	0.5	1.1	3.3	3.0	-0.8	14.5
Net operating surplus	44.9	49.1	53.7	39.2	45.4	52.0	36.0	36.4	52.3

11.   Observations and Conclusions

During the course of the project it became evident that there were institutional differences between housing markets in the United States versus Eastern and Western Europe. These differences affect international comparisons of income and product. In the United States, housing markets are well developed and highly competitive. Individuals can easily buy or sell existing homes, rent out homes they live in, or purchase new homes. Loans to finance the purchase of homes are readily obtainable. Mortgages are now offered in a bewildering array of products, some of which require virtually no down payment. There are so many products that the purchaser can effectively customize his loan, having the interest rate fixed for whatever term he desires. The population is very mobile. The average family moves every seven years. If one does not like the size of one's home, one can readily obtain a different one that is larger or smaller. Moves are readily made to distant cities because obtaining housing is generally not a problem. As a result, all of the opportunities discussed in the user cost model represent true opportunities to owner occupiers and the user cost model can give an accurate measure of the value of housing services.

The converse holds true in Eastern Europe. Because homes are rarely sold, many of the sales are at distressed prices, mortgage loans are difficult to obtain, new homes are difficult to acquire and so on, many of the opportunities postulated in the theoretical derivation of the user costs do not represent true opportunities. Thus, in a theoretical sense, the user cost model is less applicable. Nevertheless, estimates of the value of housing services need to be made and appropriate market prices do not exist. The results of the project demonstrate that the user cost measure does give reasonable estimates of the value of these services. Some critical assumptions were made: i.e., that the real rate of return is 2.5 percent. Also, the valuation of land is problematical. The difference between land being five percent of the value of dwellings and fifty percent could alter the measure of GDP by as much as two percent. However, by assuming the same real rate of return across countries, the relative magnitude of housing services is made more strictly a function of the relative sizes of the net stock of housing.

The project demonstrated that the CCs have a wealth of data on the characteristics of dwellings from censuses that can be used to make estimates of the net stock of dwellings. Given the damage to the housing stock during World War II, estimates made using variants of the physical inventory method may give more accurate estimates than those based on the perpetual inventory method. In devising the examples for the templates using U.S. data, it proved difficult to reconcile stock estimates obtained with the perpetual and physical inventory methods.

The data from the project suggest that there may be significant institutional differences between the markets for owner-occupied dwellings in the United States and those of the CCs and Western Europe. In the United States, a large part of the services of these dwellings goes toward the payment of property taxes and mortgage interest. In Europe, the share of output spent on these costs is much lower but expenditures on maintenance and repair as well as depreciation are relatively higher. The true extent of these differences is difficult to determine because of the lack of underlying detail and differences in the statistical methodologies used.

Appendix A. Derivation of the User Cost Measure

The user cost of capital measure provides an estimate of the market rental price based on costs of owners. It is directly derived from the principle that, in equilibrium, the purchase price of a durable good will equal the discounted present value of its expected net income (or benefits); i.e., it will equal the discounted present value of its expected future services less the discounted present value of its expected future operating costs. To see this, let $P_{s,t}$ denote the purchase price of an s year old durable at the beginning of year t; $P^e_{s+1,t+1}$ denote its expected purchase price at the beginning of year t+1 when the durable is one year older; $C^e_{s,t}$ denote the expected value of the services of this s year old durable in year t; $O^e_{s,t}$ denote the expected operating expenses for this s year old durable in year t; and r^e_t denote the expected nominal discount rate (i.e., the rate of return on the best alternative investment) in year t. Expected variables are measured as of the beginning of year t. Assume that the entire value of the durable's services in any year will be received at the end of the year, and that the durable is expected to have a service life of m years. From the definition of discounted present value,

$$
\begin{aligned}
P_{s,t} = &\frac{C^e_{s,t}}{1+r^e_t} + \frac{C^e_{s+1,t+1}}{(1+r^e_t)(1+r^e_{t+1})} + \ldots + \frac{C^e_{m-1,t+m-s-1}}{\prod_{i=t}^{t+m-s-1}(1+r^e_i)} \\
&-\frac{O^e_{s,t}}{1+r^e_t} - \frac{O^e_{s+1,t+1}}{(1+r^e_t)(1+r^e_{t+1})} - \ldots - \frac{O^e_{m-1,t+m-s-1}}{\prod_{i=t}^{t+m-s-1}(1+r^e_i)}
\end{aligned}
$$

(A1)

When the durable is one year older, the services it renders in year t will have been received and the operating expenses of year t already incurred. Consequently, the expected price of the durable at the beginning of year t+1 is given by

(A2)
$$P_{s+1,t+1} = \frac{C^e_{s+1,t+1}}{1+r^e_{t+1}} + \frac{C^e_{s+2,t+2}}{(1+r^e_{t+1})(1+r^e_{t+2})} + \ldots + \frac{C^e_{m-1,t+m-s-1}}{\Pi^{t+m-s-1}_{i=t+1}(1+r^e_i)}$$
$$- \frac{O^e_{s+1,t+1}}{1+r^e_{t+1}} - \frac{O^e_{s+2,t+2}}{(1+r^e_{t+1})(1+r^e_{t+2})} \cdots - \frac{O^e_{m-1,t+m-s-1}}{\Pi^{t+m-s-1}_{i=t+1}(1+r^e_i)}$$

Dividing both sides of (A2) by $(1+r^e_t)$ and subtracting the result from equation (A1) yields

(A3)
$$P_{s,t} - \frac{P^e_{s+1,t+1}}{1+r^e_{t+1}} = \frac{C^e_{s,t}}{1+r^e_t} - \frac{O^e_{s,t}}{1+r^e_t}$$

Multiplying both sides of equation (A3) by $(1+r^e_t)$ and combining terms, one obtains the standard user cost measure:

(A4)
$$C^e_{s,t} = r^e_t P_{s,t} + (P_{s,t} - P^e_{s+1,t+1} + O^e_{s,t})$$

Equation (A4) expresses the expected value of the durable's services as the sum of three components: the expected nominal net operating surplus, the expected decline in the price of the durable during the year, and the expected value of operating expenses. Because it is measured as an opportunity cost, the first of these components, the expected nominal net operating surplus, is measured by the product of the expected nominal discount rate and the price of the durable as of the beginning of the year. As explained in footnote 13, this return to capital is gross of any interest payments made on debt used to finance the purchase of the durable. The expected decline in the price of the durable is usually partitioned into two components: consumption of fixed capital (i.e., depreciation) and the expected capital loss on the durable. The expected capital loss component can be summed with the nominal net operating surplus to yield an expected real net operating surplus. When this is done, the expected value of the durable's services is, consequently, expressed as the sum of the expected real net operating surplus, depreciation, and the expected value of operating expenses.

References

Bureau of Labor Statistics (BLS), U.S. Department of Labor (1983), *Trends in Multifactor Productivity, 1948-81*, Bulletin 2178, September.

Christensen, L.R. and D.W. Jorgenson (1973), "Measuring Economic Performance in the Private Sector," in M. Moss (ed.), *The Measurement of Economic and Social Performance*, Studies in Income and Wealth 38, Columbia University Press for the National Bureau of Economic Research.

Commission of the European Communities, International Monetary Fund, Organisation for Economic Co-operation and Development, United Nations, and World Bank (1993), *System of National Accounts 1993*, Brussels/Luxembourg, New York, Paris, Washington DC.

Diewert, W.E. (2002), "Harmonized Indexes of Consumer Prices: Their Conceptual Foundations," *Swiss Journal of Economics and Statistics*, 138, 547-637. http://www.econ.ubc.ca/diewert/harindex.pdf

Diewert, .W.E. (2003), "The Treatment of Owner Occupied Housing and Other Durables in a Consumer Price Index" Discussion Paper 03-08, Dept. of Economics, University of British Columbia, Canada, available at http://www.econ.ubc.ca/discpapers/dp0308.pdf. Forthcoming in W.E. Diewert, J. Greenless and C. Hulten (eds.), *Price Index Concepts and Measurement*, NBER Studies in Income and Wealth, U. of Chicago Press.

Diewert, W.E. (2005a), "Issues in the Measurement of Capital Services, Depreciation, Asset Price Changes, and Interest Rates," in C. Corrado, J. Haltiwanger and D. Sichel (eds.), *Measuring Capital in the New Economy*, paper presented at the Conference On Research in Income and Wealth held in Washington, D.C., on April 26, 2002. http://www.econ.ubc.ca/discpapers/dp0411.pdf

Diewert, W.E. (2005b), "A Note on Schreyer's Model for Depreciation and Welfare," http://www.econ.ubc.ca/diewert/schreyer.pdf.

Diewert, W.E. and A.O. Nakamura (2011), "Accounting for Housing in a CPI," chapter 2, pp. 7-32 in Diewert, W.E., B.M. Balk, D. Fixler, K.J. Fox and A.O. Nakamura (2011), *PRICE AND PRODUCTIVITY MEASUREMENT: Volume 1 -- Housing*. Trafford Press.

European Commission (2001), Eurostat Projects on Non-financial National Accounts With the Candidate Countries, 1998-2000, Luxembourg: Office for Official Publications of the European Communities.

Eurostat B1 (2002), "Task Force Report on Alternative Estimation Methods for Dwelling Services in the Candidate Countries," Document NA-PPP 02/6 presented to the Meeting of the Working Parties on National Accounts and Purchasing Power Parities, Luxembourg, November 19. This paper was also presented by Eurostat at the Regional Coordinator's Workshop of the International Comparison Program 2003-2005 held in Luxembourg, March 24-28, 2003

Faucett, J. (1980), "Comment", in D. Usher (ed.), *The Measurement of Capital*, Studies in Income and Wealth 45, University of Chicago Press for the National Bureau of Economic Research, 68-81.

Hartmann, N. (2003), "Net Operating Surplus (NOS) of Owner-occupied Dwellings – The User Cost Method Applied to Germany," Calculations in the Frame of the Task Force "Estimation Methods for Dwelling Services in the Candidate Countries."

Hill, P. (1999), "Capital Stocks, Capital Services and Depreciation, " Document No. 1 presented at the meetings of the Canberra Group on Capital Stock Statistics, Washington, D.C., November 8-10. http://www.oecd.org/dataoecd/12/47/2549891.pdf

Hill, P. (2000), "Economic Depreciation and the SNA"; paper presented at the Conference of the International Association for Research on Income and Wealth, Krakow.

Hotelling, H. (1925), "A General Mathematical Theory of Depreciation," *Journal of the American Statistical Association* 20, September, 340-353.

Katz, A.J. (1982), "The Value of Services Provided by the Stock of Consumer Durables, 1947-79: Alternative User Cost Measures," in BEA Working Paper No. 2: *Measuring Nonmarket Economic Activity*, National Technical Information Service, December, Accession No. PB 83-167-395.

Katz, A.J. (1983), "Valuing the Services of Consumer Durables," *Review of Income and Wealth*, Series 29, December, 405-427.

Katz, A.J. (2003a), "Template and Notes to Accompany the Template for Deriving Estimates with the User Cost of Capital Measure," paper presented by Eurostat at the Regional Coordinator's Workshop of the International Comparison Program 2003-2005 held in Luxembourg, March 24-28.

Katz, A.J. (2003b), "Estimating Dwelling Services in the Candidate Countries: Theory and Application of the User Cost Measure" paper presented by Eurostat at the Regional Coordinator's Workshop of the International Comparison Program 2003-2005 held in Luxembourg, March 24-28.

Katz, A.J. and J. Peskin (1980), "The Value of Services Provided by the Stock of Consumer Durables, 1947-77: An Opportunity Cost Measure," *Survey of Current Business* 60, July, 22-31.

Martin, F.D., J.S. Landefeld, and J. Peskin (1984), "The Value of Services Provided by the Stock of Government-Owned Fixed Capital in the United States, 1948-79," *Review of Income and Wealth 30*, Sept., 331-349.

Mohr, M.F. (1984), "The Theory and Measurement of the Rental Price of Capital in Industry-Specific Productivity Analysis: A Vintage Rental Price of Capital Model," BIE-SP84-1, Bureau of Industrial Economics, U.S. Department of Commerce, January.

OECD (2002), *Measuring Capital: A Manual on the Measurement of Capital Stocks, Consumption of Fixed Capital, and Capital Services.*

Wykoff, F.C. (1980), "A Deflator for Consumer Durable Services in Theory and Practice," unpublished paper written under contract to BEA, January.

Chapter 4

HEDONIC ESTIMATES OF THE COST OF HOUSING SERVICES: RENTAL AND OWNER OCCUPIED UNITS

Theodore M. Crone, Leonard I. Nakamura and Richard P. Voith[1]

1. Introduction

Housing services account for a seventh of U.S. personal consumption expenditures. For rental units, housing costs are directly observed in the form of market rents. For owner occupied housing (OOH) services, many economists feel that the preferred measure of housing costs is the user cost of capital.[2] Since 1983, the U.S. Bureau of Labor Statistics (BLS) has measured the inflation rate for rental units similar to owner occupied units and has used this as a proxy for the inflation rate for the OOH service flow: the rental equivalent way of measuring the user cost of capital for OOH.[3]

In this study, we compare the BLS estimates of increases in rents and owner occupied housing costs to hedonic regression based estimates based on data from the American Housing Survey (AHS). We argue that our hedonic regression based method represents an alternative to the current BLS method. The method is applied to renter and owner occupied housing over the period from 1985 to 1999. Our empirical results suggest that for the period of 1985-1999 in the United States, the CPI component for housing may have slightly underestimated rental increases and significantly overestimated increases in housing costs for homeowners.

Section 2 outlines the BLS rental equivalent method. Section 3 presents our hedonic method. Section 4 describes the data used. Section 5 compares our measures of owner occupied housing services inflation with those of the BLS. Section 6 concludes.

---

[1] Leonard Nakamura is with the Research Department of the Federal Reserve Bank of Philadelphia and can be reached at leonard.nakamura@phil.frb.org. Theodore Crone was with the Research Department, Federal Reserve Bank of Philadelphia and can be reached at tedcrone@gmail.com. Richard Voith is Senior VP and Principal, Econsult Corporation and can be reached at voith@econsult.com. The views expressed are those of the authors and do not necessarily represent those of the Federal Reserve Bank of Philadelphia or the Federal Reserve System.

[2] For more on user costs, see for example Diewert (1974, 2003). See also Diewert and Nakamura (2011).

[3] See Smith, Rosen and Fallis (1988) on implicit rent as a measure of the user cost of capital for the marginal homeowner.

Crone, T.M., L.I. Nakamura and R.P. Voith (2011), "Hedonic Estimates of the Cost of Housing Services: Rental and Owner Occupied Units," chapter 4, pp. 51- 68 in
W.E. Diewert, B.M. Balk, D. Fixler, K.J. Fox and A.O. Nakamura (2011),
PRICE AND PRODUCTIVITY MEASUREMENT: Volume 1 -- Housing. Trafford Press.

2.   The BLS Methods for Measuring Inflation in Housing Services

Households derive a service flow from the dwellings they inhabit. In exchange for this service flow, renters pay an explicit rent and owners pay an implicit "equivalent" rent. What we have data on are rents in the first case and dwelling prices in the second.

Beginning in 1978, the BLS estimated rental increases by sampling rental units on a six month rotation. By 1999, the BLS was collecting rent data for about 25,000 units. Rent data are transactions prices, as reported in tenant surveys and interviews rather than posted prices. Evaluating measured rental inflation by survey is complicated by at least three factors: (1) the quality of a given apartment or house can change over time because of imperfect maintenance or through improvements made by the landlord or tenants;[4] (2) tenants' reports of changes in rents may be inaccurate;[5] and (3) tenants move and vacant apartments, where rents are not recorded, may have different inflation rates.[6] The methods used by the BLS to measure rental inflation for individual units have evolved over time to correct for various measurement problems.[7]

Prior to 1983, the BLS arrived at estimates of homeowner expenses by making estimates of individual cost components including mortgage interest costs, home purchase prices, insurance costs, and so forth. In 1983, the BLS adopted the concept of owners' equivalent rent for the CPI (Gillingham and Lane, 1982). For the period of 1983 to 1986, owners' equivalent rent was calculated by reweighting the rent sample to better represent owner occupied units, since the typical owner occupied housing unit has many characteristics that differ from a typical rental unit. For example, owner occupied units are predominantly single-family detached units, while rental units are predominantly in multiple unit buildings.

In January 1987, the BLS changed methodology again and began imputing owners' equivalent rent to a sample of owner occupied units by matching each one to a number of rental units in the same neighborhood and with the same structural attributes. Unfortunately, the rental units to which the owner occupied units were matched were aggregated using the Sauerbeck formula, a formula that was shown to cause a systematic overstatement of inflation (Armknecht

---

[4] The quality issue is complicated further by vintage effects or unmeasured quality differences that are proxied by the age of the unit. All vintage effects are not necessarily negatively related to age; e.g., older units may be located closer to the center of a metro area or surviving older units may represent the highest quality units built in their time (see Randolph, 1988a and 1988b).

[5] When the new formula for estimating changes in rents was introduced in 1978, the tenant was asked what the current month's rent was and what the previous month's rent had been. Two changes -- the current month change and the six-month change -- were then used to estimate the current month change in rent. Research by the BLS found that the reported one-month changes tended to underestimate rental increases. One reason for the underestimation is apparently that rent changes often occur when the tenant changes and the new tenant may not be aware that a rent change has taken place. However, even reports of one-month changes by tenants who had occupied the unit in the previous month tended to be underreported. The recall bias was corrected in 1995. Now the BLS estimates the one-month change by the sixth root of the six-month change. See Crone, Nakamura, and Voith (2008).

[6] The vacancy effect resulted in a major change in methodology in 1983. Changes in prices for vacant apartments are now imputed (Rivers and Sommers, 1983; and Genesove, 1999).

[7] Note that the BLS does not attempt to make the CPI a consistently measured series; i.e., changes in methodology are not retroactively applied to the series. Stewart and Reed (1999) discuss this issue and construct a version of the CPI that is intended to be consistently measured from 1978 on. For a discussion of the issues associated with the BLS methodology for collecting rental data, see Crone, Nakamura, and Voith (2008).

et al., 1995). This overstatement is estimated by the BLS to have been about half a percentage point annually. A correction for this problem was implemented in 1995. However, difficulties were encountered in finding rental units in neighborhoods in which homes are predominantly owner occupied.[8] Thus the BLS returned in 1998 to the method used between 1983 and 1986 of reweighting rental units to obtain owners' equivalent rent.

The main concerns that have been raised about the BLS methods center on whether changes in rental rates are measured accurately and, if they are, whether they accurately reflect changes in the user cost of capital for residents of owner occupied housing. The issue of maintaining constant quality illustrates these concerns. The CPI is meant to reflect *pure* inflation; that is, it is meant to reflect the change in rent or owner occupied housing costs holding the quality of the unit constant. It is an established fact for rental properties that the rent charged is negatively related to the age of the housing unit. This economic depreciation can be interpreted in either or both of two ways: rental properties physically deteriorate over time as a result of imperfect maintenance, and embodied technological progress makes existing rental properties increasingly economically obsolete over time. Randolph (1988a and 1988b) estimated that, at the national level, rental units depreciate between 0.3 percent and 0.4 percent per year. In 1988, the BLS began applying an aging adjustment to the rental index. In contrast, homeowners are thought to maintain their properties more fully and upgrade them more frequently to compensate for obsolescence. Thus, increases in reported rents adjusted for depreciation from a sample of rental units may overstate the rate of increase of the *implied* rental rates for owner occupied housing because rental properties depreciate faster than owner occupied housing.

3. The Hedonic Approach to Measuring Inflation in Housing Services

There is a vast literature on hedonic techniques applied to the housing market to estimate the underlying prices of various elements of the housing bundle.[9] There is almost as large a literature devoted to constructing indexes of house price appreciation, and many of these papers use hedonic techniques to control for changes in house quality over time.[10] Surprisingly, there is a dearth of studies using hedonic methods to construct indexes of price changes for housing services. House price appreciation indexes are not indexes of the change in the price of the flow of housing services for owner occupied houses because they do not distinguish between gains in the value of the capital asset and changes in the underlying value of the service flow. In other words, house price appreciation indexes do not control for changes in the capitalization rate.

Estimating changes in the price of housing service flows requires estimating the market rent of constant quality rental housing, the market price of constant quality owner occupied

---

[8] In general, the market for these units is relatively thin, so that the observed rents may not be good proxies for the implicit value of the housing service flows for owner occupied units. Also, the rental units that have characteristics most like owner occupied dwellings are often temporary rentals; that is, they are in the rental sample for only short time periods. The rent for such units may be unusually high or low depending on the circumstances under which they are temporarily in the rental market. A different sort of problem is that rental units in general are often subject to long-term contracts or price regulation.

[9] See Sheppard (1999) for a review and references to the empirical literature.

[10] See Malpezzi, Chun, and Green (1998), for example. Further discussion of this issue, alternative empirical approaches, and references can also be found in Diewert and Nakamura (2011).

housing, and the capitalization rate of owner occupied housing. Consumers presumably make tenure choices based on individual optimization, and the capitalization rate makes the marginal consumer indifferent between renting and owning. Using hedonic techniques, we can identify the capitalization rate that yields renter and owner indifference while statistically controlling for differences in housing unit traits.

In this paper, we develop separate price indexes for rental and owner occupied units using hedonic methods and a data set that contains both rental and owner occupied units. We estimate capitalization rates and then compute alternative estimates of the rate of inflation of housing services. These alternative estimates are compared with measures of housing inflation from the CPI to help assess possible bias problems in the CPI measures.

The basic procedure is as follows. We estimate hedonic prices for each trait in a bundle of traits providing housing services (bathrooms, garage, etc.) and construct separate constant quality price indexes for rental and owner occupied housing. We estimate a capitalization rate for owner occupied housing that yields an estimate of the value of the service flow from owner occupied housing.[11] Implied capitalization rates are important for measuring inflation in housing because changes in capitalization rates result in changes in the user cost of capital and hence in the inflation rate for owner occupied housing services. Increases in capitalization rates will increase the measured rate of inflation for owner occupied housing services even if the prices of housing traits remain unchanged from one period to the next. While there is little reason to expect major changes in the capitalization rate over one or two year intervals, it is quite possible for capitalization rates to change significantly over longer periods of time. Indeed, over the 1985-1999 period, we find that the capitalization rates of owner occupied housing ranged from 8.1 percent to 9.0 percent.

To construct measures of change in the price and the quantity of constant quality housing services, we estimate the market prices of the component housing traits. Then, using the estimates of the quantities of these traits, we estimate the change in the value of an average constant quality house.

For owner occupied housing, a typical hedonic regression takes the form:[12]

$$(1) \qquad \ln V_{it} = \beta_t X_{it} + e_{it} \quad \text{for} \quad i = 1, \ldots, I.$$

V_{it} is the value for house i in period time t, X_i is a K element row vector of traits of house i, and β_t is a vector of the estimated percentage contributions to the house value of the housing traits.

The stream of housing services that implicitly is equal to the rent, R_{it}, is hypothesized to depend on the value of housing, V_{it}, and a capitalization rate, C_t, in the following manner: $R_{it} = C_t V_{it}$. Thus equation (1) can be rewritten as $\ln(R_{it} / C_t) = \beta_t X_{it} + e_{it}$, or as

$$(2) \qquad \ln(R_{it}) = \beta_t X_{it} + \ln(C_t) + e_{it} \quad \text{for} \quad i = 1, \ldots, I.$$

A corresponding hedonic regression for the rent for rental units is given by:

---

[11] Linneman (1980), Linneman and Voith (1991), and Crone, Nakamura, and Voith (2000) develop these methods.

[12] There is a large literature on the appropriate choice of functional form for the hedonic price function (see Linneman, 1980, for example), but the simple semi log form generally performs well.

(3) $\qquad \ln(R_{jt}) = \gamma_t X_{jt} + u_{jt} \ \text{ for } \ j = 1, \ldots, J,$

where R_{jt} is the rent for unit j in time t, X_j is a K element row vector of traits of rental unit j, and γ_t is a vector of traits for the individual rental unit. Unlike the case of owner occupied units, the capitalization rate does not appear in the equation for rental units since the price of the service flow is observed directly for rentals. Note, moreover, that in the semi-log functional form, if owners and renters value housing traits similarly, then we will have $\beta_t = \gamma_t$ and the owner and renter hedonic equations will differ only by the constant, $\ln(C_t)$.

Let $W_{it} = Z_{it}^{-1}$ where Z_{it} is the sampling probability of house i. Also, let X_{ot} be an I by K matrix whose i^{th} row consists of values for the traits of the ith house in the sample, and let W_{ot} be a 1 by I vector of weights that blows the sample up to the universe. Then $C_t W_{ot} \exp(B_t X_{ot})$ is a measure of the nominal value of rental services in period t, where B_t is an estimator of β_t. Using the matrix of characteristics of homes in period $t+n$ and using base-year trait prices, we can represent the real output of the services in period $t+n$, evaluated in terms of period t prices, by the expression $C_t W_{ot+n} \exp(B_t X_{ot+n})$.

A Laspeyres quantity index of housing services is given by:

(4) $\qquad W_{ot+n} \exp(B_t X_{ot+n}) / W_{ot} \exp(B_t X_{ot}),$

since the capitalization terms cancel out. Similarly, a Paasche quantity index of housing services is given by:

(5) $\qquad W_{ot+n} \exp(B_{t+n} X_{ot+n}) / W_{ot} \exp(B_{t+n} X_{ot}).$

We can construct a Fisher index of the quantity of housing services as the square root of the product of the Laspeyres and Paasche indexes; e.g., the Fisher index is given by:

(6) $\qquad [\{W_{ot+n} \exp(B_t X_{ot+n}) / W_{ot} \exp(B_t X_{ot})\} \\ \{W_{ot+n} \exp(B_{t+n} X_{ot+n}) / W_{ot} \exp(B_{t+n} X_{ot})\}]^{1/2}.$

Holding the matrix of characteristics of homes constant, we can determine the price of the same bundle of services in period t+n by $C_{t+n} W_{ot} \exp(B_{t+n} X_{ot})$.

If C_t can be estimated, then we can construct indexes of the price of owner occupied housing services using estimates of the parameters of (2). A Laspeyres price index of owner occupied housing services is given by

(7) $\qquad W_{ot} \exp(B_{t+n} X_{ot}) C_{t+n} / W_{ot} \exp(B_t X_{ot}) C_t.$

A Paasche price index of owner occupied housing services is:

(8) $\qquad W_{ot+n} \exp(B_{t+n} X_{ot+n}) C_{t+n} / W_{ot+n} \exp(B_t X_{ot+n}) C_t.$

And the Fisher index of the price of owner occupied housing services is given by:

$$(9) \qquad [\{W_{ot}\exp(B_{t+n}X_{ot})C_{t+n} \,/\, W_{ot}\exp(B_t X_{ot})C_t\}$$
$$\{W_{ot+n}\exp(B_{t+n}X_{ot+n})C_{t+n} \,/\, W_{ot}\exp(B_t X_{ot+n})\}C_t]^{1/2}.$$

Unfortunately, however, the capitalization rate C_t, which is a scale parameter, cannot be estimated from a sample of owner occupied units alone.[13]

If we are constructing an index for the total flow of housing services, it is important that we have an estimate of the capitalization rate for two reasons. First, the capitalization rate, as shown above, affects the measured inflation index of owner occupied housing. Second, the capitalization rate, in part, determines the size of the service flow of owner occupied housing relative to that of renter occupied housing and other goods and hence its weight in the CPI. This is clear if the total flow of housing services in a given year from rental housing is $W_{rt} \cdot \exp(\gamma_t X_{rt})$ where X_{rt} is the quantity of rental traits and is defined analogously to X_{ot} and W_{rt} is defined analogously to W_{ot}. Thus, the total flow of housing services is the sum of the flow to owners and renters:

$$(10) \qquad C_t W_{ot}\exp(\beta_t X_{ot}) + W_{rt}\exp(\gamma_t X_{rt}).$$

Note that changes in the price indexes for the same bundles of housing services based on this sum will depend on the capitalization rate even if the capitalization rate is unchanged between the two periods. For example, the Laspeyres price index of total housing services is given by

$$(11) \qquad \{W_{rt}\exp(\gamma_{r+n}X_{rt}) + W_{ot}C_{t+n}\exp(\beta_{t+n}X_{ot})\} / \{W_{rt}\exp(\gamma_{rt}X_{rt}) + W_{ot}C_t\exp(\beta_t X_{ot})\}.$$

If we assume that $\beta_t = \gamma_t$, we can combine the owner and rental samples to estimate the capitalization rate as well as the trait prices.[14] We use owner occupied and rental dummies to formulate the estimating equation,

$$(12) \qquad \ln(C_t V_{it})D_o + \ln(R_{it})D_r = \beta_t X_{it} + e_{it} \quad \text{for } i = 1,\ldots,I+J,$$

where $D_o = 1$ if the unit is owner occupied and 0 if it is rented, $D_r = 1$ if the unit is rented and 0 if it is owner occupied, and where X_{it} is the matrix of characteristics of the homes of owners and renters. (The subscript i runs from 1 to I+J, the total number of dwelling units including both the owner occupied and the rental ones.) We can rewrite (12) as

$$(13) \qquad \ln(V_{it})D_o + \ln(R_{it})D_r = -\ln(C_t)D_0 + \beta_t X_{it} + e_{it} \quad \text{for } i = 1,\ldots,I+J.$$

Since V_{it} is zero when D_o is zero and R_{it} is zero when D_r is zero, we can rewrite (13) as

$$(14) \qquad \ln(V_{it} + R_{it}) = \alpha_t D_0 + \beta_t X_{it} + e_{it} \quad \text{for } i = 1,\ldots,I+J.$$

---

[13] The capitalization rate is also likely to change over time because it is a function of the user cost of capital, which in turn depends on the tax advantages of owner occupied housing, mortgage rates, depreciation, and the expected future value of residential properties.

[14] It is not necessary to assume that all components of β and γ are the same in order to obtain this identification. Linneman (1980) includes some characteristics only for rental units, thus constraining the coefficients on those variables to be zero for owner occupied units. Linneman and Voith (1991) investigate the appropriateness of pooling owners and renters.

The capitalization rate $C_t = \exp(-\alpha_t)$ can be estimated from the regression (14). Estimating (14) separately for two time periods allows the calculation of price indexes for the total flows of owner occupied housing (OOH) services. In the pages that follow, we present hedonic estimates of price indexes for housing services. The data used are from the 1985 to 1999 national cross sections of the American Housing Survey (AHS). We compare the hedonic estimates with the official CPI measures by the BLS of the change in the price of housing services.

4.   The American Housing Survey (AHS) Data

Every two years, the U.S. Bureau of the Census conducts a survey of 50,000 to 60,000 rental and owner occupied houses known as the American Housing Survey (AHS). The current panel for the survey dates from 1985, with some units disappearing from the survey every two years and new units being added. We restricted our estimation sample to the years 1985 to 1999 so the estimates would be based on data from the same basic panel.

The cross sections from the national AHS are useful for evaluating changes in the price of U.S. housing services for two reasons. First, they have data on housing attributes, prices, and rental rates that can be used to estimate hedonic equations and capitalization rates. Second, each cross sectional sample has associated weights that can be used to expand the sample to the housing universe. Theoretically, these weights allow the calculation of the total flow of housing services, given a set of estimated trait prices and capitalization rates.

There are, however, a number of problems with the AHS data, including missing values. Although every observation in the AHS sample has an associated weight that can be used to expand the sample to national totals, some observations have missing values for the dependent variables in our hedonic equation (rent and house value). We could not use these observations in the hedonic estimation, but we did use them to calculate the Fisher indexes for rents and owner occupied housing costs as long as they had values for the traits in our regressions. A number of observations in the AHS had missing values for housing traits used in the regressions. These observations could not be used to estimate the trait prices or to calculate implied rents or owner occupied housing costs.

We calculate the change in owner occupied housing (OOH) costs and rents based on the normalized weighted values for the available observations in each year. Each element i of the vector W_{ot} is set equal to $w_{iot} / \sum_{i=1}^{I} w_{iot}$ where I is the number of observations in period t that have no missing values for the housing traits included in the regression equation. We apply an analogous weighting scheme to the rental units to produce a vector W_{rt} of normalized weights. Our annual samples contain approximately 32,000 to 45,000 observations that we can use to estimate the Fisher index of housing costs.

Table A1 in appendix A displays the sample means and standard deviations of the variables used to estimate the Fisher price index for the years of 1985, 1993 and 1999.

Truncation is another problem with the AHS data. The rent and house value data have upper bounds that change over the survey years. Any rent or house value that exceeds the upper bound is coded at the upper limit. In order to avoid systematic mismeasurement of larger and more expensive units, we eliminated from our regression sample any observation that was coded at the upper bound.[15] As a consequence, however, the rent and house value samples are not representative of the underlying housing populations. Since our purpose is to estimate increases in market rents, we also eliminated from our regression sample any rental units where the rent was subsidized.[16] Our regression samples range from approximately 29,000 to 40,000 observations.

Appendix table A2 displays the sample means and standard deviations of the variables used in the regression analysis for the 1985, 1993 and 1999 cross sections.

5. Hedonic Estimates of Rents, the Cost of OOH Services, and Capitalization Rates

The assumption that $\beta_t = \gamma_t$ in equation (12) constrains the choice of traits that we can use in our regression analysis. Kurz and Hoffmann (2011) use owners' estimates of the rental value of their property and market rents for rental properties in West Germany to examine the accuracy of the German CPI for owner occupied housing. In a pooled regression of renters and owners they find that for most of the coefficients on the hedonic characteristics there is no statistically significant difference between the two groups.

The fact that not all the coefficients are statistically the same is not surprising. Linneman (1980) and Linneman and Voith (1991) argue that F-tests that reject the equality of coefficients across samples do not provide conclusive evidence that the samples should not be pooled. They argue that the implicit prices derived from a hedonic price function estimated on either owners or renters alone will be biased for two reasons. First, the owners and renters each are likely to be non-random samples of the population in the housing market. Thus, hedonic price functions estimated on either owners or renters alone will be subject to sample selection bias. Second, because owners and renters typically purchase houses that have different quantities of each trait, non-linearity in the underlying hedonic price function suggests that predicted trait prices outside of the normal range for either owners or renters will not reflect the actions of all participants in the housing market.

Unlike Kurz and Hoffmann's data set, our data set does not include owners' estimates of the rental value of their units but only an estimate of the asset value: the dwelling price. We ran separate owner and renter equations on various sets of variables from the AHS for each of our cross sections to check for similarity in the coefficients for owners and renters. The results of the separate owner and renter equations using the traits that we included in our final estimation are shown in tables A3 and A4 in appendix A.

With one exception, we included in our combined estimates only those traits for which the statistically significant coefficients (at the 5 percent level) had the same sign across years and

---

[15] Square footage was also truncated at an upper bound and was missing for a large number of observations. Therefore, we used the number of rooms as our measure of unit size. This variable has many fewer missing values and is not truncated.

[16] We also did not use for our regressions any rental units with recorded rent less than $10 or any homeowner unit with a recorded value less than $1000. We considered such low values the result of miscoding.

for both renters and owners. In some cases, the magnitudes of the coefficients were also close (central air, unit in a multi-unit building, number of bathrooms, and if the unit is in a metropolitan statistical area (MSA)). In other cases, the magnitudes were not close (number of rooms, garage dummy, satisfaction with the neighborhood) even though the signs were the same. Building age was the one exception to our rule for choosing for the combined equation only those traits that had the same sign in the separate renter and owner equations. The coefficient on building age for renters was negative for every year of AHS data from 1985 to 1999. For homeowners the coefficient on building age was positive and significant in five of the regressions, positive and insignificant in one, and negative and insignificant in two of the regressions. Because of the importance of age in the hedonic literature on house values and rents, we included it in our combined equation.

Our estimates of trait prices from the combined sample of rental and owner occupied units are based on equation (14). Table A5 presents the estimates for 1985, 1993, and 1999. We impose the constraint that $\beta_t = \gamma_t$ for all traits. All the significant coefficients on the independent variables except the regional dummies have the same sign across all the years in our sample. The fact that a regional dummy changes sign from one year to the next simply indicates that housing services inflation has been faster or slower in that region relative to other regions.

The coefficient on the owner dummy variable (α) is the basis for our estimation of the capitalization rate. Since the rents used in the estimating equations are monthly rents, the annual capitalization rate C_t in percentage terms is equal to ($12 \times 100 \times \exp(-\alpha)$). The estimated capitalization rates for all the AHS sample years between 1985 and 1999 are shown in figure 1. They range from 8.1 percent to 9.0 percent, and the average is 8.6 percent.[17] This average capitalization rate represents a rental equivalent of $1433 per month for an owner occupied house valued at $200,000.[18] These are gross capitalization rates, so they include any property taxes or maintenance costs that are passed on to renters.

Based on the capitalization rates and trait prices estimated using the bi-annual AHS data, we calculated Fisher price indexes and inflation rates for both rented and owner occupied housing services. Table 1 compares these inflation rates with the reported CPI inflation for rent and for owners' equivalent rent for the entire 1985-1999 period. Several differences are immediately apparent. According to the CPI, owners' equivalent rent increased more than 11 percent faster than rents over this 14-year period. According to the Fisher indexes based on our hedonic estimates, the cost of owner occupied housing services increased less than 2 percent faster than rents. Our hedonic estimates suggest that the CPI slightly underestimated inflation for rental units (-0.8 percent) and significantly overestimated inflation in the cost of owner occupied housing (9.1 percent).[19] The Boskin Commission estimated that the upward bias for shelter costs for both rental and owner occupied housing from 1976 to 1996 averaged 0.25 percent per year.

---

[17] These capitalization rates are very similar to those estimated for apartment units by Sivitanides and Sivitanidou (1997). Linneman and Voith (1991) show that capitalization rates may differ systematically across homeowners as a result of tax and life cycle considerations. We abstract from these issues.

[18] $1433 = (.086 \times \$200,000)/12$

[19] If we allow the coefficient on age to vary between owners and renters, the difference between the CPI and the hedonic estimate for rents over this 14-year period would be -3.3 percent and the difference between the CPI and the hedonic estimate for owner occupied housing services would be 21.1 percent. The estimated capitalization rates in that model range from 9.4 percent to 9.8 percent with an average of 9.6 percent.

Our estimates suggest that there was a much larger upward bias for owner occupied housing costs from 1985 to 1999 but little, if any, bias for rental housing.

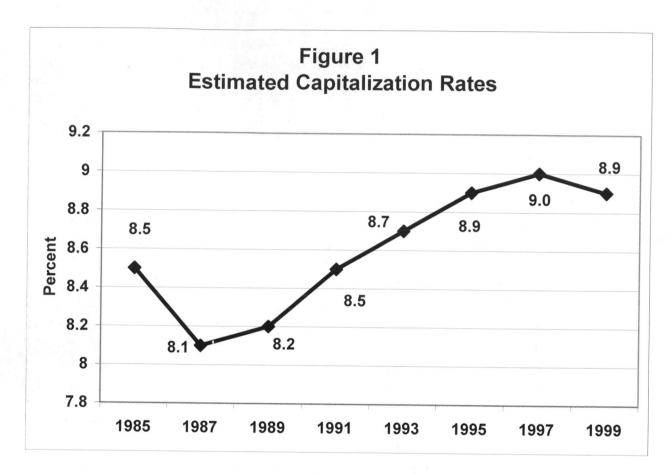

Figure 1
Estimated Capitalization Rates

Table 1. Inflation in Housing Services: 1985-1999

Housing segment	CPI	Hedonic estimates	Difference (CPI minus hedonic)
Rental Units	56.8%	57.7%	-0.8%
Owner occupied units (Owners' equivalent rent)	68.4%	59.3%	9.1%

Table 2a shows the annualized inflation rates for rental units over successive two-year periods from 1985 to 1999 based on the CPI and our hedonic estimates, and table 2b shows the annualized cumulative rates since 1985. The period-by-period changes in the CPI for rents are much smoother than the changes in the Fisher indexes based on the hedonic model. Moreover, the differences between the two measures fluctuate in sign (table 2a, column 3 and figure 2a), suggesting that any imprecision in the hedonic based estimates is corrected over time.

Since 1993 the annualized cumulative difference between the CPI and the hedonic based measure has ranged between 0.1 percent and -0.2 percent (table 2b and figure 2b). In a separate paper (Crone, Nakamura, and Voith, 2008), we estimate that methodological issues accounted for an underestimate of rental increase of about 0.1 percent a year between 1985 and 1999.

Table 2a. Rental Inflation (Annualized Rates)

Years	CPI	Hedonic estimates	Difference (CPI minus hedonic)
85-87	4.5	5.3	-0.9
87-89	3.9	2.9	1.0
89-91	3.6	5.0	-1.4
91-93	2.3	1.7	0.7
93-95	2.5	3.2	-0.7
95-97	2.5	1.4	1.1
97-99	1.5	3.8	-2.3

Table 2b. Cumulative Rental Inflation (Annualized Rates)

Years	CPI	Hedonic estimates	Difference (CPI minus hedonic)
85-87	4.5	5.3	-0.9
85-89	4.2	4.1	0.1
85-91	4.0	4.4	-0.4
85-93	3.6	3.7	-0.1
85-95	3.4	3.6	-0.2
85-97	3.3	3.2	0.1
85-99	3.3	3.3	-0.0

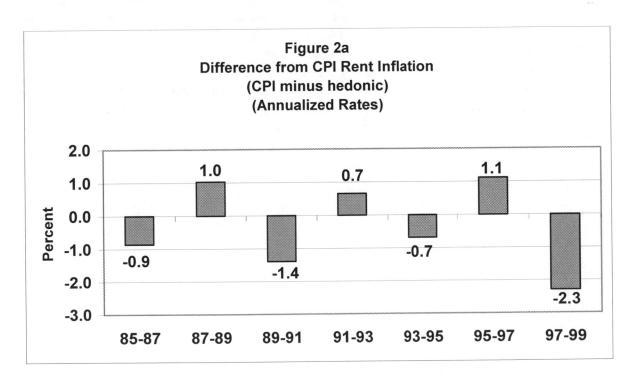

Figure 2a
Difference from CPI Rent Inflation
(CPI minus hedonic)
(Annualized Rates)

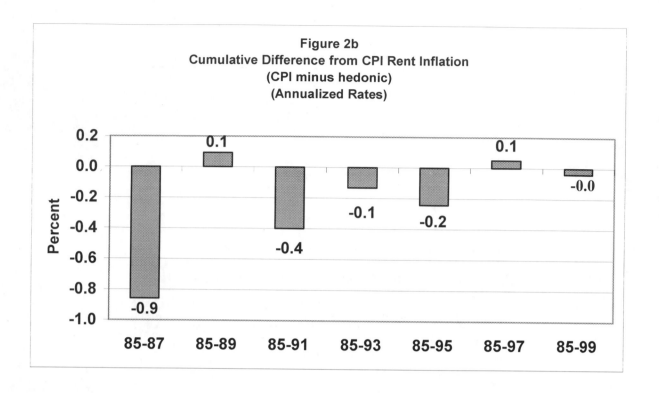

Table 3a shows the annualized inflation rates for the cost of owner occupied housing over successive two-year periods from 1985 to 1999. These estimates are based on the CPI owners' equivalent rent and our hedonic estimates, and table 3b shows the annualized cumulative rates since 1985. The hedonic estimate is higher than the CPI inflation measure in four of the two-year periods for which we estimate our index. On the other hand, it is lower than the CPI in three of the periods (table 3a and figure 3a). On an annualized basis, the cumulative difference between the CPI and our hedonic measure has been between 0.4 percent and 0.9 percent since 1991. If the hedonic estimates are a good measure of inflation in owner occupied housing over the longer term, this suggests that the CPI has overestimated owner occupied housing inflation (table 3b and figure 3b). This overestimation is explained primarily by the use, prior to 1995, of the Sauerbeck formula for matching rental and homeowner units that resulted in an overestimation of inflation for OOH costs (Armknecht et al., 1995).

6.   Conclusion

In this paper we have used hedonic techniques to overcome some of the problems of measuring changes in the cost of constant quality housing services. Using American Housing Survey (AHS) data, we estimated hedonic parameters for the characteristics of rental and owner occupied units separately at two-year intervals over the period 1985 to 1999. We then combined the rental and owner occupied units to estimate the capitalization rate for homeowner units and the costs of housing services for both renters and homeowners. Using these estimates, we calculated Fisher indexes for the increase in rents and the costs of owner occupied housing services for constant quality units.

Hedonic methods are helpful in estimating rental increases, but they are even more useful for estimating changes in the cost of housing services for homeowners. Even though the U.S. Bureau of Labor Statistics (BLS) attempts to construct a sample of rental units that are similar to owner occupied houses, we have listed several reasons why this sample may not yield a good estimate of the rental equivalent of owner occupied housing. Using hedonic methods we estimate the market value (but not the rental equivalent) of a constant quality owner occupied house in two different periods. With an estimated capitalization rate, the change in the value of the house can be translated directly into the change in the user cost of capital for the homeowner.

We estimated that the capitalization rate ranged from 8.1 percent to 9.0 percent over the period of 1985 through 1999. Our hedonic estimates imply a 59.3 percent increase in the cost of housing services for homeowners over this period, which is considerably less than the 68.4 percent increase estimated by the BLS. We estimate a 57.7 percent increase in rents over this period, which is just slightly higher than the 56.8 percent increase estimated by the BLS. We offer several possible explanations for an overestimation by the BLS of inflation for owner occupied housing services and an underestimation of rental inflation. In many cases, these explanations are based on flaws in the CPI methodology already recognized by the BLS and in some cases already remedied. However, the BLS may want to consider collecting more detailed traits on the housing units in their sample to check the inflation rates calculated using the CPI methodology against a hedonic measure.

Table 3a. Inflation for OOH Services (Annualized Rates)

Years	CPI	Hedonic estimates	Difference (CPI minus hedonic)
85-87	4.9	1.5	3.4
87-89	5.0	3.0	1.9
89-91	4.3	7.1	-2.7
91-93	3.1	2.7	0.4
93-95	3.5	4.3	-0.9
95-97	2.9	1.9	1.0
97-99	2.9	3.2	-0.4

Table 3b. Cumulative Inflation for OOH Services (Annualized Rates)

Years	CPI	Hedonic estimates	Difference (CPI minus hedonic)
85-87	4.9	1.5	3.4
85-89	4.9	2.3	2.7
85-91	4.7	3.8	0.9
85-93	4.3	3.6	0.8
85-95	4.2	3.7	0.4
85-97	4.0	3.4	0.5
85-99	3.8	3.4	0.4

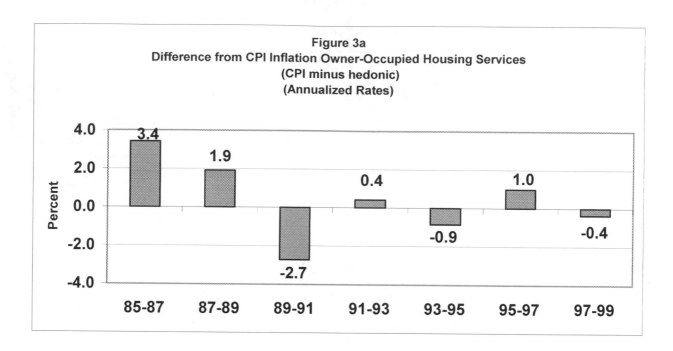

Figure 3a
Difference from CPI Inflation Owner-Occupied Housing Services
(CPI minus hedonic)
(Annualized Rates)

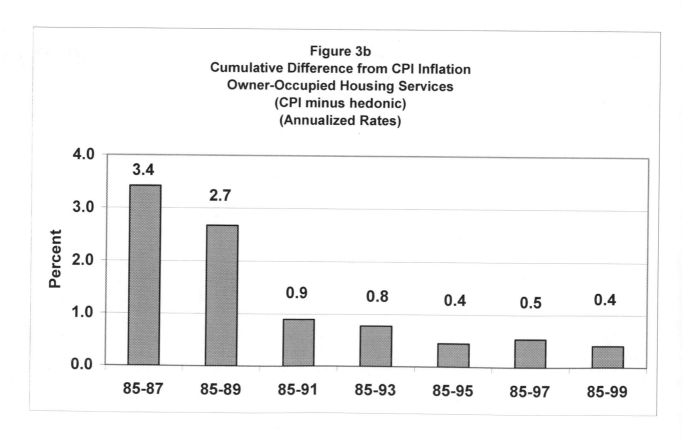

Figure 3b
Cumulative Difference from CPI Inflation
Owner-Occupied Housing Services
(CPI minus hedonic)
(Annualized Rates)

Appendix A. Estimation Results

Table A1. Samples for Calculating Fisher Index

Variable	1985 Mean	1985 Std. Dev.	1993 Mean	1993 Std. Dev.	1999 Mean	1999 Std. Dev.
rent	316	163	455	215	581	342
house value	72491	53187	106430	80856	141805	117513
owner dummy	0.650	0.477	0.647	0.478	0.663	0.473
number of rooms	5.5	1.8	5.6	1.9	5.6	1.8
number of bathrooms	1.4	0.6	1.5	0.6	1.6	0.6
age of structure	30	21	35	23	40	24
in a multi-unit building	0.299	0.458	0.298	0.457	0.241	0.428
garage dummy	0.555	0.497	0.572	0.495	0.605	0.489
central air dummy	0.335	0.472	0.438	0.496	0.525	0.499
holes in floor dummy	0.015	0.120	0.012	0.107	0.011	0.105
mice or rats dummy	0.046	0.210	0.027	0.161	0.177	0.382
satisfied with neighborhood (1 to 10)	8.1	2.2	8.0	2.2	7.8	2.2
MSA dummy	0.779	0.415	0.780	0.414	0.871	0.336
midwest dummy	0.248	0.432	0.241	0.428	0.267	0.442
south dummy	0.331	0.471	0.334	0.472	0.313	0.464
west dummy	0.191	0.393	0.196	0.397	0.222	0.416
Number of observations	32320		33986		45234	

Notes: MSA stands for metropolitan statistical area.

Table A2. Regression Samples

Variable	1985 Mean	1985 Std. Dev.	1993 Mean	1993 Std. Dev.	1999 Mean	1999 Std. Dev.
rent	323	142	450	188	545	219
house value	67660	45000	97492	67235	118326	70962
owner dummy	0.694	0.461	0.689	0.463	0.695	0.460
number of rooms	5.6	1.8	5.6	1.8	5.6	1.7
number of bathrooms	1.4	0.5	1.5	0.6	1.6	0.6
age of structure	31	21	35	23	41	24
in a multi-unit building	0.274	0.446	0.274	0.446	0.226	0.418
garage dummy	0.572	0.495	0.589	0.492	0.612	0.487
central air dummy	0.340	0.474	0.445	0.497	0.533	0.499
holes in floor dummy	0.014	0.117	0.011	0.106	0.011	0.105
mice or rats dummy	0.044	0.205	0.025	0.155	0.175	0.380
satisfied with neighborhood (1 to 10)	8.1	2.2	8.0	2.1	7.7	2.2
MSA dummy	0.776	0.417	0.776	0.417	0.866	0.340
midwest dummy	0.254	0.435	0.248	0.432	0.276	0.447
south dummy	0.336	0.472	0.340	0.474	0.323	0.468
west dummy	0.186	0.389	0.189	0.392	0.209	0.406
Number of observations	29434		30702		40434	

Notes: MSA stands for metropolitan statistical area.

Table A3. Regression Results for Rental Units

Dependent variable: Ln(Rent)	1985	1993	1999
number of rooms	0.041[a]	0.036[a]	0.052[a]
number of bathrooms	0.233[a]	0.250[a]	0.204[a]
age of structure	-0.005[a]	-0.003[a]	-0.002[a]
in a multi-unit building	0.209[a]	0.196[a]	0.122[a]
garage dummy	0.129[a]	0.092[a]	0.080[a]
central air dummy	0.157[a]	0.110[a]	0.105[a]
holes in floor dummy	-0.091[a]	-0.070[b]	-0.065[b]
mice or rats dummy	-0.086[a]	-0.016	-0.033[a]
satisfied with neighborhood (1 to 10)	0.001	0.005[b]	0.007[a]
MSA dummy	0.309[a]	0.337[a]	0.387[a]
midwest dummy	-0.237[a]	-0.338[a]	-0.240[a]
south dummy	-0.325[a]	-0.418[a]	-0.351[a]
west dummy	-0.035[b]	-0.105[a]	-0.038[a]
Constant	5.041[a]	5.355[a]	5.455[a]
Number of observations	9001	9567	12329
Adjusted R-squared	0.302	0.304	0.242
Sum of Squared Residuals	9047	10188	12600

Notes: A superscript a or b denotes a coefficient significant with a 0.99 or 0.95 level of confidence, respectively, with a two-tailed critical region. MSA stands for metropolitan statistical area.

Table A4. Regression Results for Owner Occupied Units

Dependent variable: Ln(House Value)	1985	1993	1999
number of rooms	0.114[a]	0.121[a]	0.129[a]
number of bathrooms	0.293[a]	0.312[a]	0.261[a]
age of structure	-0.0001	0.002[a]	0.001[a]
in a multi-unit building	0.168[a]	0.284[a]	0.170[a]
garage dummy	0.429[a]	0.429[a]	0.377[a]
Central air dummy	0.141[a]	0.135[a]	0.116[a]
holes in floor dummy	-0.407[a]	-0.462[a]	-0.295[a]
mice or rats dummy	-0.182[a]	-0.130[a]	-0.094[a]
satisfied with neighborhood (1 to 10)	0.031[a]	0.039[a]	0.028[a]
MSA dummy	0.330[a]	0.350[a]	0.233[a]
midwest dummy	-0.355[a]	-0.456[a]	-0.223[a]
south dummy	-0.305[a]	-0.468[a]	-0.347[a]
west dummy	0.031	-0.044[a]	0.063[a]
Constant	9.040[a]	9.172[a]	9.565[a]
Number of observations	20433	21147	28105
Adjusted R-squared	0.378	0.391	0.332
Sum of squared residuals	1796	1770	2151

Notes: A superscript a or b denotes a coefficient significant with a 0.99 or 0.95 level of confidence, respectively, with a two-tailed critical region. MSA stands for metropolitan statistical area.

Table A5. Regression Results for Renter and Homeowner Units Combined

Dependent Variable: Ln(Rent) or Ln(House Value)	1985	1993	1999
owner dummy	4.949[a]	4.922[a]	4.909[a]
number of rooms	0.100[a]	0.105[a]	0.115[a]
number of bathrooms	0.297[a]	0.314[a]	0.259[a]
age of structure	-0.002[a]	0.0003	0.00003
in a multi-unit building	0.260[a]	0.298[a]	0.214[a]
garage dummy	0.338[a]	0.321[a]	0.274[a]
central air dummy	0.154[a]	0.139[a]	0.125[a]
holes in floor dummy	-0.212[a]	-0.255[a]	-0.154[a]
mice or rats dummy	-0.130[a]	-0.068[a]	-0.078[a]
satisfied with neighborhood (1 to 10)	0.020[a]	0.026[a]	0.021[a]
MSA dummy	0.331[a]	0.356[a]	0.274[a]
midwest dummy	-0.316[a]	-0.419[a]	-0.225[a]
south dummy	-0.318[a]	-0.463[a]	-0.356[a]
west dummy	-0.005	-0.081[a]	0.016
Constant	4.370[a]	4.567[a]	4.883[a]
Number of observations	29434	30714	40434
Adjusted R-squared	0.940	0.937	0.941
Sum of squared residuals	11220	12394	15159

Notes: A superscript a or b denotes a coefficient significant with a 0.99 or 0.95 level of confidence, respectively, with a two-tailed critical region. MSA stands for metropolitan statistical area.

References

Armknecht, P.A., B.R. Moulton, and K.J. Stewart (1995), "Improvements to the Food at Home, Shelter, and Prescription Drug Indexes in the U.S. Consumer Price Index," BLS Working Paper 263.

Boskin, M.J., E. Dulberger, R. Gordon, Z. Griliches, and D. Jorgenson (1996), "Toward a More Accurate Measure of the Cost of Living," Final Report to the Senate Finance Committee, December 4.

Crone, T.M., L.I. Nakamura, and R.P. Voith, (2000), "Measuring Housing Services Inflation," *Journal of Economic and Social Measurement* 26, 153-171.

Crone, T.M., L.I. Nakamura, and R.P. Voith (2008), "Rents Have Been Rising, Not Falling, in the Postwar Period," *Review of Economics and Statistics*, forthcoming.

Diewert, W.E. (1974), "Intertemporal Consumer Theory and the Demand for Durables," *Econometrica* 53, 497–516.

Diewert, .W.E. (2003), "The Treatment of Owner Occupied Housing and Other Durables in a Consumer Price Index" Discussion Paper 03-08, Department of Economics, University of British Columbia, Vancouver, Canada, available at http://www.econ.ubc.ca/discpapers/dp0308.pdf. This paper is forthcoming in W.E. Diewert, J. Greenless and C. Hulten (eds.), *Price Index Concepts and Measurement,* NBER Studies in Income and Wealth, U. of Chicago Press.

Diewert, W.E. and A.O. Nakamura (2011), "Accounting for Housing in a CPI," chapter 2, pp. 7-32 in Diewert, W.E., B.M. Balk, D. Fixler, K.J. Fox and A.O. Nakamura (2011), *PRICE AND PRODUCTIVITY MEASUREMENT: Volume 1 -- Housing.* Trafford Press.

Diewert, E.W. and K.J. Fox (1999), "Can Measurement Error Explain the Productivity Paradox?" *Canadian Journal of Economics* 32, 251-280.

Genesove, D. (1999), "The Nominal Rigidity of Apartment Rents," NBER Working Paper 7137, May.

Gillingham, R. and W. Lane (1982), "Changing the Treatment of Shelter Costs for Homeowners in the CPI," *Monthly Labor Review* 105 (June), 9-14.

Gordon, R.J. (1990), *The Measurement of Durable Goods Prices*, NBER Studies in Income and Wealth, University of Chicago.

Gordon, R.J., and T. van Goethem, (2003), "A Century of Housing Shelter Prices: How Big Is the CPI Bias?" presented at the CRIW Conference in Memory of Zvi Griliches. Bethesda, MD, September 19-20.

Griliches, Z. (1994), "Productivity, R&D, and the Data Constraint," *American Economic Review* 84, 1-23.

Hoffmann, J. and C. Kurz (2002), "Rent Indices for Housing in West Germany 1985 to 1998," Economic Research Centre of the Deutsche Bundesbank Discussion Paper No. 01/02.

Kurz, C. and J. Hoffmann (2011), "A Rental Equivalence Index for Owner Occupied Housing in West Germany," chapter 5, pp. 69-86 in Diewert, W.E., B.M. Balk, D. Fixler, K.J. Fox and A.O. Nakamura (2011), *PRICE AND PRODUCTIVITY MEASUREMENT: Volume 1 -- Housing.* Trafford Press.

Linneman, P. (1980), "Some Empirical Results on the Nature of the Hedonic Price Function for the Urban Housing Market," *Journal of Urban Economics* 8, 47-68.

Linneman, P. and R.P. Voith (1991), "Housing Price Functions and Ownership Capitalization Rates," *Journal of Urban Economics* 30, 100-111.

Malpezzi, S., G.H. Chun, and R.K. Green (1998), "New Place-to-Place Housing Price Indexes for U.S. Metropolitan Areas and Their Determinants," *Real Estate Economics*, 26, 235-274.

Moulton, B.R. (1997), "Issues in Measuring Price Changes for Rent of Shelter," paper presented at Conference on Service Sector Productivity and the Productivity Paradox, Ottawa. http://www.csls.ca/events/confers/moulton.pdf

Nakamura, L.I. (1996), "Is U.S. Economic Performance Really That Bad?" Federal Reserve Bank of Philadelphia, Working Paper No. 95-21/R, April.

Nakamura, L.I. (1999), "The Measurement of Retail Output and the Retail Revolution," *Canadian Journal of Economics*, 32, 408-425.

Price Statistics Review Committee (1961), *The Price Statistics of the Federal Government*, NBER, New York.

Randolph, W.C. (1988a) "Estimation of Housing Depreciation: Short-Term Quality Change and Long-Term Vintage Effects," *Journal of Urban Economics* 23, 162-178.

Randolph, W.C. (1988b) "Housing Depreciation and Aging Bias in the Consumer Price Index," *Journal of Business and Economic Statistics* 6, 359-371.

Reinsdorf, M. (1993), "The Effect of Outlet Price Differentials on the U.S. Consumer Price Index," in Murray F. Foss et al. eds., *Price Measurements and Their Uses*, NBER Studies in Income and Wealth No. 57, University of Chicago Press, 227-254.

Rivers, J.D. and J.P. Sommers (1983), "Vacancy Imputation Methodology for Rents in the CPI," *Proceedings of the ASA Economics and Business Section*, 201-205.

Sheppard, S. (1999), "Hedonic Analysis of Housing Markets," in P.C. Cheshire and E.S. Mills (eds.), *Handbook of Regional and Urban Economics Volume 3*, Elsevier.

Sivitanides, P.S. and R.C. Sivitanidou (1997), "Exploring Capitalization Rate Differentials across Property Types," *Real Estate Issues* 22, 47-54.

Stewart, K.J., and S.B. Reed (1999), "Consumer Price Index Research Series Using Current Methods, 1978-1998," *Monthly Labor Review*, 122 (June), 29-38 .

Smith, L.B., K.T. Rosen and G. Fallis (1988), "Recent Developments in Economic Models of Housing Markets," *Journal of Economic Literature* 26, 29-64.

Chapter 5

A RENTAL EQUIVALENCE INDEX FOR OWNER OCCUPIED HOUSING IN WEST GERMANY

Claudia Kurz and Johannes Hoffmann[1]

1.   Introduction

Determining the appropriate treatment in official economic statistics of owner occupied housing (OOH) services is a complex problem.[2] Besides the heterogeneity of residential structures and the importance of location, their long lived nature causes difficulties.[3] In the context of a cost-of-living index, the traditional acquisitions approach, which does not differentiate between the period of purchase and the period of consumption, does not seem to be satisfactory.[4] Instead, a distribution of the initial cost of purchase over the life of the residential structure or the expected period of ownership seems called for. Period specific user costs are the theoretically implied solution to this inter-temporal distribution problem. However, user costs have proved problematical to compute. If there is a well developed rental market that is not distorted by taxes, rents can be viewed as representing the opportunity costs for owners of living in the homes they own.[5] This line of reasoning suggests that the use of data on actual rents for

---

[1] Claudia Kurz is with the University of Applied Sciences Mainz (claudia.kurz@wiwi.fh-mainz.de). Johannes Hoffmann is with the Economics Department of the Deutsche Bundesbank (johannes.hoffmann@bundesbank.de)..
An earlier version of this paper was published in the Discussion Paper series of the Economic Research Centre of the Deutsche Bundesbank as No. 08 in 2004. The paper benefited from discussions with colleagues at the Bundesbank and participants of the ZEW conference "Price Indices and the Measurement of Quality Changes," Mannheim, April 25-26, 2002, and of the SSHRC International Conference on Index Number Theory and the Measurement of Prices and Productivity, Vancouver, June 30-July 3, 2004. We are particularly grateful to Erwin Diewert, Heinz Herrmann, Hans-Albert Leifer, Ian McLoughlin, Alice Nakamura, Gerd Ronning, Harald Stahl and Richard Voith. Any remaining errors (and incorrect assessments) are our own. Furthermore, the paper represents the authors' personal opinions and does not necessarily reflect the views of the Deutsche Bundesbank or its staff.

[2] On this issue, see Blinder (1980) and Blackley and Follain (1995). See also Gillingham (1983).

[3] For an authoritative discussion of the problems at hand and alternative approaches, see Triplett (2001), Diewert (2003) and ILO et al. (2004, chapter 23). See also Diewert and Nakamura (2011) in this volume.

[4] However, if the purpose of the CPI is more restricted as for the European Harmonised Index of Consumer Prices (HICP), an acquisitions approach may be considered to be appropriate. See, for example, Leifer (2001).

[5] Darrough (1983), however, argues that rents and user costs are inherently different because of the distortions caused by taxes. Ayuso and Restoy (2003) report substantial but temporary deviations of property prices from rents and vice versa with the dynamics of the rental prices generally found to be smoother. Schulz and Werwatz (2004) find that rents in the German capital of Berlin reacted more slowly to changing market conditions than house prices. Verbrugge (2008) and Garner and Verbrugge (2011) also observe that user costs are more volatile than rents, and furthermore that for the period of 1978 to 2001, U.S. rents and user costs do not appear to share a common trend.

Kurz, C. and J. Hoffmann (2011), "A Rental Equivalence Index for Owner Occupied Housing in West Germany," chapter 5, pp. 69-86 in
W.E. Diewert, B.M. Balk, D. Fixler, K.J. Fox and A.O. Nakamura (2011),
PRICE AND PRODUCTIVITY MEASUREMENT: Volume 1 -- Housing. Trafford Press.

dwellings that closely match owner occupied dwellings in terms of characteristics is a suitable alternative to directly calculating user cost measures.

The importance of owner occupied housing in Germany is less than in most other industrialised economies.[6] Nevertheless, more than 40% of households live in their own residential properties. In the German consumer price index (CPI), as in the U.S. CPI, actual rents are used for the imputation of the cost of owner occupied housing, which is done by increasing the relative weight of the rent subindex. Approximating the costs of owner occupied housing by means of the rent index is said to be a valid method for Germany because the German housing market is lightly regulated, the tax system is not severely distorting and the share of rental housing is quite substantial.[7] However, the distribution of types of owner occupied housing differs substantially from that for rental housing. In Germany, rental housing typically takes the form of flats in apartment buildings, whereas single family houses and terraced houses predominate in the owner occupied segment. Only a restricted sample of dwelling types are used for the rent sample for the official German CPI. Price trends might differ between various segments of the housing market, creating a potential for bias. Given the substantial weight of housing, any bias in the housing component raises concerns about the accuracy of the total CPI.

For assessing the appropriateness of the German rental equivalence imputation method, we estimate alternative indexes of the costs of owner occupied housing using the German Socio Economic Panel (GSOEP). The GSOEP is a yearly household panel that reports on housing conditions in Germany including actual rents for renters. Each owner is asked to estimate the monthly rent they would need to pay to rent their own dwelling. This is a promising strategy for obtaining rental equivalents provided that owners have a good knowledge of market conditions.

We assess the quality of owner estimates of rental equivalents by estimating separate hedonic functions for rents and for rental equivalents and then comparing the estimated coefficients for the functions. The estimation strategy follows our companion paper on dwelling rents (Hoffmann and Kurz 2002). We find, in general, that the estimated coefficients do not differ significantly between rental and owner occupied housing. This finding implies that the variation in the marginal valuation of characteristics across markets, and between actual rents and reported rental equivalents, is not significant. This, in turn, implies that it is reasonable to use the estimated hedonic functions as a basis for the compilation of price indexes for OOH.

In section 2, we describe the peculiarities of the subindex for housing in the German CPI. In section 3, the German Socio Economic Panel (GSOEP) is introduced. In section 4, a hedonic analysis is performed of rental equivalents and actual rents as reported in the GSOEP. The hedonic functions from which the quality adjusted price indexes are derived are estimated for each period separately to allow for changing relative prices of characteristics. We calculate fixed based traditional Laspeyres and superlative indexes. In section 5, we discuss alternative indexes for owner occupied housing based on rental equivalents. Section 6 merges our new findings with those of our previous paper on the developments of actual rents. Section 7 concludes.[8]

---

[6] See the European Central Bank (2003).

[7] For a comparative analysis of European housing markets, see European Central Bank (2003).

[8] In some respects, our paper resembles Arévalo and Ruiz-Castillo (2006). They discuss the feasibility of the rental equivalence approach in the context of the Spanish housing market that is dominated by owner occupied housing. However, the Arévalo and Ruiz-Castillo study uses cross sectional data whereas we have panel data. Also, they use a procedure due to Heckman (1979) to allow for the interdependence of tenure mode and housing characteristics.

2. The Housing Subindex of the Official German CPI

The official German CPI subindex for housing covers rental and owner occupied housing.[9] For the German CPI (as for the U.S. CPI), the price component for owner occupied dwellings is currently produced using the index for rents.[10] The rent index itself is calculated as a matched models index. Quality adjustments are performed only when major renovations take place. No adjustments are made for the creeping changes in quality that stem from wear and tear. As no adjustments are made for ongoing maintenance investments either, the hope is that, on average, these omissions cancel out. In regions with substantial construction activity, the matched models sample is supplemented with data on new dwellings, for which rudimentary quality adjustments for differences in size are performed.

For the German CPI, rent data are collected for a restricted selection of dwelling types: three narrowly defined types of apartments from the privately financed segment of the market, and three from the subsidised segment. Only three and four room apartments are covered, so single and two room flats and also single family and terraced houses are missing.

The relative weight of owner occupied housing, which is not published separately, is derived from the share of rental equivalents in household consumption expenditures as estimated for the national accounts. This practice results in more than doubling the weight of the subindex for rented flats in the German CPI to take account of owner occupied housing. This reflects the fact that larger proportions of the owner occupied dwellings are of higher priced types.[11]

The German imputation practice implicitly assumes that the housing cost dynamics are similar for rented and owner occupied dwellings. This could be misleading.[12] Firstly, the distribution of owner occupied dwellings by type differs substantially from that of rental dwellings. This is especially a worry in the German case as the subindex for rents in the CPI is based on a very restricted list of dwelling types (given at the left in table 1). Furthermore, the regulation of the rental market and the differences in taxation could introduce biases.[13]

---

[9] For details, see Hoffmann and Kurz (2002).

[10] However, the German CPI rent index is derived from a dwelling sample and not a renter sample, and since prices at the lower level are aggregated by means of a Dutot index, it is not prone to the non-response-bias described by Crone, L.I. Nakamura and Voith (2001).

[11] In 1985, in the national accounts, West German actual rents amounted to 37 billion euro and estimated rental equivalents to 42 billion euro. In 1991, the corresponding figures were 50 and 59 billion euro.

[12] For further discussion in the context of the U.S. CPI, see Crone, L.I. Nakamura and Voith (2000, 2008, 2011).

[13] On these issues, see Hoffmann and Kurz (2002) and the European Central Bank (2003).

Table 1. Dwelling Types in the German CPI

Dwelling type	CPI expenditure weights (including imputed rent for owner occupied dwellings) as a % in the base year:		
	1985	1991	1995
All dwelling types	177.77	191.93	185.02
Privately financed apartments	143.99	163.45	166.33
3 room apartment (including kitchen), with bathroom, furnace heating, built by 1948	3.91	2.96	3.89
3 room apartment (including kitchen), with bathroom, furnace heating, built by 1948	16.71	12.15	35.53
4 room apartment (including kitchen), with bathroom, central heating, built after 1948	123.37	148.34	126.91
Subsidised apartments, built after 1948	33.78	28.48	18.69
3 room apartment (including kitchen), with bathroom, furnace heating	5.51	5.03	1.30
3 room apartment (including kitchen), with bathroom, central heating	28.27	18.91	13.13
4 room apartment (including kitchen), with bathroom, central heating	---	4.54	4.26

3.   Owner Occupied Housing in the German Socio-Economic Panel (GSOEP)

The GSOEP is an annual household panel that assembles information about living and working conditions in Germany.[14] Among other information, the GSOEP reports major physical and locational characteristics of dwellings, rents actually paid by households, and rental equivalents as estimated by owners. The panel started in 1984 with nearly 6,000 households, 65% of which were tenants and 35% owners.

In the GSOEP, owners are asked: "And if you lived in this flat or house as a tenant: what do you estimate would be the monthly rent without heating costs?" The wording implies that the equivalent rents reported in the GSOEP include some housing related expenses such as water supply and refuse collection. Up until 1998, the same was true of the rents collected for the compilation of the German CPI. Since 1998, however, rent data for the CPI excludes any additional expenses. As we want to compare the development of rental equivalents in the GSOEP to the rent measure in the CPI, this analysis is restricted to rented and owner-occupied dwellings in West Germany for 1985 to 1997.[15]

---

[14] For a detailed description of the GSOEP, see the SOEP Group (2001). Foreigners are deliberately oversampled.

[15] In 1990, the coverage of the GSOEP was extended to East Germany. However, most dwellings in East Germany were still state-owned. Rents were adjusted towards market values in phases. Owner occupied housing was marginal, and even at the end of the 1990s, the share of owner occupied housing was substantially below western levels. Also, in estimating the hedonic equations, an enlargement of the sample in 1998 was found to cause difficulties.

Sampling weights are provided together with the GSOEP. Estimates based on weighted GSOEP data can be regarded as approximately representative of Germany. All figures and results reported in this study are derived from the weighted sample.[16]

Although the focus in this paper is on dwellings rather than households, we cannot generate a true dwellings panel from the GSOEP. In the case of a move, the GSOEP follows the household. For the period under review, we observe a total of 10,000 different households, but 14,000 different dwellings. The greater number of dwellings reflects household moves.

A comparison of the structure of the housing expenditure shares in the GSOEP with that of the German CPI basket reveals that while nearly 40% of the rental expenditures reported in the GSOEP are for types of dwellings that correspond to CPI specifications, this is the case for less than 15% of the estimated rent expenditures for owner occupied housing, as can be seen from the second row of figures in table 2. This finding raises some doubts about the suitability of the CPI sample for the imputation of housing costs for owner occupied housing.

A closer look at the structure of rental and owner occupied housing (tables 3a and 3b) reveals that renters predominately live in apartment buildings whereas single family and terraced houses are the most common dwelling types for owners. There are further differences in the structure of rental and owner occupied housing. Owner occupied dwellings are on average larger and (slightly) better equipped than rented ones.[17] Owners also live more often in dwellings built after 1971. Rental housing is predominately located in big cities, whereas ownership is more evenly spread across various types of places of residence.

There are striking differences in the mobility of renters and owners. Between 6% and 11% of the renters move into the sample each year, whereas the corresponding figure for owners is less than 1%.[18] The average occupancy duration in owner occupied housing is almost twice as high as for rented dwellings.

However, even though the distribution of types of rental housing clearly differs from that of owner occupied housing, there are some important overlaps. About one fifth of renters live in single family or terraced houses, and about one fifth of owners live in flats. The quite substantial standard deviations for size for rented and owner occupied dwellings imply that there is no strict delineation of owner occupied and rental housing in terms of size. Also, we find both forms of tenure in all locations.

---

[16] When extracting the housing sample from the GSOEP, we found evidence of misreporting. For some dwellings, the reported occupancy duration is not consistent with the vintage. Also, some rents and rental equivalents seem to be excessively volatile. We used the panel structure of the data and developed procedures for deciding whether to keep observations and for adjusting inconsistent data. For a more detailed description of the adjustments made, see Hoffmann and Kurz (2002). About 1% of the observations each year were adjusted.

[17] The list of amenities reported in the GSOEP is a bit outdated since, as long ago as the 1980s, nearly all dwellings had a kitchen, a bathroom and a toilet. A cellar was available in more than nine out of ten dwellings. Substantial differences can be found only for central heating, galleries and gardens.

[18] These figures do not include those households that enter the sample after having moved recently or those households that were not contacted successfully by the GSOEP in the year immediately following the move.

Table 2. Housing as a Percentage of Household Expenditures

Dwelling type	1985	1991	1997
Owner occupied dwellings: all	**50.0**	**55.0**	**52.0**
Owner occupied dwellings, by type:			
Dwellings included in the CPI specifications	**11.0**	**13.1**	**12.9**
3 room apartment (including kitchen), without bathroom, furnace heating, built by 1948	0.1	0.0	0.0
3 room apartment (including kitchen), with bathroom, central heating, built by 1948	0.8	0.2	0.1
4 room apartment (including kitchen), with bathroom, central heating, built after 1948	10.1	12.9	12.8
Other dwellings	89.0	86.9	87.1
Rented dwellings: all	**50.0**	**45.0**	**48.0**
Rented dwellings, by type:			
Privately financed dwellings	**74.9**	**78.9**	**82.9**
Dwellings included in the CPI specification	**24.0**	**25.9**	**26.3**
3 room apartment (including kitchen), without bathroom, furnace heating, built by 1948	0.6	0.1	0.0
3 room apartment (including kitchen), with bathroom, central heating, built by 1948	4.6	5.7	4.3
4 room apartment (including kitchen), with bathroom, central heating, built after 1948	18.8	20.1	22,0
Other dwellings	51.0	53.0	56.6
Subsidised dwellings, built after 1948	**25.1**	**21.1**	**17.1**
Dwellings including in the CPI specification	**15.3**	**13.9**	**11.8**
3 room apartment (including kitchen), with bathroom, furnace heating	0.8	0.9	0.3
3 room apartment (including kitchen), with bathroom, central heating	5.3	5.1	4.4
4 room apartment (including kitchen), with bathroom, central heating	9.2	7.9	7,1
Other apartments	9.9	7.2	5.3

Note: Housing expenditure includes imputed rent for owners. All calculations use weighted GSOEP data.

Over the period covered, both rented and owner occupied dwellings became somewhat larger, slightly better equipped and more modern. The average size of dwellings increased by about 8% for rental units and by 13% for owner occupied dwellings. Throughout the period under review, the locational distribution of dwellings did not change much.

In each year, estimated equivalent rents were higher than actual rents, both in absolute terms and per square meter. Up to 1992, the equivalent rents also increased substantially faster than actual rents. In the years following 1992, the increase in actual rents was strong whereas the estimated equivalent rents nearly stagnated, albeit at a high level. Over the full period, these differences nearly cancel out and both the mean of the actual rents and the mean of the estimated equivalent rents (per square meter) go up by about 70%, or 4½% per year.

Table 3a. Characteristics of Dwellings in the 1985 GSOEP

Variable	Rented		Owner occupied	
	Mean	**Std dev**	**Mean**	**Std dev**
Rent (DM)	438.2	206.8	743.1	376.8
Occupancy duration (years)	10.9	11.3	22.4	17.6
Subsidised apartment	0.27	0.44		
Physical characteristics				
Vintage				
Built 1918 or earlier	0.14	0.35	0.20	0.40
Built between 1918 and 1948	0.21	0.41	0.16	0.37
Built between 1949 and 1971	0.49	0.50	0.40	0.49
Built 1972 or later	0.16	0.37	0.24	0.43
Built between 1972 and 1980				
Built between 1981 and 1990				
Built 1991 or later				
Size (square meters)	66.7	24.8	104.8	37.8
Furnishing				
Kitchen	0.98	0.14	1.00	0.00
Bathroom	0.95	0.22	0.98	0.14
Toilet	0.97	0.17	0.98	0.14
Central heating	0.78	0.41	0.84	0.37
Cellar	0.93	0.26	0.97	0.17
Gallery	0.60	0.49	0.76	0.43
Garden	0.26	0.44	0.88	0.32
Property type				
Farm house or other	0.01	0.10	0.07	0.26
Single family houses	0.09	0.29	0.45	0.50
Terraced house	0.08	0.27	0.30	0.46
Apartment house (3-8 flats)	0.57	0.50	0.13	0.34
Apartment house (more than 8 flats)	0.22	0.41	0.04	0.20
Multi storey building	0.03	0.17	0.00	0.00
Locational characteristics				
Type of quarter				
Residential area	0.65	0.48	0.75	0.43
Downtown district	0.01	0.10	0.00	0.00
Industrial area	0.00	0.00	0.00	0.00
Mixed area	0.32	0.47	0.21	0.41
Other	0.02	0.14	0.03	0.17
Conurbation type (inhabitants)				
500,000 and more (central area)	0.48	0.50	0.15	0.36
500,000 and more (other area)	0.13	0.34	0.19	0.39
100,000 - 500,000 (central area)	0.11	0.31	0.08	0.27
100,000 - 500,000 (other area)	0.04	0.20	0.08	0.27
50,000 - 100,000	0.03	0.17	0.02	0.14
20,000 - 50,000	0.06	0.24	0.09	0.29
5,000 - 20,000	0.10	0.30	0.21	0.41
2,000 - 5,000	0.03	0.17	0.10	0.30
Less than 2,000	0.01	0.10	0.08	0.27
State				
West Berlin	0.08	0.27	0.01	0.10
Baden-Württemberg	0.12	0.32	0.18	0.38
Bavaria	0.15	0.36	0.20	0.40
Bremen	0.02	0.14	0.01	0.10
Hamburg	0.05	0.22	0.01	0.10
Hesse	0.09	0.29	0.10	0.30
Lower Saxony	0.10	0.30	0.13	0.34
North Rhine-Westphalia	0.30	0.46	0.20	0.40
Rhineland-Palatinate / Saarland	0.05	0.22	0.10	0.30
Schleswig-Holstein	0.03	0.17	0.06	0.24

Table 3b. Characteristics of Dwellings in the 1997 GSOEP

Variable	Rented		Owner occupied	
	Mean	Std dev	Mean	Std dev
Rent (DM)	776.8	375.6	1365.9	591.9
Occupancy duration (years)	10.8	11.6	19.0	17.6
Subsidised apartment	0.20	0.40		
Physical characteristics				
Vintage				
Built 1918 or earlier	0.09	0.29	0.16	0.37
Built between 1918 and 1948	0.17	0.38	0.09	0.29
Built between 1949 and 1971	0.45	0.50	0.31	0.46
Built 1972 or later	0.29	0.45	0.45	0.50
Built between 1972 and 1980	0.15	0.36	0.22	0.41
Built between 1981 and 1990	0.06	0.24	0.12	0.32
Built 1991 or later	0.08	0.27	0.11	0.31
Size (square meters)	71.9	26.1	117.9	40.1
Furnishing				
Kitchen	0.99	0.10	1.00	0.00
Bathroom	0.99	0.10	0.99	0.10
Toilet	0.99	0.10	0.99	0.10
Central heating	0.90	0.30	0.96	0.20
Cellar	0.95	0.22	0.98	0.14
Gallery	0.66	0.47	0.89	0.31
Garden	0.31	0.46	0.89	0.31
Property type				
Farm house or other	0.02	0.14	0.07	0.26
Single family houses	0.12	0.32	0.42	0.49
Terraced house	0.08	0.27	0.29	0.45
Apartment house (3-8 flats)	0.54	0.50	0.15	0.36
Apartment house (more than 8 flats)	0.22	0.41	0.06	0.24
Multi-storey building	0.02	0.14	0.01	0.10
Locational characteristics				
Type of quarter				
Residential area	0.64	0.48	0.79	0.41
Downtown district	0.01	0.10	0.00	0.00
Industrial area	0.01	0.10	0.00	0.00
Mixed area	0.34	0.47	0.19	0.39
Other	0.01	0.10	0.01	0.10
Conurbation type (inhabitants)				
500,000 and more (central area)	0.50	0.50	0.20	0.40
500,000 and more (other area)	0.08	0.27	0.14	0.35
100,000 - 500,000 (central area)	0.11	0.31	0.09	0.29
100,000 - 500,000 (other area)	0.06	0.24	0.07	0.26
50,000 - 100,000	0.02	0.14	0.03	0.17
20,000 - 50,000	0.08	0.27	0.11	0.31
5,000 - 20,000	0.10	0.30	0.19	0.39
2,000 - 5,000	0.03	0.17	0.11	0.31
Less than 2,000	0.02	0.14	0.06	0.24
State				
West Berlin	0.07	0.26	0.01	0.10
Baden-Württemberg	0.13	0.34	0.19	0.39
Bavaria	0.16	0.37	0.19	0.39
Bremen	0.02	0.14	0.00	0.00
Hamburg	0.04	0.20	0.01	0.10
Hesse	0.08	0.27	0.06	0.24
Lower Saxony	0.10	0.30	0.14	0.35
North Rhine-Westphalia	0.32	0.47	0.26	0.44
Rhineland-Palatinate / Saarland	0.06	0.24	0.08	0.27
Schleswig-Holstein	0.03	0.17	0.06	0.24

4.   Hedonic Analysis of Estimated Equivalent Rents

The analysis in section 3 reveals that estimated equivalent rents are higher than actual rents, and moreover that owner occupied dwellings on average are of higher quality than rented dwellings. Here we ask whether the higher level of the rental equivalents found in the GSOEP is related to micro level differences in quality. Furthermore, we investigate whether the valuation of characteristics differs between rental and owner occupied housing. The technique on which our analysis is based is the hedonic regression approach. In Hoffmann and Kurz (2002) we show that for rental housing, taking the logs of the dependent variable, rent, and the one continuous explanatory variable, size of the dwelling, and adding dummy variables for other characteristics, works well.[19] Here we use the same functional form for owner reported equivalent rent:

$$(3\text{-}1) \quad \ln\text{rent} = c_0 + c_1 \ln\text{size} + \sum\nolimits_{i=2}^{n} c_i x_i + u,$$

where the dwelling traits are given by $X = (x_1, x_2, \ldots, x_i, \ldots, x_n)$ and u denotes an error term.

Using ordinary least squares, equation (3-1) was estimated separately for each year for renters (with actual rent), for owners (with equivalent rent), and for pooled renter-owner samples. The constant term gives the estimated rent for the baseline dwelling (without size effects). It is located in a residential area in the central district of a city of more than 500,000 inhabitants in North Rhine-Westphalia. The property is in an apartment house with up to eight flats, built before 1949. It is equipped with a bathroom/toilet, central heating, and a gallery or garden. It was privately financed, and the current household has been there for more than ten years. For most of the regressions, the Cook-Weisberg test showed evidence of heteroscedasticity. Thus, heteroscedasticity consistent robust standard errors were computed.

The occupancy duration that proved important in the Hoffmann and Kurz (2002) hedonic study of actual rents for rental dwellings is insignificant in the case of owner occupied housing. This means that the length-of-stay discounts found for rental housing either stem from unmeasured quality deterioration related to the length of occupancy, which does not take place in owner occupied housing, or the discounts are a consequence of the peculiarities of the landlord-tenant relationship. Here we drop the length-of-occupancy variable from the model.

Table 4 reports the regression results for the first and the last year in our sample.[20] The adjusted R squared values for owner occupied housing range from 0.43 to 0.56, and those for rented housing range from 0.53 to 0.65.[21] Most of the estimated coefficients are statistically significant and have the expected signs. Most parameter estimates are similar for rental and owner occupied dwellings. However, differences are evident in the valuation of different property types and for location.

---

[19] The occupancy duration is split into several dummy variables to allow for non-linearity in tenancy discounts. Furthermore, the occupancy duration variables have been interacted with the dummy variable for social housing. For details, see Hoffmann and Kurz (2002).

[20] For a fuller exposition and discussion of the regression set-up and the results including the issues of flexibility of the functional form, interaction between variables, heteroscedasticity, multicollinearity, misspecification and missing variables, see Hoffmann and Kurz (2002).

[21] The R-squared values are, however, still larger than those reported by Crone, L.I. Nakamura and Voith (2000).

To test the statistical significance of the differences between the coefficients of rental and owner occupied housing, for a pooled sample covering both segments of the housing market, the explanatory variables were interacted with dummy variables for owner occupied dwellings and for rented housing.[22] We used Wald tests to determine the significance of differences in the influence of the characteristics on rents versus the rental equivalents. Statistically significant differences were found in some years for the size variable, the property type, and the location. For example, typically, the estimated elasticity of equivalent rents with respect to dwelling size is somewhat lower than that of actual rents. Also, for owners, we find that single and terraced houses are more valuable than flats in apartment buildings, whereas the opposite is found sometimes for rental dwellings. Perhaps the tenure choice is not fully separable from the decision about dwelling type. However, the differences in the estimated impacts of the characteristics for rents versus rental equivalents are mostly found to be insignificant. Whereas differences in marginal valuations tend to be quite small and restricted to a few characteristics, the overall dummy for owner occupied housing, in almost all periods, is statistically significant and greater than zero,[23] indicating a higher valuation of owner occupied housing even after controlling for differences in quality and the length of stay for renters. Heston and Nakamura (2011) suggest two reasons for this discrepancy that is also observed in U.S. data. The first is what they term the pride factor: owners may value distinctive features of their dwellings more than the market does.[24] Secondly, there might be unmeasured characteristics. As the GSOEP reports only a restricted number of characteristics, this could explain some of the observed differences.

In line with our earlier finding for rental units (Hoffmann and Kurz 2002), we find here too that quality adjusted rents are on average lower for existing contracts than for new ones. However, looking at our results for each of the nine years, we find that these discounts display a cyclical pattern. These phenomena are believed to be the result of the peculiarities of contracting on the rental market (Francois 1989).[25] Genesove (2003) reports U.S. evidence of nominal rent rigidity for sitting tenants. The difference between estimated rental equivalents and actual rents might result from a tendency of owners to form their ideas about what their homes would rent for on the basis of new rental contracts (Francois 1989).

Of course, if the hypothesis is true that owners tend to base their rental equivalent estimates on new rental contracts, then the (quality adjusted) estimated equivalent rents should mirror actual rents for new contracts closely. Francois (1989), in a study for the United States, found that while estimated equivalent rents were typically above the average level of actual rents, they were close to rents for new contracts. Figures on rents in new contracts derived from the GSOEP also give some support to this hypothesis. Rents in new contracts tend to be higher than those for sitting tenants, display a more cyclical pattern, and more nearly resemble the pattern for the estimated equivalent rents for owners.

---

[22] Alternatively, a SUR estimator could be applied to take account of cross correlations in the regressions.

[23] It is only in 1985 and 1986 that the coefficient is not significantly different from zero.

[24] Linneman and Voith (1991) argue that many owners have a preference for homeownership. See also Goodman and Ittner (1992).

[25] In Germany, rents for sitting tenants generally can only be increased up to the level of rents for comparable dwellings in the vicinity. The level of rents for comparable dwellings is typically assessed by reference to a rent survey published by local authorities. The representative list of rents has to be compiled for new contracts and for contracts for which rents have been adjusted within four years. This means that rents for sitting tenants adjust to changing market conditions with a delay. See Hoffmann and Kurz (2002) and the European Central Bank (2003).

Table 4. Cross Section Hedonic Regressions

Variable	1985		1997	
	Rented	Owner occupied	Rented	Owner occupied
Constant	2.733[a]	2.983[a]	3.066[a]	4.031[a]
Physical characteristics				
Vintage				
Between 1949 and 1971	0.139[a]	0.072[a]	0.072[a]	0.062[c]
1972 or later	0.315[a]	---	---	---
Between 1972 and 1980		0.136[a]	0.136[a]	0.153[a]
Between 1981 and 1990		0.257	0.257[a]	0.176[a]
1991 or later		0.333	0.333[a]	0.248[a]
ln size (square meters)	0.772	0.776	0.809[a]	0.658[a]
Furnishing				
Without bathroom/toilet	-0.126[a]	-0.212	-0.212[a]	-0.352[a]
Without central heating	-0.226[a]	-0.156[a]	-0.156[a]	-0.116[b]
Without garden/gallery	-0.064[a]	-0.030	-0.030	-0.114
Property type				
Farm house or other	-0.097	-0.174	-0.174[a]	-0.094
Single-family house	-0.162[a]	-0.047[a]	-0.047	0.097[b]
Terraced house	-0.043	-0.061[a]	-0.061	0.127[a]
Apartment house (more than eight flats)	0.054[a]	0.009[a]	0.009	0.028
Multi-storey building	0.109[a]	0.083[a]	0.083[c]	0.105
Locational characteristics				
Type of quarter				
Downtown district	0.221[a]	0.013	0.013	0.093
Industrial area	-0.238	0.109	0.109	0.155
Mixed area	0.017	0.014[b]	0.014	-0.053c
Other	0.101	-0.052	-0.052	-0.081
Conurbation				
500,000 and more (other area)	-0.069[b]	-0.072[a]	-0.072[b]	-0.153[a]
100,000 to 500,000 (central area)	-0.140[a]	-0.171[a]	-0.171[a]	-0.135[a]
100,000 to 500,000 (other area)	-0.224[a]	-0.276[a]	-0.276[a]	-0.190[a]
50,000 to 100,000	-0.058	-0.206[a]	-0.206[a]	-0.205[a]
20,000 to 50,000	-0.210[a]	-0.130[a]	-0.130[a]	-0.249[a]
5,000 to 20,000	-0.290[a]	-0.280[a]	-0.280[a]	-0.263[a]
2,000 to 5,000	-0.256[a]	-0.293[a]	-0.293[a]	-0.297[a]
Less than 2,000	-0.289[a]	-0.553[a]	-0.553	-0.303[a]
State				
West Berlin	-0.095[a]	-0.040	-0.040	0.408[a]
Baden-Württemberg	0.032	0.125	0.125[a]	0.092[b]
Bavaria	0.030	0.095	0.095[a]	0.002
Hamburg/Bremen/ Lower Saxony/ Schleswig-Holstein	0.068[a]	0.116	0.116[a]	0.002
Hesse	0.046	0.109	0.109[a]	0.126[b]
Rhineland-Palatinate/ Saarland	-0.036	0.098	0.098[b]	-0.122[a]
Adjusted R-squared	0.58	0.55	0.62	0.62
Number of observations	2752	1552	2237	2237

Note: A superscript a, b or c indicates that, statistically, the coefficient is significantly different from zero at the 99, 95 or 90% level of confidence, respectively. Heteroscedasticity robust standard errors were used.

With our data, a formal test of the hypothesis proposed by Francois (1989) is not feasible since the number of new rental contracts in the GSOEP is too small. As an alternative, we define the baseline dwelling differently. Instead of referring to households with a length of stay of more than ten years, we re-estimate the hedonic model for a baseline household with an occupancy duration of up to two years. It turns out that the size of the estimated dummy for owner occupied housing shrinks. However, it stays statistically different from zero in nearly all years. Even after quality adjustments, there is, on average, a difference between the predicted rental equivalence and actual rents that can be only partly explained by the hypothesis that owners base the rental equivalence values they provide on the rents in new contracts. Still, in our view, these findings indicate that the owners' estimates of equivalent rents are, by and large, consistent with actual rents and that the markets for rental and owner occupied housing are interrelated in Germany.

Regarding the development over time, the estimated coefficients are quite stable, both for actual and equivalent rents. To test for stability, we pool the sample over adjacent periods and interact each regressor with a time dummy. A Wald test rejects the null hypothesis that the interactive terms are jointly significantly different from zero, implying that the parameter estimates can be regarded as stable over adjacent periods. For longer time spans, parameter stability is rejected; instead we find evidence of slow moving trends for some parameters.

5.   Alternative Rental Equivalence Indexes for Owner Occupied Housing

In this section, we present various rental equivalence indexes for owner occupied housing. We start with non-hedonic indexes: both simple statistical measures and matched models indexes. We then compare the results to indexes that are quality adjusted using hedonic techniques. In this part of our study, we replicate the research approach of our study of actual rents (Hoffmann and Kurz 2002). All measures have been calculated using GSOEP weights, so they can be regarded as being approximately representative for West Germany.

As measured by the geometric mean, non-adjusted rental equivalents increased by 90%, or 5.5% per year, over the period under review (table 5). Equivalent rent per square meter increased at a substantially slower pace: 72% over the review period, or 4.6% a year.

Table 5. Average Measures of the Change in Equivalent Rents (1985=100)

	1988	1991	1994	1997
Without quality adjustment				
Ratio of arithmetic means	112.8	139.9	172.0	183.8
Ratio of geometric means	114.9	142.5	175.2	189.9
Per square meter				
Ratio of arithmetic means	114.8	138.5	162.2	169.8
Ratio of geometric means	113.0	136.4	162.4	172.2

As the GSOEP is a household panel, household moves cause a fixed base index to become less and less representative over time. Hence, we also calculate chained matched model indexes (table 6).[26] The matched models indexes indicate that the true quality adjusted increase in estimated equivalent rents is perhaps even smaller than suggested by the rent-per-square-meter measure. Only the linked Carli index exhibits a strongly deviating trend, thus confirming the poor reputation of this type of index.

Over the full period, the fixed base geometric mean matched models index gives nearly the same estimate of price change as the chained geometric mean index (though in the medium term there are greater differences between the fixed base and chained measures). It shows a lower rate of increase than the table 5 estimate for the simple rent-per-square-meter measure.

Table 6. Matched Models Indexes (1985=100)

	1988	1991	1994	1997
Fixed base matched models				
Ratio of arithmetic means (Dutot)	107.5	124.1	149.8	159.0
Ratio of geometric means (Jevons)	108.6	126.0	151.6	161.6
Arithmetic mean of changes (Carli)	115.6	133.3	158.5	169.0
(Number of observations)	(992)	(634)	(309)	(168)
Chained matched models				
Ratio of arithmetic means (Dutot)	109.0	129.1	153.5	156.5
Ratio of geometric means (Jevons)	**111.0**	**131.8**	**157.5**	**160.8**
Arithmetic mean of changes (Carli)	126.0	162.5	210.0	237.6
(Number of observations)	(1314)	(1213)	(1034)	(1028)

Turning to quality adjusted indexes based on hedonic regression techniques, we start with the time dummy method.[27] A Wald test reveals that the estimated coefficients of the hedonic equations are stable over adjacent periods. Hence we pool the samples for adjacent years and calculate a biannual price index by exponentiating the coefficient of the time dummy. The resulting annual indexes are multiplied to form chain time series.[28]

From table 7, it can be seen that over the period of 1988 through 1997, according to the adjacent year index, rental equivalents for owner occupied housing increased by 63.1% for the review period, or 4.2% per year. This is less than indicated by the measures based on average rental equivalents or rental equivalents per square meter, reflecting the improvement in the quality of owner occupied housing. The estimate is, however, close to that of the chained variant of the geometric means matched models index suggesting that, for the data under review, matched models indexes deliver reasonable results.

---

[26] For the various elementary index number formulae, we refer the reader to ILO et al. (2004, chapters 9 and 20).

[27] On hedonic indices see ILO et al. (2004, chapter 21) and Diewert and Nakamura (2011).

[28] We made extensive checks to explore whether the type of bias analysed by van Dalen and Bode (2007), which results from the fact that least-squares estimates of x are biased estimates of e^x, is of empirical relevance in our calculations. We find that our time dummy estimates are not affected at the level of precision reported in the tables.

Table 7. Hedonic Indexes Based on Adjacent Year Regressions (1985=100)

	1988	1991	1994	1997
Owner occupied housing	111.1	131.7	154.7	163.1

Table 8 shows the results for three alternative index number formulae evaluated with and without chaining and making use of the parameter estimates from the cross section hedonic equations. According to the fixed base Fisher formula (Fisher 1985=100), equivalent rents increased by 63.6% for the review period, or 4.2% per year. This is slightly above the estimated rate of increase for the time dummy method that was also used (table 7). The chained Fisher index yields a slightly higher estimated increase of 65.9% for the review period, or 4.3% per year. Overall, the differences among the various indexes appear to be quite small.[29]

Table 8. Explicit Hedonic Indexes (1985=100)

	1988	1991	1994	1997
Laspeyres (1985=100)	109.2	128.2	154.2	164.7
Laspeyres, chained	110.0	130.3	154.4	164.2
Paasche (1985=100)	108.5	127.4	150.7	162.5
Paasche, chained	109.9	131.8	156.4	167.6
Fisher (1985=100)	108.9	127.8	152.4	163.6
Fisher, chained	110.0	131.1	155.4	165.9

Over the same period, the official CPI subindex for housing increased by just 48% or 3.3% per year (table 9). For privately financed four room apartments, which are mainly employed for the imputation of rental equivalents in the CPI, the recorded rate of change is only marginally higher (48.4%). This finding suggests that the official CPI housing subindex might be biased downwards.

Table 9. CPI Measures of Rent Inflation (1985=100)

	1988	1991	1994	1997
Total	105.0	117.0	136.0	148.0
4 room apartments (privately financed)	105.1	116.7	135.8	148.4

One might suspect that this downward bias originates from the lack of representativity of the CPI sample for owner occupied housing, since the official CPI measure of housing cost

---

[29] The explicit indexes suffer a bit more strongly from the bias mentioned in the previous footnote than the time-dummy indexes. However, up to 1997, the cumulated bias amounts to just 0.8%. In most years, the bias is significantly smaller than 1%.

inflation is derived from a restricted sample of dwellings. Our earlier research on the measurement of housing rents (Hoffmann and Kurz 2002) revealed, however, that actual rents, as measured by a chained hedonic Fisher index, increased by 59.2%, or 4.0% per year over the period under review giving only a slightly lower estimate of long run price change compared with the corresponding index based on rental equivalents that is developed in this paper. Also, we found for rental housing that the differences in price trends between a sample restricted to flats matching the CPI specifications and a sample covering other dwellings are trivial.

Our new findings also suggest that, for the period under review, no substantial changes occurred in relative prices between owner occupied and rental housing.

A closer look at the data reveals that while, in the long run, quality adjusted estimated rental equivalents for owners display exactly the same trend as quality adjusted actual rents for renters, nevertheless, important differences exist in the short to medium term. Whereas rental equivalents increased more sharply in the period up to 1992, opening a gap versus actual rents, afterwards actual rents increased substantially faster and nearly made up the gap. The rents for new contracts increased steeply in this period, responding to the inflow of population from East Germany and other countries in Eastern Europe and the unification boom in Germany.[30] Hence, the equivalent rents mirror the present state of the housing market more closely, whereas the actual rents echo developments in the (recent) past.

6. Price Indexes for Overall Housing

The findings in the earlier sections of this paper, and in our earlier paper, show how we can calculate an index for total housing and examine its effects versus the official CPI index for Germany. In principle, there are two ways of calculating indexes for total housing from our earlier findings. Using appropriate weights, we may calculate a weighted average of the indexes for rental and owner occupied housing. Alternatively we can pool the renter and the owner samples and then proceed as for the separate samples.

We start with a regression model including a full set of interaction terms between rental and owner occupied housing. Statistically insignificant interaction terms have been dropped from this model, with the result that only interaction terms for the length of stay, the size of the dwelling, the location in states and for single and terraced houses are kept. Taking the estimated marginal valuations and the average levels of the traits, we calculate fixed base and chained Laspeyres, Paasche and Fisher indexes in two variants. In the first variant we stay with our original specification for owners, whereas in the second variant we adjust for the length of stay and the time varying tenancy discounts.

For this purpose, we need to stipulate a distribution of the length-of-stay for owners that would be relevant in a fictional universe of renters. As mentioned before, there are substantial differences in the average occupancy duration between renters and owners, the latter being much longer than the former. The longer occupancy duration of owners is probably related to the relatively high transaction costs for owner occupied housing. On the other hand, there is clearly a kind of sorting effect as the transaction costs are also an important argument in the tenure

---

[30] On these issues, see Deutsche Bundesbank (2002, 2003).

decision of households. Therefore, we expect households with potential needs for mobility to be more likely to rent and households without mobility to be more likely to own. Based on these arguments, we take the average of the owner and the renter durations as the length-of-stay in a fictional world exclusively populated by renters.

According to our calculations for the period under review, total housing costs increased by 63.4%, or 4.2% per year. Adjusting the owner occupied segment for the effect of the occupancy duration on actual rents over the period of years covered by this analysis reduces the estimated rate of price increase only slightly, to 61.3%, or 4.1% per year (see table 10). Whereas the differences between the length-of-stay-adjusted and the non-adjusted Fisher indexes are rather small, there is a substantial discrepancy versus the official CPI housing cost inflation measures (table 9). Over the full period of 12 years, the difference versus the adjusted Fisher index amounts to about 13 percentage points, or 0.7 percentage points per year.

A closer inspection of the dynamics of the various indexes reveals that until 1988, the CPI measures are rather close to the hedonic indexes. Starting in 1989, the rates of increase for the hedonic indexes are substantially higher than for the CPI rent subindex. But from 1994 on, the CPI and the hedonic measures by and large again display the same rate of change. These findings, which resemble those of our earlier paper on rents,[31] may be interpreted as evidence of a time related bias in the German CPI housing cost measure. Probably it is no coincidence that major divergences appear for the first time in the year in which immigration started to put pressure on the German housing market.[32] In our earlier paper we discuss a list of potential causes, but conclude that none of these is fully convincing. Probably the divergence stems from hidden differences in the CPI and GSOEP dwelling samples that are unrelated to the types of dwellings. Such differences can, however, not be explored without a detailed examination of the CPI sample which is beyond the scope of this paper.

7. Conclusions

We find that the official German imputation method for owner occupied housing basically seems to be sound on the whole. However, we find some evidence of a downward bias in the German housing cost measure, though the causes remain unclear.

Our results seem to indicate that the equivalent rents reported in the GSOEP, as estimated by owners, are by and large reasonable. It is true that we find evidence of an overestimation of the level of estimated rental equivalents that can be only partly explained by a presumed tendency of owners to be aware primarily of rents for new contracts, and for this to affect their estimates of what their homes would rent for. In addition, probably the relatively higher expected rental values reported by owners for their homes reflect characteristics not reported in the GSOEP. To the extent that the latter is true, the higher values reported by owners could be an indication that the range of characteristics reported in the GSOEP, which is obviously limited, is not fully adequate to support the use of hedonic methods for making adjustments for quality differences.

---

[31] See Hoffmann and Kurz (2002).

[32] See Deutsche Bundesbank (2002) and Deutsche Bundesbank (2003).

Table 10. Explicit Hedonic Indexes for Total Housing (1985=100)

	1988	1991	1994	1997
Non-adjusted				
Laspeyres 1985	107.1	123.7	149.9	162.8
Laspeyres, chained	107.2	124.3	149.9	162.1
Paasche 1985	106.8	124.0	148.1	161.4
Paasche, chained	107.2	125.3	151.4	164.8
Fisher 1985	106.9	123.8	149.0	162.1
Fisher, chained	107.2	124.8	150.7	163.4
Adjusted for length of occupation				
Laspeyres 1985	105.9	121.5	148.4	161.6
Laspeyres, chained	105.8	121.5	147.1	159.2
Paasche 1985	105.7	121.6	146.7	159.8
Paasche, chained	105.9	122.5	149.5	163.5
Fisher 1985	105.8	121.5	147.5	160.7
Fisher, chained	105.8	122.0	148.3	161.3

References

Ayuso, J. and F. Restoy (2003), "House Prices and Rents: An Equilibrium Asset Pricing Approach," *Banco de Espana Documento de Trabajo* No. 0304.

Arévalo, R. and J. Ruiz-Castillo (2006), "On the Imputation of Rental Prices to Owner-Occupied Housing," *Journal of the European Economic Association* 4 (4), June, 830-860.

Blackley, D.M. and J.R. Follain (1995), "In Search of Empirical Evidence That Links Rent and User Costs," NBER Working Paper No. 5177.

Blinder, A.S. (1980), "The Consumer Price Index and the Measurement of Recent Inflation," *Brookings Papers on Economic Activity* No. 2, 539-565.

Crone, T.M., L.I. Nakamura and R.P. Voith (2000), "Measuring Housing Services Inflation," *Journal of Economic and Social Measurement* 26, 153-171.

Crone, T.M., L.I. Nakamura and R.P. Voith (2001), "Measuring American Rents: A Revisionist History," Federal Reserve Bank of Philadelphia Working Paper No. 01-8.

Crone, T.M., L.I. Nakamura, and R.P. Voith (2008), "Rents Have Been Rising, Not Falling, In the Postwar Period," *Review of Economics and Statistics*, forthcoming.

Crone, T.M., L.I. Nakamura and R.P. Voith (2011), "Hedonic Estimates of the Cost of Housing Services: Rental and Owner Occupied Units," chapter 4 in W.E. Diewert, B.M. Balk, D. Fixler, K.J. Fox and A.O. Nakamura (eds.), *Price and Productivity Measurement, Volume 1: Housing* Trafford Press.

Darrough, M.N. (1983), "The Treatment of Housing in a Cost-Of-Living Index: Rental Equivalence and User Cost," in W.E. Diewert and C. Montmarquette (eds.), *Price Level Measurement,* Proceedings from a Conference Sponsored by Statistics Canada, Statistics Canada, Ottawa, 599-618.

Deutsche Bundesbank (2002), "The Housing Market During the Nineties," *Monthly Report* January 2002, 27-37.

Deutsche Bundesbank (2003), "Price Indicators for the Housing Market," *Monthly Report* September 2003, 45-58.

Diewert, .W.E. (2003), "The Treatment of Owner Occupied Housing and Other Durables in a Consumer Price Index" Discussion Paper 03-08, Department of Economics, University of British Columbia, Vancouver, Canada, available at http://www.econ.ubc.ca/discpapers/dp0308.pdf. This paper is published in W.E.

Diewert, J. Greenless and C. Hulten (eds.), *Price Index Concepts and Measurement,* NBER Studies in Income and Wealth, University of Chicago Press.

Diewert, W.E. and A.O. Nakamura (2011), "Accounting for Housing in a CPI," chapter 2, pp. 7-32 in Diewert, W.E., B.M. Balk, D. Fixler, K.J. Fox and A.O. Nakamura (2011), *PRICE AND PRODUCTIVITY MEASUREMENT: Volume 1 -- Housing.* Trafford Press.

European Central Bank (2003), *Structural Factors in the EU Housing Markets,* Frankfurt am Main.

Francois, J.F. (1989), "Estimating Homeownership Costs: Owners' Estimates of Implicit Rents and the Relative Importance of Rental Equivalence in the Consumer Price Index," *AREUEA Journal* 17, 87-99.

Garner, T.I. and R. Verbrugge (2011), "The Puzzling Divergence of Rents and User Costs, 1980-2004: Summary and Extensions," chapter 8, pp. 125-146 in Diewert, W.E., B.M. Balk, D. Fixler, K.J. Fox and A.O. Nakamura (2011), *PRICE AND PRODUCTIVITY MEASUREMENT: Volume 1 -- Housing.* Trafford Press.

Genesove, D. (2003), "The Nominal Rigidity of Apartment Rents," *Review of Economics and Statistics* 85, 844-853.

Gillingham, R. (1983), "Measuring the Cost of Shelter for Homeowners: Theoretical and Empirical Considerations," *Review of Economics and Statistics* 65, 254-265.

Goodman, J.L. and J.B. Ittner (1992), "The Accuracy of Home Owners' Estimates of House Value," *Journal of Housing Economics* 2, 339-357.

Heckman, J.J. (1979), "Sample Selection Bias as a Specification Error," *Econometrica* 47, 153-161.

Heston, A. and A.O. Nakamura (2011),"On the Treatment of Owner Occupied Housing in Spatial and Temporal Price Indexes and in National Accounts," chapter 7, pp. 117-124 in Diewert, W.E., B.M. Balk, D. Fixler, K.J. Fox and A.O. Nakamura (2011), *PRICE AND PRODUCTIVITY MEASUREMENT: Volume 1 -- Housing.* Trafford Press.

Hoffmann, J. and C. Kurz (2002), "Rent Indices for Housing in West Germany 1985 to 1998," Economic Research Centre of the Deutsche Bundesbank Discussion Paper No. 01/02.

International Labour Office (ILO), International Monetary Fund, Organisation for Economic Co-operation and Development, Eurostat, United Nations, and The World Bank (2004), *Consumer Price Index Manual: Theory and Practice.* http://www.ilo.org/public/english/bureau/stat/guides/cpi/index.htm

Leifer, H.-A. (2001), "Zur Behandlung dauerhafter Güter in einem Verbraucherpreisindex und in einem Lebenshaltungskostenindex," *Allgemeines Statistisches Archiv* 85, 301-318.

Linneman, P. and R.P. Voith (1991), "Housing Price Functions and Ownership Capitalization Rates," *Journal of Urban Economics* 30, 100-111.

Schulz, R. and A. Werwatz (2004), A State Space Model for Berlin House Prices: Estimation and Economic Interpretation, Journal of Real Estate Finance and Economics 28, 37-57.

SOEP Group (2001), "The German Socio-Economic Panel (GSOEP) after More than 15 Years - Overview," in Elke Holst, Dean R. Lillard and Thomas A. DiPrete (eds.), Proceedings of the 2000 Fourth International Conference of German Socio-Economic Panel Study Users (GSOEP2000), *Vierteljahreshefte zur Wirtschaftsforschung* 70, 7-14.

Triplett, J.E. (2001), "Should the Cost-of-Living Index Provide the Conceptual Framework for a Consumer Price Index?" *Economic Journal* Vol. 111, F311-F334.

van Dalen, J. and B. Bode (2011), "Estimation Biases in Quality-Adjusted Hedonic Price Indices," in W.E. Diewert, B.M. Balk, D. Fixler, K.J. Fox and A.O. Nakamura (eds.), *Price and Productivity Measurement, Volume 5: Hedonics,* Trafford Press.

Verbrugge, R. (2008), "The Puzzling Divergence of Rents and User Costs, 1980-2004", paper presented at the OECD-IMF Workshop on Real Estate Price Indexes held in Paris, November 6-7, 2006. http://www.oecd.org/dataoecd/42/57/37612870.pdf Published in *Review of Income and Wealth* 54 (4), 671-699.

Chapter 6

THE PARIS OECD-IMF WORKSHOP
ON REAL ESTATE PRICE INDEXES:
CONCLUSIONS AND FUTURE DIRECTIONS

W. Erwin Diewert[1]

1.   Introduction

This paper highlights some of the themes that emerged from the OECD-IMF Workshop on Real Estate Price Indexes which was held in Paris, November 6-7, 2006. The paper discusses possible uses and target indexes for real estate price indexes and notes that a major problem is that it is not possible to exactly match the quality of dwelling units over time due to the fact that the housing stock changes in quality due to renovations and depreciation. Four alternative methods for constructing real estate price indexes are discussed: the repeat sales model; the use of assessment information along with property sale information; stratification methods and hedonic methods. The paper notes that the typical hedonic regression method may suffer from specification bias and suggests a way forward. Problems with the user cost method for pricing the services of owner occupied housing are also discussed. The paper is organized as follows.

Section 2 discusses the question: what are appropriate target indexes for Real Estate Prices? This section argues that the present System of National Accounts is a good starting point for a systematic framework for Real Estate Price indexes but the present SNA has to be augmented somewhat to meet the needs of economists who are interested in measuring consumption on a more comprehensive service flow basis and who are interested in measuring the productivity of an economy.

Section 3 notes the fundamental problem that makes the construction of constant quality real estate price indexes very difficult: namely depreciation and renovations to structures make the usual matched model methodology for constructing price indexes inapplicable.

Section 4 discusses four classes of methods that were suggested at the workshop to deal with the above problem and section 5 discusses some additional technical difficulties.

[1] This paper is an extended written version of my Discussion at the Concluding Overview session of the OECD-IMF Workshop on Real Estate Price Indexes held in Paris, November 6-7, 2006. The financial assistance of the OECD and the Australian Research Council is gratefully acknowledged, as is the hospitality of the Centre for Applied Economic Research at the University of New South Wales. The author thanks Paul Armknecht, Stephan Arthur, David Fenwick, Jan de Haan, Johannes Hoffmann, Anne Laferrère, Alice Nakamura, Marc Prud'homme, David Roberts, Mick Silver, Paul Schreyer and Kam Yu for helpful comments. None of the above individuals or organizations is responsible for any opinions expressed in this paper.

Diewert, W.E. (2011), "The Paris OECD-IMF Workshop on Real Estate Price Indexes: Conclusions and Future Directions," chapter 6, pp. 87-116 in
W.E. Diewert, B.M. Balk, D. Fixler, K.J. Fox and A.O. Nakamura (2011),
PRICE AND PRODUCTIVITY MEASUREMENT: Volume 1 -- Housing, Trafford Press.

Section 6 discusses the problems raised by Verbrugge's (2006) contribution to the Workshop; i.e., why do user costs diverge so much from rents?

Finally, section 7 summarizes suggestions for moving the agenda forward, including a proposal for a new approach to accounting for real estate in measures of inflation.

2.   What Are Appropriate Target Indexes?

There are many possible target real estate price indexes that could be constructed. Thus it is useful to consider alternative *uses* for real estate price indexes that were suggested at the workshop since these uses will largely determine what type of indexes should be constructed.

Fenwick (2006; 6) suggested the following list of possible uses for house price indexes:

- As a general macroeconomic indicator (of inflation);

- As an input into the measurement of consumer price inflation;

- As an element in the calculation of household (real) wealth, and

- As a direct input into an analysis of mortgage lender's exposure to risk of default.

Arthur (2006) also suggested some (related) uses for real estate price indexes:

- Real estate price bubbles (and the subsequent collapses) have repeatedly been related to financial crises and thus it is important to measure these price bubbles accurately and in a way that is comparable across countries, and

- Real estate price indexes are required for the proper conduct of monetary policy.

Fenwick also argued that various real estate price indexes are required for deflation purposes in the System of National Accounts (SNA):

"The primary focus of a national accountant seeking an appropriate deflator for national accounts will be different. Real estate appears in the National Accounts in several ways;

- the imputed rental value received by owner occupiers for buildings, as opposed to land, is part of household final consumption,

- the capital formation in buildings, again as opposed to land, is part of gross fixed capital formation, depreciation, and the measurement of the stock of fixed capital,

- and land values are an important part of the National stock of wealth."

David Fenwick (2006; 7-8)

Fenwick (2006; 6) also argued that it would be useful to develop a coherent conceptual framework for an appropriate *family* of real estate price indexes[2] and he provides such a framework towards the end of his paper.[3]

Diewert, in his oral presentation to the Workshop, followed Fenwick and argued that in the first instance, real estate price statistics should serve the needs of the SNA. The reason for this is that (with one exception to be discussed later) the SNA provides a quantitative framework where value flows and stocks are systematically decomposed in an economically meaningful way into price and quantity (or volume) components. The resulting p's and q's are the basic building blocks which are used in virtually all macroeconomic models. Hence it seems important for price statisticians to do their best to meet the deflation needs of the SNA.

Before the main problem area with the present SNA treatment of real estate is discussed, it is useful to review a bit of basic economics. There are two main paradigms in economics:

- Consumers or households maximizing utility subject to their budget constraints, and

- Producers maximizing profits subject to their production function (or more generally, their technology) constraints.

There are one period "static" and many period "intertemporal" versions of the two paradigms. However, for our purposes, it suffices to say that the SNA provides the necessary data to implement both models *except* for the fact that the SNA does not deal adequately with the consumption of consumer durables for the needs of either consumer or producer modeling. The problem is that when a consumer or producer purchases a good that provides services over a number of years, it is not appropriate to charge the entire purchase cost to the quarter or month when the durable is purchased; the purchase cost should be spread out over the useful life of the durable. However, with the important exception of residential housing, the SNA simply charges the entire cost of the durable to the period of purchase.[4] This is not an appropriate treatment of durables for many economic purposes. Thus, for the SNA household accounts, in addition to the usual *acquisitions approach* treatment of consumer durables (which simply charges the entire purchase cost to the period of purchase), it would be useful to have alternative measures of the service flows generated by household holdings of consumer durables. There are two alternative approaches to constructing such flow measures:

- An *imputed rent approach* which imputes market rental prices for the same type of service (if such prices are available), and

- A *user cost approach* which forms an estimate of what the cost would be of buying the durable at the beginning of the period, using the services of the durable during the period and then selling it at the end of the period. This estimated cost also includes the interest cost that is

---

[2] "It can be seen that user needs will vary and that in some instances, more than one measure of house price or real estate inflation may be required. It can also be seen that coherence between different measures and with other economic statistics is important and that achieving this will be especially difficult as statisticians are unlikely to have an ideal set of price indicators available to them." David Fenwick (2006, p. 8).

[3] See Fenwick (2006, pp. 8-11).

[4] More specifically, for owner occupied residential housing, the SNA incorporates estimates of the period by period flow of housing services. One reason this is done is to improve the comparability of the SNA between nations where the percentage of households living in owner occupied versus rental housing is very different.

[5] However, if most owners of some sort of durable, in fact, continue to hold it for multiple periods, then the buy-use-sell sequence might be priced out as a per-year average over the expected holding period, using the available information on the beginning and end of period prices and the transaction costs that would be involved in buying and then selling once over the expected holding period.

We discuss the relative merits of the above two service flow methods for valuing housing services in section 6 below. For additional material on the various economic approaches to the treatment of durables and housing in particular, see Diewert (2002; 611-622), (2003), Verbrugge (2006), and Chapter 23, "Durables and User Costs", in the International Labour Organization (ILO) Consumer Price Index Manual (2004).

On the producer side of the SNA, the service flows generated by durable inputs that are used to produce goods and services are buried in Gross Operating Surplus. Jorgenson and Griliches (1967) (1972) showed how gross operating surplus could be decomposed into price and quantity components using the user cost idea and their work led directly to the first national statistical agency productivity program; see the Bureau of Labor Statistics (1983).[6] Schreyer, Diewert and Harrison (2005) argued that this *productivity oriented approach to the System of National Accounts* could be regarded as a natural extension of the present SNA where the extended version provides a decomposition of a value flow (Gross Operating Surplus) into price and quantity (or volume) components.

We will argue below that if the SNA is expanded to exhibit the service flows that are associated with the household and production sectors' purchases of durable goods, then the resulting *Durables Augmented System of National Accounts* (DASNA)[7] provides a natural framework for a family of real estate price indexes.

In this augmented system of national accounts, household wealth and consumption will be measured in real and nominal terms. This will entail measures of the household sector's stock of residential wealth and it will be of interest to decompose this value measure into price and quantity (or volume) components. It will also be useful to decompose the residential housing stock aggregate into various subcomponents such as:

- by type of housing,

- by location or region,

- by the proportion of land and structures in the aggregate value,

- by age (in particular, new housing should be distinguished), and

- by whether the residence is rented or owned.

[5] The user cost idea can be traced back to Walras in 1874; see Walras (1954).

[6] The list of countries that now have official productivity programs includes the United States, Canada, the United Kingdom, Australia, New Zealand and Switzerland. The EU KLEMS project (for the EU KLEMS database and related information, see http://www.euklems.net/) is developing productivity accounts for many European countries using the Jorgenson and Griliches methodology, which is described in more detail in Schreyer (2001). For recent extensions and modifications, see Schreyer (2006).

[7] Such an accounting system is laid out and implemented for the United States by Jorgenson and Landefeld (2006).

Each of these subaggregates should be decomposed into price and volume components if possible. The DASNA will also require a measure of the flow of services from households' consumption of the services of their long lived consumer durables such as motor vehicles and owner occupied housing.[8] Thus it will be necessary to either implement the rental equivalence approach (as is currently recommended in the SNA) or the user cost approach (or some alternative) for valuing the services of Owner Occupied Housing in this extended system of accounts.[9]

Turning now to the producer side of the DASNA, for productivity measurement purposes, we will want user costs for owned commercial, industrial and agricultural properties. In order to form wealth estimates, we will require estimates for the value of commercial, industrial and agricultural properties and decompositions of the values into price and volume components. The price components can be used as basic building blocks to form user costs for the various types of property. It will also be useful to decompose the business property stock aggregates into various subcomponents such as:

- by type of structure,
- by location or region,
- by the proportion of land and structures in the aggregate value,
- by age (in particular, new structures should be distinguished), and
- by whether the structure is rented or owned.

If we think back to the list of uses for real estate price indexes suggested by Fenwick and Arthur earlier in this section, it can be seen that if we had all of the price indexes for implementing the DASNA as suggested above, then virtually all of the user needs could be met by this family of national accounts type real estate price indexes. The Durables Augmented SNA is a natural framework for the development of real estate price indexes that would meet comprehensive user needs.

We turn now to a discussion of the many technical issues that arise when trying to construct a property price index.

3. Failure of the Traditional Matched Model Methodology in the Real Estate Context

Consider the problems involved in constructing a constant quality price index for a class of residential dwelling units or business structures. The starting point for constructing any price

---

[8] For short lived household durables, it is not worth the bother of capitalizing these stocks; the usual acquisitions approach will suffice for these assets.

[9] We will return to this topic in section 6 below.

index between two time periods is to collect prices on exactly the same product or item for the two time periods under consideration; this is the standard *matched model* methodology.[10]

The *fundamental problem* that price statisticians face when trying to construct a real estate price index is that *exact matching of properties over time is often not possible* for two reasons:

- The property depreciates over time (*the depreciation problem*), and

- The property may have had major repairs, additions or remodeling done to it between the two time periods under consideration (*the renovations problem*).

Because of the above two problems, some form of imputation or indirect estimation will be required. A third problem that faces many European countries is the *problem of low turnover of properties*; i.e., if the sales of properties are very infrequent, then even if the depreciation and renovations problems could be solved, there would still be a problem in constructing a satisfactory property price index because of the low incidence of resales.[11]

A fourth problem should be mentioned at this point. For some purposes, it is desirable to decompose the real estate price index into two separate constant quality components:

- A component that measures the change in the price of the structure, and

- A component that measures the change in the price of the underlying land.

In the following section, we will look at some of the methods that were suggested by conference participants to construct constant quality real estate price indexes for the land and structures taken together. The problem of decomposing a real estate price index into its structure and land components is deferred until section 5 below.

4. Suggested Methods for Constructing Constant Quality Real Estate Price Indexes

4.1 The Repeat Sales Method

The *repeat sales approach* is due to Bailey, Muth and Nourse (1963), who saw their procedure as a generalization of the *chained matched model methodology* that was used by the early pioneers in the construction of real estate price indexes like Wyngarden (1927) and Wenzlick (1952). We will not describe the technical details of the method; we simply note that the method uses information on real estate properties which trade on the market more than once over the sample period.[12] By utilizing information on properties that are legally the same that

---

[10] For a detailed description of how this methodology works, see Chapter 20, "Elementary Indices", in the ILO (2004).

[11] Related problems are that the mix of transactions can change over time and in fact entirely new types of housing can enter the market.

[12] See Case and Shiller (1989) and Diewert (2003, pp. 31-39) for detailed technical descriptions of the method. Diewert showed how the repeat sales method is related to Summers' (1973) country product dummy model used in international price comparisons and the product dummy variable hedonic regression model proposed by Aizcorbe, Corrado and Doms (2001).

trade more than one period, the repeat sales method attempts to hold the quality of the properties constant over time.

We now discuss some of the advantages and disadvantages of the repeat sales method.[13]

The *main advantages* of the repeat sales model are:

• The availability of source data from administrative and real estate industry records on property sales, so that no imputations are involved (if no adjustments are made for renovations), and

• Reproducibility of the results; i.e., different statisticians given the same data on the sales of real estate properties will come up with the same estimate of quality adjusted price change.[14]

The *main disadvantages* of the repeat sales model are:

• It does not use all of the available information on property sales; it uses only information on properties that have sold more than once during the sample period.[15]

• It cannot deal adequately with depreciation of the dwelling unit or structure.

• It cannot deal adequately with units that have undergone major repairs or renovations.[16] In contrast, a general hedonic regression model for housing or structures can adjust for the

---

[13] Throughout this section, we will discuss the relative merits of the different methods that have been suggested for constructing property price indexes. For a similar (and perhaps more comprehensive) discussion, see Hoffmann and Lorenz (2006, pp. 2-6).

[14] Hedonic regression models suffer from a reproducibility problem; i.e., different statisticians will use different characteristics variables, different functional forms and different stochastic specifications, possibly leading to quite different results. However, in actual applied use, the repeat sales model is not as reproducible in practice as indicated in the main text because, in some variants of the method, houses that are "flipped" (sold very rapidly) and houses that have not sold for long periods are excluded from the regressions or regression-based adjustments are made to try to allow for changes in properties in the intervals between resale. The exact methods for making these sorts of adjustments vary among analysts and over time to time, leading to a lack of reproducibility.

[15] Some of the papers presented at the workshop suggested that the repeat sales method might lead to estimates of price change that were biased upwards, since often sellers of properties undertake major renovations and repairs just before putting their properties on the market, leading to a lack of comparability of the unit from its previous sale if the pure repeat sales approach is used. For example, Erna van der Wal, Dick ter Steege and Bert Kroese (2006, p. 3) write that: "The repeat sales method does not entirely adjust for changes in quality of the dwellings. If a dwelling undergoes a major renovation or even an extension between two transaction moments, the repeat sales method will not account for this. The last transaction price may in that case be too high, which results in an overestimation of the index." Andrew Leventis (2006, p. 9) writes that: "Research has suggested that appreciation rates for houses that sell may not be the same as appreciation rates for the rest of the housing stock." Leventis goes on to cite material by Stephens, Li, Lekkas, Abraham, Calhoun and Kimner (2005) on this point. Finally, Gudnason and Jonsdottir (2006) observe that: "The problem with this method is the risk for bias; e.g., when major renovation and other changes have been made on the house which increases the quality or if the wear of the house has been high, causing a decrease in the quality. Such changes are not captured by this method. Furthermore, in Iceland, this method cannot be used because the numbers of housing transactions are too few and thus there are not enough repeated sales to enable calculation of the repeated sales index."

[16] Case and Shiller (1989) used a variant of the repeat sales method with U.S. data on house sales in four major cities over the years 1970-1986. They attempted to deal with the depreciation and renovation problems as follows: "The tapes contain actual sales prices and other information about the homes. We extracted from the tapes for each city a file of data on houses sold twice for which there was no apparent quality change and for which conventional

effects of renovations and extensions if (real) expenditures on renovations and extensions are known and can be temporally matched with the data on property transactions.[17]

- The method cannot be used if indexes are required for very fine classifications of the type of property, due to insufficient observations. For example, if monthly property price indexes are required, the method may fail due to a lack of market sales for smaller categories of property.

- In principle, estimates for past price change obtained by the repeat sales method should be updated as new transaction information becomes available.[18] Thus the Repeat Sales property price index is subject to never ending revision.

We turn now to another class of methods suggested by workshop participants for forming constant quality property price indexes.

4.2 The Use of Assessment Information

Most countries tax real estate property. Hence, most countries have some sort of official valuation office that provides periodic appraisals of all taxable real estate property. The paper by van der Wal, ter Steege and Kroese (2006) presented at the Workshop describes how Statistics Netherlands uses appraisal information in order to construct a property price index. In particular, the *SPAR (Sales Price Appraisal Ratio) Method* is described as follows:[19]

> "This method has been used in New Zealand since the early 1960s. It also uses *matched pairs*, but unlike the Repeat Sales method, the SPAR method relies on nearly all transactions that have occurred in a given housing market, and hence should be less prone to sample selection bias. The first measure in each pair is the official government appraisal of the property, while the second measure is the matching transaction price. The ratio of the sale price and the appraisal of all sold dwellings in the base period, $t=0$, serves as the denominator. The numerator is the ratio of the selling price in the reference period, $t=t$, and the appraisal price in the base period for all dwellings that were sold in the reference period," van der Wal, ter Steege and Kroese (2006, p. 3).

We will follow the example of van der Wal, ter Steege and Kroese and describe the SPAR method algebraically. Denote the number of sales of a certain type of real estate in the

---

mortgages applied" (Karl E. Case and Robert J. Shiller, 1989, pp. 125-126). It is sometimes argued that renovations are approximately equal to depreciation. While this may be true in the aggregate, it certainly is not true for individual dwelling units because, over time, many units are demolished.

[17] However, usually information on maintenance and renovation expenditures is not available in the context of estimating a hedonic regression model for housing. Malpezzi, Ozanne and Thibodeau (1987, pp. 375-376) comment on this problem as follows: "If all units are identically constructed, inflation is absent, and the rate of maintenance and repair expenditures is the same for all units, then precise measurement of the rate of depreciation is possible by observing the value or rent of two or more units of different ages.... To accurately estimate the effects of aging on values and rents, it is necessary to control for inflation, quality differences in housing units, and location. The hedonic technique controls for differences in dwelling quality and inflation rates but cannot control for most differences in maintenance (except to the extent that they are correlated with location)."

[18] "Another drawback on the RS method is the fact that previously published index numbers will be revised when new data are added to the sample," Erna van der Wal, Dick ter Steege and Bert Kroese (2006, p. 3).

[19] van der Wal, ter Steege and Kroese (2006, p. 3) noted that this method is described in more detail in Bourassa, Hoesli and Sun (2006). The conference presentation by Statistics Denmark indicated that a variant of this method is also used in Denmark. Jan de Haan brought to my attention that a more comprehensive analysis of the SPAR method (similar in some respects to the analysis in this section) may be found in de Haan, van der Wal, ter Steege and de Vries (2006).

base period by N(0), let the sales prices be denoted as $[S_1^0, S_2^0, ..., S_{N(0)}^0] \equiv S^0$ and denote the corresponding official appraisal prices as $[A_1^{00}, A_2^{00}, ..., A_{N(0)}^{00}] \equiv A^{00}$. Similarly, denote the number of sales of the same type of property in the current period by N(t), let the sales prices be denoted as $[S_1^t, S_2^t, ..., S_{N(t)}^t] \equiv S^t$ and denote the corresponding official appraisal A^{0t} prices in the base period as $[A_1^{0t}, A_2^{0t}, ..., A_{N(t)}^{0t}] \equiv A^{0t}$. The reason for the double superscript on the appraisals is that we are assuming here that the appraisals are only made periodically; i.e., in period 0 but not period t. Thus the first superscript 0 indicates that the appraisal was made in period 0 and the second superscript, 0 or t, indicates that the property was sold either in period 0 or t. The *value weighted SPAR index* defined by van der Wal, ter Steege and Kroese (2006; 4) in our notation is defined as follows:

(1) $\qquad P_{DSPAR}(S^0, S^t, A^{00}, A^{0t}) \equiv [\sum_{i=1}^{N(t)} S_i^t / \sum_{i=1}^{N(t)} A_i^{0t}] / [\sum_{n=1}^{N(0)} S_n^0 / \sum_{n=1}^{N(0)} A_n^{00}]$.

We have labeled the index defined by (1) as P_{DSPAR} where the D stands for Dutot, since the index formula on the right hand side of (1) is closely related to the Dutot formula that occurs in the theory for the elementary price index components, which are the lowest level of aggregation for the components used in compiling a price index.[20]

What is the intuitive justification for formula (1)? One way to justify (1) is to suppose that the value S_n^0 for each property transaction in period 0 is equal to a period 0 common price level for the type of property under consideration, P^0 say, times a quality adjustment factor, Q_n^0 say, so that:

(2) $\qquad S_n^0 = P^0 Q_n^0, \qquad\qquad\qquad\qquad n = 1, 2, ..., N(0)$.

Next, we assume that the period 0 assessed value for transacted property n, A_n^{00}, is equal to the common price level P^0 times the quality adjustment factor Q_n^0 times an error term, which we write as $1 + \varepsilon_n^{00}$, and which is assumed to be independently distributed with zero mean.[21] Thus we have

(3) $\qquad A_n^{00} = P^0 Q_n^0 (1 + \varepsilon_n^{00}), \qquad\qquad\qquad n = 1, 2, ..., N(0)$,

with

(4) $\qquad E[\varepsilon_n^{00}] = 0, \qquad\qquad\qquad\qquad\qquad n = 1, 2, ..., N(0)$.

where E is the expectation operator.

---

[20] If the term $\sum_{n=1}^{N(0)} S_n^0 / \sum_{k=1}^{N(0)} A_n^{00}$ on the right hand side of (1) is equal to 1, then the index reduces to a Dutot index. For the properties of Dutot indexes, see Chapter 20, "Elementary Indices", in ILO (2004) or IMF (2004).

[21] This stochastic specification reflects the fact that the errors are more likely to be multiplicative than additive.

Turning now to a model for the period t property price transactions, we suppose that the value S_n^t for each property transaction in period t is equal to a period t common price level for the given property type, P^t say, times a quality adjustment factor, Q_i^t say, so that:

$$(5) \qquad S_i^t = P^t Q_i^t, \qquad\qquad i = 1,2,\ldots,N(t).$$

Next, we assume that the period 0 assessed value for property i transacted in period t, A_i^{0t}, is equal to the period 0 price level P^0 times the quality adjustment factor Q_i^t times an independently distributed error term, which we write as $1 + \varepsilon_i^{0t}$.[22] Thus we have:

$$(6) \qquad A_i^{0t} = P^0 Q_i^t (1 + \varepsilon_i^{0t}) \qquad\qquad i = 1,2,\ldots,N(t).$$

Our goal is to obtain an estimator for the level of property prices in period t relative to period 0, which is P^t / P^0. Define the share of transacted property n in period 0 to the total value of properties transacted in period 0, s_n^0, as follows:

$$(7) \qquad s_n^0 \equiv S_n^0 / \sum_{k=1}^{N(0)} S_k^0 \qquad\qquad n = 1,2,\ldots,N(0).$$

Similarly, define the share of transacted property i in period t to the total value of properties transacted in period t, s_i^t, as:

$$(8) \qquad s_i^t \equiv S_i^t / \sum_{k=1}^{N(t)} S_k^t \qquad\qquad i = 1,2,\ldots,N(t).$$

Substituting (2)-(6) into definition (1), and using definitions (7) and (8), and we obtain the following expression for the Dutot type SPAR price index:

$$(9) \qquad P_{DSPAR}(S^0, S^t, A^{00}, A^{0t})$$
$$= [\sum_{i=1}^{N(t)} P^t Q_i^t / \sum_{i=1}^{N(t)} P^0 Q_i^t (1 + \varepsilon_i^{0t})] / [\sum_{n=1}^{N(0)} P^0 Q_n^0 / \sum_{n=1}^{N(0)} P^0 Q_n^0 (1 + \varepsilon_n^{00})]$$
$$= [P^t / P^0][1 + \sum_{i=1}^{N(0)} s_i^0 \varepsilon_i^{00}] / [1 + \sum_{n=1}^{N(t)} s_n^t \varepsilon_n^{0t}].$$

Thus the Dutot type SPAR index will be unbiased for the "true" property price index, P^t / P^0, provided that the share weighted average of the period 0 and t quality adjustment errors are equal to zero; i.e., there will be no bias if

$$(10) \qquad \sum_{n=1}^{N(0)} s_n^0 \varepsilon_n^{00} = 0 \text{ and}$$

$$(11) \qquad \sum_{n=1}^{N(t)} s_n^t \varepsilon_n^{0t} = 0.$$

It is likely that the weighted sum of errors in period 0 is equal to zero (at least approximately) because it is likely that the official assessed values for period 0 are

_____

[22] It is no longer likely that the expected value of the error term ε_i^{0t} is equal to 0 since the base period assessments cannot pick up any depreciation and renovation biases that might have occurred between periods 0 and t.

approximately equal to the market transaction values in the same period; i.e., it is likely that (10) is at least approximately satisfied. However, it is not so likely that (11) would be satisfied since the period 0 assessed values will not reflect depreciation and renovations done between periods 0 and t. If the economy is growing strongly, then it is likely that the value of renovations will exceed the value of depreciation between periods 0 and t and hence the error terms ε_i^{0t} will tend to be less than 0 and $P_{DSPAR}(S^0, S^t, A^{00}, A^{0t})$ will be biased upwards. On the other hand, if there is little growth (or a declining population), then it is likely that the value of renovations will be less than the value of depreciation between periods 0 and t and hence the error terms ε_i^{0t} will tend to be greater than 0 and $P_{DSPAR}(S^0, S^t, A^{00}, A^{0t})$ will be biased downwards.

Variants of the Dutot type SPAR index can be defined; i.e., *the equal weighted SPAR index* defined by van der Wal, ter Steege and Kroese (2006; 4) in our notation is defined as follows:

$$(12) \quad P_{CSPAR}(S^0, S^t, A^{00}, A^{0t}) \equiv [\textstyle\sum_{i=1}^{N(t)}(S_i^t / A_i^{0t}) / N(t)] / [\textstyle\sum_{n=1}^{N(0)}(S_n^0 / A_n^{00}) / N(0)]$$

$$= [\textstyle\sum_{i=1}^{N(t)}\{P^t Q_i^t / P^0 Q_i^t (1+\varepsilon_i^{0t})\} / N(t)] / [\textstyle\sum_{n=1}^{N(0)}\{P^0 Q_n^0 / P^0 Q_n^t (1+\varepsilon_n^{0t})\} / N(0)]$$

$$\text{using (2)-(6)}$$

$$= [P^t / P^0][\textstyle\sum_{i=1}^{N(t)}(1+\varepsilon_i^{0t})^{-1} / N(t)] / [\textstyle\sum_{n=1}^{N(0)}(1+\varepsilon_n^{00})^{-1} / N(0)].$$

We have labeled the index as P_{CSPAR} since looking at the first line of (12), it can be seen that the index is a ratio of two equally weighted indexes of price relatives; i.e., the index is a ratio of two Carli indexes.[23] By looking at (12), it can be seen that if all of the error terms ε_i^{0t} and ε_i^{00} are equal to zero, then $P_{CSPAR}(S^0, S^t, A^{00}, A^{0t})$ will be equal to the target index, P^t / P^0. Of course, it is much more likely that the period 0 error terms, ε_i^{00}, are close to zero than the period t terms, ε_i^{0t}. If, in fact, all of the period 0 error terms are equal to 0, then it can be seen that $S_n^0 = A_n^{00}$ for all n and P_C reduces to the ordinary Carli index, $\sum_{i=1}^{N(t)}(S_i^t / A_i^{0t}) / N(t)$, which is known to be biased upwards.[24]

The last equation in (12) gives us an expression that could be helpful in determining the bias in this Carli type SPAR index in the general case of errors in both periods. However, it proves to be useful to approximate the reciprocal function, $f(\varepsilon) \equiv (1+\varepsilon)^{-1}$, by the following second order Taylor series approximation around $\varepsilon = 0$:

$$(13) \quad f(\varepsilon) \equiv (1+\varepsilon)^{-1} \approx 1 - \varepsilon + \varepsilon^2.$$

Substituting (13) into the last line of (12), we find that the Carli type SPAR index is approximately equal to:

---

[23] For the properties of Carli indexes, see Chapter 20, "Elementary Indices", in ILO (2004).

[24] See Chapter 20, "Elementary Indices", in ILO (2004).

(14) $P_{CSPAR}(S^0, S^t, A^{00}, A^{0t})$

$$\approx [P^t/P^0][\sum_{i=1}^{N(t)}(1-\varepsilon_i^{0t}+[\varepsilon_i^{0t}]^2)/N(t)]/[\sum_{n=1}^{N(t)}(1-\varepsilon_0^{00}+[\varepsilon_n^{00}]^2)/N(0)]$$

$$= [P^t/P^0][1+\sum_{i=1}^{N(t)}(-\varepsilon_i^{0t}+[\varepsilon_i^{0t}]^2)/N(t)]/[1+\sum_{n=1}^{N(t)}(-\varepsilon_0^{00}+[\varepsilon_n^{00}]^2)/N(0)]$$

$$\approx [P^t/P^0][1+\sum_{i=1}^{N(t)}(-\varepsilon_i^{0t}+[\varepsilon_i^{0t}]^2)/N(t)]/[1+\sum_{n=1}^{N(0)}[\varepsilon_n^{00}]^2)/N(0)]$$

where the last approximation follows from the (likely) assumption that

(15) $\sum_{n=1}^{N(0)}\varepsilon_n^{00}=0$;

i.e., that the sum of the assessment measurement errors in period 0 is zero. Now we can use the last line in (14) in order to assess the likely size of the bias in P_{CSPAR}.

If the economy is growing strongly, then it is likely that the value of renovations will exceed the value of depreciation between periods 0 and t and hence the error terms ε_i^{0t} will tend to be less than 0 so that $\sum_{n=1}^{N(t)}-\varepsilon_i^{0t}$ will be positive. The terms $\sum_{i=1}^{N(t)}[\varepsilon_i^{0t}]^2/N(t)$ and $\sum_{n=1}^{N(0)}[\varepsilon_i^{00}]^2/N(0)$ will both be positive but the period t squared errors most likely will be much larger than the period 0 squared errors so, overall, $P_{CSPAR}(S^0,S^t,A^{00},A^{0t})$ is likely to have a strong upward bias.

If there is little growth (or a declining population), then the upward bias is likely to be smaller. However, an upward bias is still likely because the term $\sum_{i=1}^{N(t)}[\varepsilon_i^{0t}]^2/N(t)$ is likely to be very much larger than the terms $-\sum_{n=1}^{N(t)}\varepsilon_n^{0t}/N(t)$ and $\sum_{n=1}^{N(0)}[\varepsilon_n^{00}]^2/N(0)$.

What about the relative sizes of the bias in the Dutot SPAR formula defined by the last line in (9) versus the Carli SPAR formula defined by the last line in (14)? Assuming that (10) holds and using a second order approximation analogous to (13) for $[1+\sum_{n=1}^{N(t)}s_n^t\varepsilon_n^{0t}]^{-1}$, we obtain the following approximation for the Dutot type SPAR formula:

(16) $P_{DSPAR}(S^0,S^t,A^{00},A^{0t})$

$$\approx [P^t/P^0]/[1+\sum_{n=1}^{N(t)}s_n^t\varepsilon_n^{0t}]$$

$$\approx [P^t/P^0]/\{1-\sum_{n=1}^{N(t)}s_n^t\varepsilon_n^{0t}+[\sum_{k=1}^{N(t)}s_n^t\varepsilon_n^{0t}]^2\}.$$

Comparing (14) with (16), it can be seen that the upward bias in the Carli type index will generally be *much greater* than the corresponding bias in the Dutot type index, since the sum of the individual period t errors divided by the number of observations, $\sum_{i=1}^{N(t)}[\varepsilon_i^{0t}]^2/N(t)$, will usually be very much greater than the square of the period t weighted sum of errors, $[\sum_{n=1}^{N(t)}s_n^t\varepsilon_n^{0t}]^2$.

It is evident that instead of using arithmetic averages of price relatives as in the Carli type formula (12), geometric averages could be used, leading to the following *Jevons*[25] *type SPAR index*:

$$(17) \quad P_{JSPAR}(S^0, S^t, A^{00}, A^{0t}) = [\prod_{i=1}^{N(t)}(S_i^t / A_i^{0t})]^{1/N(t)} / [\prod_{n=1}^{N(0)}(S_n^0 / A_n^{00})]^{1/N(0)}$$

$$= [\prod_{i=1}^{N(t)}\{P^t Q_i^t / P^0 Q_i^t (1+\varepsilon_i^{0t})\}]^{1/N(t)} / [\prod_{n=1}^{N(0)}\{P^0 Q_n^0 / P^0 Q_n^t (1+\varepsilon_n^{0t})\}]^{1/N(0)}$$

using (2)-(6)

$$[P^t / P^0][\prod_{n=1}^{N(0)}(1+\varepsilon_n^{00})]^{1/N(0)} / [\prod_{i=1}^{N(t)}(1+\varepsilon_i^{0t})]^{1/N(t)} .$$

Under the assumption that there are no systematic appraisal errors in period 0 so that (4) is satisfied, we can assume that $\prod_{n=1}^{N(0)}(1+\varepsilon_n^{00})$ is close. In contrast, if the value of renovations between periods 0 and t exceeds the value of depreciation, it is likely that $\prod_{i=1}^{N(t)}(1+\varepsilon_i^{0t})$ will be less than one and hence $P_{JSPAR}(S^0, S^t, A^{00}, A^{0t})$ will have an upward bias.[26]

It is evident that it is not really necessary to have the denominator terms in the right hand sides of definitions (1), (12) and (17) above, provided that the assessments are reasonably close to market values in the base period. Thus, we can define the (regular) *Dutot, Carli and Jevons Market Value to Appraisal indexes* as follows:

$$(18) \quad P_{DSPAR}(S^t, A^{0t}) \equiv [\sum_{i=1}^{N(t)} S_i^t / \sum_{i=1}^{N(t)} A_i^{0t}];$$

$$(19) \quad P_{CSPAR}(S^t, A^{0t}) \equiv [\sum_{i=1}^{N(t)}(S_i^t / A_i^{0t}) / N(t)];$$

$$(20) \quad P_J(S^t, A^{0t}) \equiv [\prod_{i=1}^{N(t)}(S_i^t / A_i^{0t})]^{1/N(t)} .$$

Using the material in Chapter 20 of the ILO *CPI Manual* (2004), it can be shown that the Jevons index $P_J(S^t, A^{0t})$ is always strictly less than the corresponding Carli index $P_C(S^t, A^{0t})$, unless all of the ratios S_i^t / A_i^{0t} are equal to the same number, in which case the indexes are equal to each other. It is also shown in the ILO Manual that the Dutot index will normally be fairly close to the corresponding Jevons index.[27]

No one of the six index number formulae discussed above is completely satisfactory because none of these can deal with the depreciation and renovations problem. However, if exogenous adjustments can be made to the indexes that constitute some sort of "average" adjustment to the index for renovations and depreciation, then appraisal methods become quite attractive. If appraisals in the base period are known to be reasonably accurate, then I would vote for the ordinary Jevons index, $P_J(S^t, A^{0t})$, defined by (20). If the appraisals in the base period

---

[25] For the properties of Jevons indexes, see Chapter 20, "Elementary Indices", in the ILO (2004) Manual.

[26] Using second order Taylor series approximation techniques, it can be shown that the upward bias in the Jevons type SPAR index will be less than in the corresponding Carli type SPAR index.

[27] The Manual does not recommend the use of the Carli formula since it fails the time reversal test with an upward bias.

are known to have a systematic bias, then the Jevons type SPAR index defined by (17), $P_{JSPAR}(S^0, S^t, A^{00}, A^{0t})$, seems to be the most attractive index.[28]

It is useful to discuss the merits of the above appraisal methods compared to other methods for constructing real estate price indexes.

The *main advantages* of methods that rely on assessment information in the base period and sales information in the current period are:

• The source data on assessment and sales are usually available from administrative records.

• These methods are reproducible conditional on the assessment information; i.e., different statisticians given the same data on the sales of housing units and the same base period assessment information will come up with the same estimate of quality adjusted price change.

• The assessment methods use much more information than the repeat sales method and hence there are fewer problems due to sparse data.

• Information on housing or structure characteristics is not required in order to implement this method.

The *main disadvantages* of the assessment methods discussed above are:

• They cannot deal adequately with depreciation of the dwelling units or structures.

• They cannot deal adequately with units that have undergone major repairs or renovations.

• These methods are entirely dependent on the quality of the base period assessment information. How exactly were the base period assessments determined? Were hedonic regression methods used? Were comparable property methods used?[29] How can we be certain that the quality of these base period assessments is satisfactory?[30]

• The methods discussed above do not deal with weighting problems.[31]

---

[28] These indexes should be further adjusted to take into account depreciation and renovations bias.

[29] Leventis (2006) discussed some of the problems with U.S. private sector assessment techniques when he discussed the work of Chinloy, Cho and Megbolugbe (1997) as follows: "Using a sample of 1993 purchase price data for which they also had the appraisal information, they compared purchase prices against appraisals to determine whether there were systematic differences. They estimated an upward bias of two percent and found that appraisals exceeded purchase price in approximately 60 percent of the cases. ... That appraisers 'extrapolate' valuations from recent results and have a vested interest in ensuring that their valuations appear reasonable (and perhaps consistent) to the originators suggest that the volatility of appraised values may be lower. At the same time, the authors believe that the appraisals' reliance on a small number of comparables 'almost surely' leads to 'more volatility than market-wide prices,'" Leventis (2006, pp. 5-6).

[30] If the assessments are used for taxation purposes and they are supposed to be based on market valuations, then the assessed values cannot be too far off the mark since the government has an incentive to make the assessments as large as possible (to maximize tax revenue) and taxpayers have the opposite incentive to have the assessments as small as possible.

[31] This is not really a major problem since the base period assessment information can be used to obtain satisfactory weights. When a new official assessment takes place, superlative indexes can be formed between any two consecutive assessment periods and interpolation techniques can be used to form approximate weights for all

● If information on housing characteristics is not available, then the method can be used to form only a single index. However, in most countries, the rate of change in real estate prices is not constant across locations[32] and different types of housing and so it is useful to be able to calculate more than one real estate price index.

● These assessment based methods cannot decompose a property price index into structure and land components.[33]

My overall evaluation of these assessment based methods is that they are quite satisfactory (and superior to repeat sales methods) if:

● The assessed values are used for taxation purposes;[34]

● The index is adjusted using other information for depreciation and renovations bias, and

● Only a single index is required and a decomposition of the index into structure and land components is not required.

We turn now to another class of methods for constructing property price indexes.

4.3 Stratification Methods

Possibly the simplest approach to the construction of a real estate price index is to *stratify* or decompose the market into separate types of property, calculate the mean (or more commonly, the median) price for all properties transacted in that cell for the current period and the base period, and then use the ratio of the means as a real estate price index.

The problem with this method can be explained as follows: if there are too many cells in the stratification, then there may not be a sufficient number of transactions in any given period in order to form an accurate cell average price. On the other hand, if there are too few cells in the stratification, then the resulting cell averages will suffer from *unit value bias*; i.e., the mix of properties sold in each period within each cell may change dramatically from period to period, and thus the resulting stratified indexes do not hold quality constant.

The stratification method can work well; for example, see Rosmundur and Jonsdottir (2006; 3-5) where they note that they work with some 8,000-10,000 real estate transactions per

---

intervening periods. For descriptions of superlative indexes and their properties, see Diewert (1976) (1978) or Chapters 15-20 of ILO (2004).

[32] The paper presented by Girouard, Kennedy, van den Noord and André (2006, p. 26) showed that there are regional differences in the rate of housing price change. This paper also showed that real estate bubbles were quite common in many OECD countries. In many countries, bubbles lead to differential rates of housing price increase; i.e., in the upward phase of the bubble, expensive properties tend to increase in price more rapidly than cheaper ones and then in the downward phase, the prices of more expensive properties tend to fall more rapidly. A single index will not be able to capture these differential rates of price change.

[33] We show later in section 5.1 that the hedonic method can deal with this problem.

[34] A bit of caution is called for here: sometimes official assessments are not very accurate for various reasons.

year in Iceland, which is a sufficient number of observations to be able to produce 30 monthly subindexes.[35] Within each cell, geometric rather than arithmetic averaging of prices is used:

> "The geometric mean replaces the arithmetic mean when averaging house prices within each stratum at the elementary level. This is in line with the calculation method used at the elementary level in the Icelandic CPI. The geometric mean is also used in hedonic calculations and the geometric mean is a typical matched model estimator (Diewert (2003b) (2003c), de Haan (2003)). Rosmundur Gudnason and Guorun Jonsdottir (2006; 5).

Even though geometric averaging is difficult to explain to some users, it has much to recommend it since it is more likely that random "errors" in a particular stratum of real estate are multiplicative in nature rather than being additive; see also Chapters 16 and 20 of ILO (2004).

The Australian Bureau of Statistics (ABS) is also experimenting with stratification techniques in order to produce constant quality housing price indexes:

> "The approach uses location (suburb) to define strata that group together (or 'cluster') houses that are 'similar' in terms of their price determining characteristics. Ideally, each suburb would form its own cluster as this would maximise the homogeneity of the cluster. However, there are insufficient numbers of observations from quarter to quarter to support this methodology. The ABS has grouped similar suburbs to form clusters with sufficient ongoing observations to determine a reliable median price. ABS research showed HPI (Housing Price Index) strata (or clusters of suburbs) were most effectively determined using an indicator of socio-economic characteristics: the median price, the percentage of three bedroom houses and the geographical location of the suburbs" Merry Branson (2006; 5).

The ABS clustering procedures are interesting and novel but caution seems merited in interpreting the resulting price changes since any individual suburb might contain a mixture of properties and thus the resulting indexes may be subject to a certain amount of unit value bias.[36]

We close this section with a discussion of the advantages and disadvantages of the stratification approach to the construction of real estate price indexes. It is useful to discuss the merits of the above appraisal methods compared to other methods for constructing real estate price indexes. The *main advantages* of the stratification method are:

- The method is conceptually acceptable, though it depends crucially on the choice of stratification variables.

- The method is reproducible, conditional on an agreed on list of stratification variables.

- Housing price indexes can be constructed for different types and locations of housing.

- The method is relatively easy to explain to users.

The *main disadvantages* of the stratification method are:

- The method cannot deal adequately with depreciation of the dwelling units or structures.

---

[35] However, the monthly index is produced as a moving average: "The calculation of price changes for real estate is a three month moving average, with a one month delay." Rosmundur Gudnason and Guorun Jonsdottir (2006, p. 4). Gudnason and Jonsdottir (2006, p. 3) also note that each year about 8-10 percent of all the housing in the country is bought and sold.

[36] However, Prasad and Richards (2006) show that the stratification method applied to Australian house price data gave virtually the same results as a hedonic model that had locational explanatory variables.

- The method cannot deal adequately with units that have undergone major repairs or renovations.

- The method requires some information on housing characteristics so that sales transactions can be allocated to the correct cells in the classification scheme.[37]

- If the classification scheme is very coarse, then there may be some unit value bias in the indexes.

- If the classification scheme is very fine, the detailed cell indexes may be subject to a considerable amount of sampling variability due to small sample sizes.

- The method cannot decompose a property price index into structure and land components.

My overall evaluation of the stratification method is that it can be quite satisfactory (and superior to the repeat sales and assessment methods[38]) if:

- An appropriate level of detail is chosen for the number of cells;

- The index is adjusted using other information for depreciation and renovations bias, and

- A decomposition of the index into structure and land components is not required.

It is well known that stratification methods can be regarded as special cases of general hedonic regressions[39] and so we now turn to this more general technique.

4.4   Hedonic Methods

Very detailed expositions of hedonic regression techniques applied to the property market can be found in some of the papers presented at this workshop; see, for example, Gouriéroux and Laferrère (2006) and Li, Prud'homme and Yu (2006). Although there are several variants of the technique, the basic model regresses the logarithm of the sale price of the property on the price determining characteristics of the property and a time dummy variable is added for each period in the regression (except the base period). Once the estimation has been completed, these time dummy coefficients can be exponentiated and turned into an index.[40]

---

[37] If no information on housing characteristics is used, then the method is potentially subject to tremendous unit value bias.

[38] The standard assessment method leads to only a single price index whereas the stratification method leads to a family of subindexes. However, if stratification variables are available, the assessment method can also be used to produce a family of indexes.

[39] See Diewert (2003b) who showed that stratification techniques or the use of dummy variables can be viewed as a nonparametric regression technique. In the statistics literature, these partitioning or stratification techniques are known as analysis of variance models; see Scheffé (1959).

[40] An alternative approach to the hedonic method is to estimate separate hedonic regressions for both of the periods compared; i.e., for the base and current period. Predicted prices can then be generated in each period using the estimated hedonic regressions based on a constant characteristics set, say the characteristics of the base period. A ratio of the geometric means of the estimated prices in each period would yield a pure price comparison based on a

Since the method assumes that information on the characteristics of the properties sold is available, the data can be stratified and a separate regression can be run for each important class of property. Thus the hedonic regression method can be used to produce a family of indexes.[41] The issues associated with running weighted hedonic regressions are rather subtle and the recent literature on this topic will not be reviewed here.[42] Here, we simply note some of the advantages and disadvantages of the hedonic approach. At the outside, it should be noted that the usual hedonic regression model is not able to separate out the land and structures components of the property class under consideration. However, in section 5.1 below, we will explain how the usual method can be modified to give us this decomposition.

It is useful to discuss the merits of the hedonic regression method compared to other methods for constructing real estate price indexes. The *main advantages* of the hedonic regression method are:

• Property price indexes can be constructed for different types and locations of the property under consideration.

• The method is probably the most efficient one for making use of the available data.

• The method can be modified to give a decomposition of property prices into land and structures components (see section 5.1 below); none of the other methods described so far can handle this decomposition.

• If the list of property characteristics is sufficiently detailed so that, for example, it can be determined whether major maintenance projects have been undertaken (such as a new roof) and when they were done, then it may be possible to deal more generally with depreciation and renovations problems.

The *main disadvantages* of the hedonic method are:

• The method is data intensive (i.e., it requires information on property characteristics) and thus it is relatively expensive to implement.

• The method is not entirely reproducible; i.e., different statisticians will enter different property characteristics into the regression,[43] assume different functional forms for the

---

constant base period set of characteristics. A hedonic index based on a constant current period characteristic could also be compiled, as could such indexes based on a symmetric use of base and current period information. Heravi and Silver (2007) outline alternative formulations, and Silver and Heravi (2007) provide a formal analysis of the difference between this approach and that of the time dummy method. The French method also does not use the time dummy method but is too complex to explain here.

[41] This property of the hedonic regression method also applies to the stratification method. The main difference between the two methods is that continuous variables can appear in hedonic regressions (like the area of the structure and the area of the lot size) whereas the stratification method can only work with discrete ranges for the independent variables in the regression.

[42] Basically, this recent literature makes connections between weighted hedonic regressions and traditional index number formula that use weights; see Diewert (2003c) (2004) (2005a) (2005b); de Haan (2003) (2004); Silver (2003), and Silver and Heravi (2005). It is worth noting that a perceived advantage of the stratification method is that *median* price changes can be measured as opposed to the *arithmetic mean* ones that are implicit in a, say, an ordinary least squares estimator. However, regression estimates can also be derived from robust estimators from which the parameter estimates for the price change will be similar to a median.

[43] Note that the same criticism can be applied to stratification methods; i.e., different analysts will come up with different stratifications.

regression equation, make different stochastic specifications and perhaps choose different transformations of the dependent variable[44], all of which can lead to perhaps different estimates of the amount of overall price change.

- The method is not easy to explain to users.

My overall evaluation of the hedonic regression method is that it may be probably the best method that could be used in order to construct constant quality price indexes for various types of property, provided that adequate data are available.[45] Note that the paper by Gouriéroux and Laferrère (2006) demonstrates that it is possible to construct a credible, official, nationwide hedonic regression model for real estate properties.

In the following two sections, we will discuss some additional technical issues that emerged from the workshop. In particular, in section 5.1 below, we will show how the hedonic regression technique can be modified to provide a structures and land price decomposition of property price movements.

5.   Other Technical Issues

5.1   The Decomposition of Real Estate Values into Land and Structure Components[46]

If we momentarily think like a property developer who is planning to build a structure on a particular property, the total cost of the property after the structure is completed will be equal to the floor space area of the structure, say A square meters, times the building cost per square meter, α say, plus the cost of the land, which will be equal to the cost per square meter, β say, times the area of the land site, B. Now think of a sample of properties of the same general type, which have prices p_n^0 in period 0 and structure areas A_n^0 and land areas B_n^0 for $n = 1, \ldots, N(0)$, with these prices equal to costs of the above type of structure times error terms η_n^0 which we assume have mean 1. This leads to the following hedonic regression model for period 0 where α and β are the parameters to be estimated in the regression:[47]

$$(21) \quad p_n^0 = [\alpha A_n^0 + \beta B_n^0]\eta_n^0, \qquad\qquad n = 1, \ldots, N(0).$$

Taking logarithms of both sides of (21) leads to the following traditional additive errors regression model:[48]

$$(22) \quad \ln p_n^0 = \ln[\alpha A_n^0 + \beta B_n^0] + \varepsilon_n^0, \qquad\qquad n = 1, \ldots, N(0),$$

---

[44] For example, the dependent variable could be the sales price of the property or its logarithm or the sales price divided by the area of the structure and so on.

[45] This evaluation agrees with that of Hoffmann and Lorenz: "As far as quality adjustment is concerned, the future will certainly belong to hedonic methods." Johannes Hoffman and Andreas Lorenz (2006, p. 15).

[46] Discussions with Anne Laferrère helped improve on the initial oral presentation of the model presented in this section.

[47] Multiplicative errors with constant variances are more plausible than additive errors with constant variances; i.e., it is more likely that expensive properties have relatively large absolute errors compared to very inexpensive properties. The multiplicative specification for the errors will be consistent with this phenomenon.

[48] However, note that this model is not linear in the unknown parameters to be estimated.

where the new error terms are defined as $\varepsilon_n^0 \equiv \ln \eta_n^0$ for $n = 1, \ldots, N(0)$ and are assumed to have 0 means and constant variances.

Now consider the situation in a subsequent period t. The price per square meter of this type of structure will have changed from α to $\alpha \gamma^t$ and the land cost per square meter will have changed from β to $\beta \delta^t$ where we interpret γ^t as the *period 0 to t price index for the type of structure* and we interpret δ^t as the *period 0 to t price index for the land that is associated with this type of structure*. The period t counterparts to (21) and (22) are:

$$(23) \qquad p_n^t = [\alpha \gamma^t A_n^t + \beta \delta^t B_n^t] \eta_n^t, \qquad\qquad n = 1, \ldots, N(t);$$

$$(24) \qquad \ln p_n^t = \ln[\alpha \gamma^t A_n^t + \beta \delta^t B_n^t] + \varepsilon_n^t, \qquad\qquad n = 1, \ldots, N(t),$$

where $\varepsilon_n^t \equiv \ln \eta_n^t$ for $n = 1, \ldots, N(t)$, the period t property prices are p_n^t, and the corresponding structure and land areas are A_n^t and B_n^t for $n = 1, \ldots, N(t)$.

Equations (22) and (24) can be run as a system of nonlinear hedonic regressions and estimates can be obtained for the four parameters, α, β, γ^t and δ^t. The main parameters of interest are, of course, γ^t and δ^t, which can be interpreted as price indexes for the price of a square meter of this type of structure and for the price per meter squared of the underlying land, respectively.

The above very basic nonlinear hedonic regression framework can be generalized to encompass the traditional array of characteristics that are used in real estate hedonic regressions. Thus suppose that we can associate with each property n that is transacted in each period t a list of K characteristics $X_{n1}^t, X_{n2}^t, \ldots, X_{nK}^t$ that are price determining characteristics for the structure and a similar list of M characteristics $Y_{n1}^t, Y_{n2}^t, \ldots, Y_{nM}^t$ that are price determining characteristics for the type of land beneath the structure. The equations which generalize (22) and (24) to the present setup are the following ones:

$$(25) \qquad \ln p_n^0 = \ln\{[\alpha_0 + \sum_{k=1}^K X_{nk}^0 \alpha_k]A_n^0 + [\beta_0 + \sum_{m=1}^M Y_{nm}^0 \beta_m]B_n^0\} + \varepsilon_n^0, \qquad n = 1, \ldots, N(0),$$

$$(26) \qquad \ln p_n^t = \ln\{\gamma^t[\alpha_0 + \sum_{k=1}^K X_{nk}^t \alpha_k]A_n^t + \delta^t[\beta_0 + \sum_{m=1}^M Y_{nm}^t \beta_m]B_n^t\} + \varepsilon_n^t, \quad n = 1, \ldots, N(t),$$

where the parameters to be estimated are now the $K+1$ quality of structure parameters, $\alpha_0, \alpha_1, \ldots, \alpha_K$, the $M+1$ quality of land parameters, $\beta_0, \beta_1, \ldots, \beta_M$, the period t price index for structures parameter γ^t, and the period t price index for the land underlying the structures parameter δ^t. Note that $[\alpha_0 + \sum_{k=1}^K X_{nk}^0 \alpha_k]$ in (25) and (26) replaces the single structures quality parameter α in (22) and (24) and $[\beta_0 + \sum_{m=1}^M Y_{nm}^0 \beta_m]$ in (25) and (26) replaces the single land quality parameter β in (22) and (24).

In order to illustrate how the X and Y variables can be formed, we consider the list of exogenous variables in the hedonic housing regression model reported by Li, Prud'homme and Yu (2006; 23). The following variables in their list of exogenous variables can be regarded as variables that affect structure quality; i.e., these are X type variables: the number of reported bedrooms, the number of reported bathrooms, the number of garages, the number of fireplaces, the age of the unit, the age squared of the unit, whether the exterior finish is brick or not, a dummy variable for new units, a dummy for whether the unit has hardwood floors or not, a dummy for whether the heating fuel is natural gas or not, a dummy for whether the unit has a patio or not, a dummy for whether the unit has a central built in vacuum cleaning system or not, a dummy for whether the unit has an indoor or outdoor swimming pool or not, a dummy for whether the unit has a hot tub unit or not, a dummy for whether the unit has a sauna or not, and a dummy for whether the unit has air conditioning or not. The following variables can be regarded as variables that affect the quality of the land; i.e., these are Y type location variables: a dummy for whether the unit is at the intersection of two streets or not (corner lot or not), a dummy for whether the unit is on a cul-de-sac or not, a dummy for whether there is a shopping center nearby or not, and a dummy for various suburb location dummy variables.[49]

The nonlinear hedonic regression model defined by (25) and (26) is very flexible and can accomplish what none of the other real estate price index construction methods were able to accomplish: namely a decomposition of a property price index into structures and land components. However, this model has a cost compared to the usual hedonic regression model discussed in section 4.4: the previous class of models was linear in the unknown parameters to be estimated whereas the model defined by (25) and (26) is highly nonlinear. It remains to be seen whether such a highly nonlinear model can be estimated successfully for large data sets.[50]

5.2   Weighting and Formula Issues

Most of the papers presented at the workshop did not delve too deeply into weighting and formula issues, with some exceptions, such as the paper by Rosmundur and Jonsdottir (2006). However, for all of the methods except the hedonic regression methods, the advice on formulae and weighting given in the ILO *CPI Manual* (2004) seems relevant and the reader is advised to consult the appropriate chapters. For hedonic methods, we noted the recent literature on weighting and the reader is advised to consult this literature.

Perhaps it is worth repeating some of Diewert's observations on weighting problems that can arise if we use the acquisitions approach to housing:

---

[49] Of course, in practice, some of the land or location variables could act as proxies for unobserved structure quality variables. There are also some interesting conceptual problems associated with the treatment of rental apartments and owner occupied apartments or condominiums. Obviously, separate hedonic regressions would be appropriate for apartments since their structural characteristics are quite different from detached housing. For rental apartments, the sale price of the apartment can be the dependent variable and there will be associated amounts of structure area and land area. For a condo sale, the price of the single unit is the dependent variable while the dependent variables in the bare bones model would be structure area of the apartment plus the apartment's share of commonly owned facilities plus the apartment's share of the lot area. In the end, we want to be able to make imputations that divide the value of the property into land and structure components, and the hedonic regression should be set up so as to accomplish this task.

[50] Of course, large data sets can be transformed into smaller data sets if we run separate hedonic regressions for various property strata!

"Some differences between the acquisitions approach and the other approaches are:

- If rental or leasing markets for the durable exist and the durable has a long useful life, then the expenditure weights implied by the rental equivalence or user cost approaches will typically be much larger than the corresponding expenditure weights implied by the acquisitions approach.

- If the base year corresponds to a boom year (or a slump year) for the durable, then the base period expenditure weights may be too large or too small. Put another way, the aggregate expenditures that correspond to the acquisitions approach are likely to be more volatile than the expenditures for the aggregate that are implied by the rental equivalence or user cost approaches.

- In making comparisons of consumption across countries where the proportion of owning versus renting or leasing the durable varies greatly,[51] the use of the acquisitions approach may lead to misleading cross country comparisons. The reason for this is that opportunity costs of capital are excluded in the net acquisitions approach whereas they are explicitly or implicitly included in the other two approaches." W. Erwin Diewert (2003a, 7-8).

5.3 The Frequency Issue and the Consistency of Quarterly with Annual Estimates

For inflation monitoring purposes, central banks would like to have property price indexes produced on a monthly or quarterly basis. Given the fact that the number of observations for a monthly index will only be approximately one third the number for a quarterly index, statistical agencies must carefully evaluate the timeliness-quality tradeoff.

Another question arises in this context: how can monthly or quarterly estimates of real estate inflation be made consistent with annual estimates?

The answer to this question is not simple because of two problems:

- The existence of seasonal factors; i.e., during some seasons (e.g., winter) real estate sales tend to be more sparse, and there may be seasonal fluctuations in prices.[52]

- For high inflation countries, the price levels in the last month or quarter can be very much higher than those prevailing in the first quarter, leading to various conceptual difficulties.

If there is high inflation within the year, then when annual unit value prices are computed (to correspond to total annual production of the commodities under consideration), "too much" weight will be given to the prices of the fourth quarter compared to the prices in the first quarter.[53] There are possible solutions to this problem but they are rather complex and there is no consensus on what the appropriate solution should be.

For possible solutions to the above problems, the reader is referred to Hill (1996), Diewert (1998) (1999), Bloem, Dippelsman and Maehle (2001), and Armknecht and Diewert (2004).

---

[51] From Hoffmann and Kurz (2002, pp. 3-4), about 60% of German households live in rented dwellings whereas only about 11% of Spaniards rent their dwellings in 1999 (private communication).

[52] Hoffmann and Kurz-Kim (2006) provide some recent evidence of seasonality in German prices.

[53] See Hill (1996) and Diewert (1998) for a discussion of these problems.

5.4   Revision Policies

Many of the papers presented at this conference noted the difficulties in assembling timely data on property sales. Since many of these difficulties seem intractable, it seems sensible to *not* apply the usual Consumer Price Index methodology to Real Estate Price indexes[54]; i.e., revisions should be allowed for Real Estate price indexes. This will create problems for CPI indexes that apply a user cost approach to Owner Occupied Housing, since the user cost will depend on accurate property price indexes, which will generally only be available with a lag. The same problem will occur if the Harmonized Index of Consumer Prices decides to implement an acquisitions approach to Owner Occupied Housing.[55] One solution might be that users will be given a flagship CPI or HICP that makes use of preliminary or forecasted data, and revised indexes will only be made available as "analytic" series. This issue requires more discussion.

5.5   The Renovations versus Depreciation Problem

Renovations increase the quality of a property and depreciation decreases the quality of a property and typically, both phenomena are not directly observed, making the construction of truly constant quality real estate price indexes difficult, if not impossible.

One way to deal with this problem is for statistical agencies to have a fairly extensive *renovations and repair survey* for both households and businesses. If renovations expenditures can be tracked over time back to a base period for individual properties that have sold in the current period and if a base period estimate for the value of the property is available, then this information can be used in a hedonic regression model along the lines indicated in section 5.1 and scientific estimates of depreciation can be obtained. On the business side of property markets, the situation is not as bad, since businesses normally keep track of major renovations in their asset registers and this information could be accessed in investment surveys that also ask questions about asset sales and retirements. Canada,[56] the Netherlands[57] and New Zealand ask such questions on retirements in their investment surveys and Japan is about to follow suit.[58] Diewert and Wykoff (2006) indicate how this type of survey can be used to obtain estimates for depreciation rates.

There are a number of technical details that remain to be explored in this area.

The final technical problem that arose out of the workshop is sufficiently important that it deserves a separate section. The question which the paper by Verbrugge (2006) raised is this: are user costs so volatile and unpredictable that they are pretty much useless in a statistical agency real estate price index?

---

[54] The usual CPI methodology is to never revise the index.

[55] For an update on how thinking is progressing on the treatment of Owner Occupied Housing in the HICP, see Makaronidis and Hayes (2006).

[56] For a description and further references to the Canadian program on estimating depreciation rates, see Baldwin, Gellatly, Tanguay and Patry (2005).

[57] Actually, since 1991, the Dutch have a separate (mail) survey for enterprises with more than 100 employees to collect information on discards and retirements: The Survey on Discards; see Bergen, Haan, Heij and Horsten (2005, p. 8) for a description of the Dutch methods.

[58] The Economic and Social Research Institute (ESRI), Cabinet Office of Japan, with the help of Koji Nomura is preparing a new survey to be implemented as of the end of 2006.

6. User Costs versus Rental Equivalence

One of the most interesting and provocative papers presented at the Workshop was the paper by Verbrugge. He summarized his paper as follows:

"I construct several estimates of *ex ante* user costs for US homeowners, and compare these to rents. There are three novel findings. First, a significant volatility divergence remains even for *ex ante* user cost measures which have been smoothed to mimic the implicit smoothing in the rent data. Indeed, the volatility of smoothed quarterly aggregate *ex ante* user cost growth is about 10 times greater than that of aggregate rent growth. This large volatility probably rules out the use of *ex ante* user costs as a measure of the costs of homeownership.

The second novel finding is perhaps more surprising: not only do rents and user costs diverge in the short run, but the gaps persist over extended periods of time. ...

The divergence between rents and user costs highlights a puzzle, explored in greater depth below: rents do not appear to respond very strongly to their theoretical determinants. ...

Despite this divergence, the third novel finding is that there were evidently no unexploited profit opportunities. While the detached unit rental market is surprisingly thick, and detached housing is readily moved between owner and renter markets ..., the large costs associated with real estate transactions would have prevented risk neutral investors from earning expected profits by using the transaction sequence *buy, earn rent on property, sell*, and would have prevented risk neutral homeowners from earning expected profits by using the transaction sequence *sell, rent for one year, repurchase*" Randal Verbrugge (2006; 3).

How did Verbrugge arrive at the above conclusions? He started off with the following expression for the user cost u_i^t of home i:[59]

$$(27) \quad u_i^t = P_i^t (i^t + \delta - E[\pi_i^t])$$

where

- P_i^t is the price of home i in period t;

- i^t is a nominal interest rate;[60]

- δ is the sum of annual depreciation, maintenance and repair, insurance, property taxes and potentially a risk premium;[61] and

- $E[\pi_i^t]$ represents the expected annual constant quality home appreciation rate for home i at period t.[62]

---

[59] See formula (1) in Verbrugge (2006, p. 11). We have not followed his notation exactly.

[60] Verbrugge (2006, p. 11) used either the current 30 year mortgage rate or the average one year Treasury bill rate and noted that the choice of interest rate turned out to be inconsequential for his analysis.

[61] Verbrugge (2006, p. 13) assumed that δ was approximately equal to 7 %. Note that the higher the volatility in house prices is, the higher the risk premium would be for a risk adverse consumer.

[62] π_i^t is the actual four quarter (constant quality) home price appreciation between the beginning of period t and one year later.

Thus the resulting user cost can be viewed as an opportunity cost measure for the annual cost of owning a home starting at the beginning of the quarter indexed by time t. Presumably, landlords, when they set an annual rent for a dwelling unit, would use a formula similar to (27) in order to determine the rent for a tenant.[63] So far, there is nothing particularly controversial about Verbrugge's analysis. What is controversial was Verbrugge's determination of the expected house price appreciation term, $E[\pi_i^t]$:

"Rather than using a crude proxy, I will construct a *forecast* for $E[\pi_i^t]$, as described below. This choice is crucial, for four reasons. First, expected home price appreciation is extremely volatile; setting this term to a constant is strongly at odds with the data, and its level of volatility will be central to this study. Second, this term varies considerably across cities, and its temporal dynamics might well vary across cities as well. Third, the properties of $(i^t - E[\pi_i^t])$ are central to user cost dynamics, yet these properties are unknown (or at least, not documented); again, setting $E[\pi_i^t]$ to a constant (or even to a long moving average) would be inappropriate for this study, since this choice obviously suppresses the correlation between i^t and $E\pi_i^t$. Finally, the recent surge in $E[\pi_i^t]$ is well above its 15 year average, and implies that the user cost/rent ratio has fallen dramatically. A *single* year appreciation rate is used since we are considering the *one year* user cost, in order to remain comparable to the typical rental contract." Randal Verbrugge (2006; 12).

Verbrugge (2006; 13) went on to use various econometric forecasting techniques to forecast expected price appreciation for his one year horizon, he inserted these forecasts into the user cost formula (27) above and obtained tremendously volatile ex ante user costs and the rest of his conclusions followed.

However, it is unlikely that landlords use econometric forecasts of housing price appreciation one year away and adjust rents for their tenants every year based on these forecasts. Tenants do not like tremendous volatility in their rents and any landlord that attempted to set such volatile rents would soon have very high vacancy rates on his or her properties.[64] It is however possible that landlords may have some idea of the long run average rate of property inflation for the type of property that they manage and this long run average annual rate of price appreciation could be inserted into the user cost formula (27).[65]

Looking at the opportunity costs of owning a house from the viewpoint of an owner occupier, the relevant time horizon to consider for working out an annualized average rate of expected price appreciation is the expected time that the owner expects to use the dwelling

---

[63] Diewert (2003a) noted that there would be a few differences between a user cost formula for an owner occupier as compared to a landlord but these differences are not important for Verbrugge's analysis.

[64] Hoffmann and Kurz-Kim find that German rents are changed only once every 4 years on average: "In Germany, as in other euro area countries, prices of most products change infrequently, but not incrementally. Pricing seems to be neither continuous nor marginal. In our sample, prices last on average more than two years—if price changes within a month are not considered—but then change by nearly 10 %. The longest price durations are found for housing rents, which, on average, are for more than four years," Hoffmann and Kurz-Kim (2006, p. 5).

[65] The paper by Girouard, Kennedy, van den Noord and André nicely documents the length of housing booms and busts: "To qualify as a major cycle, the appreciation had to feature a cumulative real price increase equaling or exceeding 15%. This criterion identified 37 such episodes, corresponding to about two large upswings on average per 35 years for English speaking and Nordic countries and to 1½ for the continental European countries," Girouard, Kennedy, van den Noord and André (2006, p. 6). Thus one could justify taking 10 to 20 year (annualized) average rates of property price inflation in the user cost formula rather than one year rates.

before reselling it. This time horizon is typically at least 6 to 12 years, so again, it does not seem appropriate to stick annual forecasts of expected price inflation into the user cost formula. Once we use annualized forecasts of expected price inflation over longer time horizons, the volatility in the ex ante user cost formula will vanish or at least be much diminished.

Another method for reducing the volatility in the user cost formula is to replace the nominal interest rate less expected price appreciation term $(i^t - E[\pi_i^t])$ by a constant or a slowly changing long run average *real interest rate*, r^t say. This is what is done in Iceland[66] and the resulting user cost seems to be acceptable to the population (and it is not overly volatile).

Verbrugge had an interesting section in his paper that helps to explain why user costs and market rentals can diverge so much over the short run. The answer is high transactions costs involved in selling or purchasing real estate properties prevent arbitrage opportunities:[67]

> "The first question is thus answered: there is no evidence of unexploited profits for prospective landlords. How about the second: was there ever a period of time in any city during which a 'median' homeowner should have sold his house, rented for a year, and repurchased his house a year later? ... In this case, it appears that for Los Angeles, there was a single year, 1994, during which a homeowner should have sold her house, rented for a year, and repurchased her house. For every other time period, and for the entire period for the other four cities, a homeowner was always better off remaining in his house," Randal Verbrugge (2006, p. 36).

Since high real estate transactions costs prevent the exploitation of arbitrage opportunities between owning and renting a property, user costs can differ considerably over the corresponding rental equivalence measures over the lifetime of a property cycle.

7.   The Way Forward

The following points emerged as a result of the Workshop:

•   The needs of users cannot be met by a single housing (or more generally, by a single real estate) price index.

•   There is a demand for official real estate price indexes that are at least roughly comparable across countries.

•   Statistical agencies should not produce multiple indexes that measure the same thing.

•   The System of National Accounts should be the starting point for providing a systematic framework for a family of real estate price indexes.[68]

---

[66] See Rosmundur (2004) and Rosmundur and Jonsdottir (2006, p. 11).

[67] Verbrugge (2006, p. 35) assumed that the transactions costs in the U.S. were approximately 8 to 10 percent of the sales price.

[68] As was noted above in section 2, it is necessary to look beyond the present SNA to the next version which will probably have a more detailed treatment of durable goods in it so that consumer service flows can be better measured and so that productivity accounts can be constructed for the business sector. A natural family of real estate price indexes emerges from this expanded SNA.

- It may well be that cooperation between the private sector and statistical agencies is the way forward in this area; the papers by Gouriéroux and Laferrère (2006) and Li, Prud'homme and Yu (2006) show that this type of cooperation is possible.

- It would be very useful for the various international agencies to cooperate in producing an international Manual or Handbook of Methods on Real Estate Price Indexes so that national real estate price indexes can be harmonized across countries (or at least be more harmonized).

- It would be useful to produce a country inventory of practices in the real estate price index area.

- The OECD should take the lead in producing the Manual and the inventory of practices.

- There is a need for the Manual writers to talk to users about their needs in this area.

- The listing of properties on the internet may well facilitate the development of high quality property price indexes and may do the same for residential property price indexes as scanner data did for ordinary consumer price indexes.[69]

We conclude this section with the following (controversial) observation: perhaps the "correct" opportunity cost of housing for an owner occupier is not his or her internal user cost but the *maximum* of the internal user cost and what the property could rent for on the rental market. After all, the concept of opportunity cost is supposed to represent the *maximum sacrifice* that one makes in order to consume or use some object and so the above point would seem to follow.[70] If this point of view is accepted, then at certain points in the property cycle, user costs would replace market rents as the "correct" pricing concept for owner occupied housing, which would dramatically affect Consumer Price Indexes and the conduct of monetary policy.[71]

References

Aizcorbe, A., C. Corrado and M. Doms (2001), "Constructing Price and Quantity Indexes for High Technology Goods," Industrial Output Section, Division of Research and Statistics, Board of Governors of the Federal Reserve System, July.

Armknecht, P.A. and W.E. Diewert (2004), "Treatment of Seasonal Products," pp. 553-593 in *Producer Price Index Manual: Theory and Practice*, Washington: International Monetary Fund. http://www.imf.org/external/np/sta/tegppi/ch22.pdf

Arthur, S.V. (2006), "Residential Property Prices—What has been Achieved since 2003?," paper presented at the OECD-IMF Workshop on Real Estate Price Indexes held in Paris, November 6-7, 2006. http://www.oecd.org/dataoecd/3/9/37583158.pdf

Bailey, M.J., R.F. Muth and H.O. Nourse (1963), "A Regression Method for Real Estate Price Construction," *Journal of the American Statistical Association* 58, 933-942.

Baldwin, J., G. Gellatly, M. Tanguay and A. Patry (2005), "Estimating Depreciation Rates for the Productivity Accounts," paper presented at the OECD Workshop on Productivity Measurement, Madrid Spain, October 17-19. http://www.oecd.org/document/27/0,2340,en_2649_34409_35100379_1_1_1_1,00.html

---

[69] Johannes Hoffmann made this point.

[70] This proposal is more fully developed in Diewert and Nakamura (2011).

[71] Woolford (2006) shows that different treatments of Owner Occupied Housing in the Australian context generate very different aggregate consumer price indexes.

Bergen, Dirk van den, M. de Haan, R. de Heij and M. Horsten (2005), "Measuring Capital in the Netherlands," paper presented at the Meeting of the OECD Working Party on National Accounts, Paris, October 11-14. www.unece.org/stats/documents/ece/ces/ge.20/2005/8.e.pdf

Bloem, A.M., R.J. Dippelsman and N.Ø. Maehle (2001), *Quarterly National Accounts Manual: Concepts, Data Sources and Compilation*, Washington: International Monetary Fund.

Bourassa, S.C., M. Hoesli and J. Sun (2006), "A Simple Alternative House Price Index," *Journal of Housing Economics* 15, 80-97.

Branson, M. (2006), "The Australian Experience in Developing an Established House Price Index," paper presented at the OECD-IMF Workshop on Real Estate Price Indexes, Paris, November 6-7. http://www.oecd.org/dataoecd/2/26/37583386.pdf

Bureau of Labor Statistics (1983), *Trends in Multifactor Productivity, 1948-81*, Bulletin 2178, U.S. Government Printing Office, Washington, D.C.

Case, K.E. and R.J. Shiller (1989), "The Efficiency of the Market for Single Family Homes," *The American Economic Review* 79, 125-137.

Chinloy, P., M. Cho and I.F. Megbolugbe (1997), "Appraisals, Transactions Incentives and Smoothing," *Journal of Real Estate Finance and Economics* 14(1), 45-55.

de Haan, J. (2003), "Direct and Indirect Time Dummy Approaches to Hedonic Price Measurement," paper presented at the 7th Ottawa Group Meeting, Paris, May 27-29. http://www.ottawagroup.org/pdf/07/Time%20dummy%20hedonics%20-%20de%20Haan%20(2003).pdf Also published in 2004 in the *Journal of Economic and Social Measurement* 29, 427-443.

de Haan, J. (2004), "Hedonic Regression: The Time Dummy Index As a Special Case of the Imputation Törnqvist Index," Paper presented at the 8th Ottawa Group Meeting, Helsinki, August 23-25. http://www.stat.fi/og2004/dehaanp_ver2.pdf

de Haan, J., E. van der Wal, D. ter Steege and P. de Vries (2006), "The Measurement of House Prices: A Review of the SPAR Method," paper presented at the Economic Measurement Group Workshop 2006, Coogee Australia, December 13-15. http://www.sam.sdu.dk/parn/EMG%20Workshop%20'06%20program.pdf

Diewert, W.E. (1976), "Exact and Superlative Index Numbers," *Journal of Econometrics* 4, 114-145.

Diewert, W.E. (1978), "Superlative Index Numbers and Consistency in Aggregation," *Econometrica* 46, 883-900.

Diewert, W.E. (1998), "High Inflation, Seasonal Commodities and Annual Index Numbers," *Macroeconomic Dynamics* 2, 456-471. http://www.econ.ubc.ca/diewert/highinfl.pdf

Diewert, W.E. (1999), "Index Number Approaches to Seasonal Adjustment," *Macroeconomic Dynamics* 3, 1-21. http://www.econ.ubc.ca/diewert/seasonal.pdf

Diewert, W.E. (2002), "Harmonized Indexes of Consumer Prices: Their Conceptual Foundations," *Swiss Journal of Economics and Statistics* 138, 547-637. http://www.econ.ubc.ca/diewert/harindex.pdf

Diewert, W.E. (2003a), "The Treatment of Owner Occupied Housing and Other Durables in a Consumer Price Index" Discussion Paper 03-08, Department of Economics, University of British Columbia, Vancouver, Canada. http://www.econ.ubc.ca/discpapers/dp0308.pdf Forthcoming in W.E. Diewert, J. Greenless and C. Hulten (eds.), *Price Index Concepts and Measurement*, NBER Studies in Income and Wealth, University of Chicago Press.

Diewert, W.E. (2003b), "Hedonic Regressions: A Consumer Theory Approach," pp. 317-348 in *Scanner Data and Price Indexes*, Studies in Income and Wealth, Volume 64, R.C. Feenstra and M.D. Shapiro (eds.), NBER and University of Chicago Press. http://www.econ.ubc.ca/diewert/scan.pdf

Diewert, W.E. (2003c), "Hedonic Regressions: A Review of Some Unresolved Issues," paper presented at the 7th Meeting of the Ottawa Group, Paris, May 27-29. http://www.ottawagroup.org/pdf/07/Hedonics%20unresolved%20issues%20-%20Diewert%20(2003).pdf

Diewert, W.E. (2004), "On the Stochastic Approach to Linking the Regions in the ICP," Discussion Paper 04-16, Department of Economics, University of British Columbia, November. http://www.econ.ubc.ca/diewert/icp.pdf

Diewert, W.E. (2005a), "Weighted Country Product Dummy Variable Regressions and Index Number Formulae," *The Review of Income and Wealth* 51:4, 561-571. http://www.econ.ubc.ca/diewert/country.pdf

Diewert, W.E. (2005b), "Adjacent Period Dummy Variable Hedonic Regressions and Bilateral Index Number Theory," Discussion Paper 05-11, Department of Economics, University of British Columbia, Vancouver, Canada, V6T 1Z1. http://www.econ.ubc.ca/discpapers/dp0511.pdf

Diewert, W.E. and Alice O. Nakamura (2011), "Accounting for Housing in a CPI," chapter 2, pp. 7-32 in Diewert, W.E., B.M. Balk, D. Fixler, K.J. Fox and A.O. Nakamura (2011), *PRICE AND PRODUCTIVITY MEASUREMENT: Volume 1 -- Housing*. Trafford Press.

Diewert, W.E. and F.C. Wykoff (2006), "Depreciation, Deterioration and Obsolescence when there is Embodied or Disembodied Technical Change," forthcoming in *Price and Productivity Measurement*, W.E. Diewert, B.M. Balk, D. Fixler, K.J. Fox and A.O. Nakamura (eds.), Canada: Trafford Press. http://www.econ.ubc.ca/diewert/dp0602.pdf

Fenwick, D. (2006), "Real Estate Prices: the Need for a Strategic Approach to the Development of Statistics to Meet User Needs," paper presented at the OECD-IMF Workshop on Real Estate Price Indexes held in Paris, November 6-7, 2006. http://www.oecd.org/dataoecd/22/49/37619259.pdf

Girouard, N., M. Kennedy, P. van den Noord and C. André (2006), "Recent House Price Developments: The Role of Fundamentals," paper presented at the OECD-IMF Workshop on Real Estate Price Indexes, Paris, November 6-7. http://www.oecd.org/dataoecd/3/6/37583208.pdf

Gouriéroux, C. and A. Laferrère (2006), "Managing Hedonic Housing Price Indexes: the French Experience," paper presented at the OECD-IMF Workshop on Real Estate Price Indexes, Paris, November 6-7.
http://www.oecd.org/dataoecd/2/24/37583497.pdf

Gudnason, R. (2004), "Simple User Costs and Rentals," Paper presented at the 8th Ottawa Group Meeting, Helsinki, August 23-25. http://www.stat.fi/og2004/gudnasonpaper.pdf

Gudnason, R. and G. Jonsdottir (2006), "House Price Index, Market Prices and Flow of Services Methods," paper presented at the OECD-IMF Workshop on Real Estate Price Indexes held in Paris, November 6-7, 2006.
http://www.oecd.org/dataoecd/2/42/37583740.pdf

Heravi, S. and M. Silver (2007) "Hedonic Indexes: A Study of Alternative Methods," forthcoming in E.R. Berndt and C. Hulten (eds.) *Hard-to-Measure Goods and Services: Essays in Honour of Zvi Griliches*, Chicago: University of Chicago Press.

Hill, T.P. (1996), *Inflation Accounting: A Manual on National Accounting Under Conditions of High Inflation*, Paris: OECD.

Hoffmann, J. and C. Kurz (2002), "Rent Indices for Housing in West Germany: 1985 to 1998," Discussion Paper 01/02, Economic Research Centre of the Deutsche Bundesbank, Frankfurt.

Hoffmann, J. and J.-R. Kurz-Kim (2006), "Consumer Price Adjustment Under the Microscope: Germany in a Period of Low Inflation," Discussion Paper Series 1, Economic Studies, No 16/2006, Deutsche Bundesbank, Wilhelm-Epstein-Strasse 14, 60431, Postfach 10 06 02, 60006, Frankfurt am Main.

Hoffmann, J. and A. Lorenz (2006), "Real Estate Price Indices for Germany: Past, Present and Future," paper presented at the OECD-IMF Workshop on Real Estate Price Indexes, Paris, November 6-7.
http://www.oecd.org/dataoecd/31/20/37625451.pdf

International Labour Organization (ILO) and others (2004), *Consumer Price Index Manual: Theory and Practice*, International Labour Organization, Geneva.
http://www.ilo.org/public/english/bureau/stat/guides/cpi/index.htm

International Monetary Fund (IMF) and others (2004), *Producer Price Index Manual: Theory and Practice*, International Monetary Fund, Washington, D.C. http://www.imf.org/np/sta/tegppi/index.htm

Jorgenson, D.W. and Z. Griliches (1967), The Explanation of Productivity Change," *The Review of Economic Studies* 34, 249-283.

Jorgenson, D.W. and Z. Griliches (1972), "Issues in Growth Accounting: A Reply to Edward F. Denison," *Survey of Current Business* 52:4, Part II (May), 65-94.

Jorgenson, D.W. and J.S. Landefeld (2006), "Blueprint for Expanded and Integrated U.S. National Accounts: Review, Assessment, and Next Steps," pp. 13-112 in D.W. Jorgenson, J.S. Landefeld and W.D. Nordhaus (eds.), *A New Architecture for the U.S. National Accounts*, Chicago, University of Chicago Press.

Leventis, A. (2006), "Removing Appraisal Bias from a Repeat Transactions House Price Index: A Basic Approach," paper presented at the OECD-IMF Workshop on Real Estate Price Indexes held in Paris, November 6-7, 2006. http://www.oecd.org/dataoecd/2/45/37583706.pdf

Li, W., M. Prud'homme and K. Yu (2006), "Studies in Hedonic Resale Housing Price Indexes," paper presented at the OECD-IMF Workshop on Real Estate Price Indexes held in Paris, November 6-7, 2006.
http://www.oecd.org/dataoecd/2/25/37583404.pdf

Makaronidis, A. and K. Hayes (2006), "Owner Occupied Housing for the HICP," paper presented at the OECD-IMF Workshop on Real Estate Price Indexes held in Paris, November 6-7, 2006.
http://www.oecd.org/dataoecd/42/60/37612322.pdf

Malpezzi, S., L. Ozanne and T. Thibodeau (1987), "Microeconomic Estimates of Housing Depreciation," *Land Economics* 63, 372-385.

Prasad, N. and A. Richards (2006), "Measuring Aggregate House Prices in Australian Capital Cities: A Review of RBA Research," paper presented at the Economic Measurement Group Workshop 2006, Coogee Australia, December 13-15. http://www.sam.sdu.dk/parn/EMG%20Workshop%20'06%20program.pdf

Schreyer, P. (2001), *OECD Productivity Manual: A Guide to the Measurement of Industry-Level and Aggregate Productivity Growth*, Paris: OECD.

Schreyer, P. (2006), "Measuring Multi-Factor Productivity when Rates of Return are Exogenous," forthcoming in *Price and Productivity Measurement*, W.E. Diewert, B.M. Balk, D. Fixler, K.J. Fox and A.O. Nakamura (eds.), Canada: Trafford Press.

Schreyer, P., W.E. Diewert and A. Harrison (2005), "Cost of Capital Services in the National Accounts," paper presented to the Meeting of the Canberra II Group on Non-financial Assets in Canberra, April.

Scheffé, H. (1959), *The Analysis of Variance*, New York: John Wiley and Sons.

Silver, M. (2003), "The Use of Weights in Hedonic Regressions: The Measurement of Quality Adjusted Price Changes," Room document for the 7th Meeting of the Ottawa Group, Paris, May.
http://www.ottawagroup.org/pdf/07/Weights%20in%20hedonics%20-%20Silver%20(2003).pdf

Silver, M. and S. Heravi (2005), "A Failure in the Measurement of Inflation: Results from a Hedonic and Matched Experiment Using Scanner Data," *Journal of Business and Economic Statistics* 23:3, 269-281.

Silver, M. and S. Heravi (2007), "The Difference Between Hedonic Imputation Indexes and Time Dummy Hedonic Indexes," forthcoming in the *Journal of Business and Economic Statistics*, also published as *IMF Working Paper Series* No. 181, 2006. http://www.imf.org/external/pubs/cat/longres.cfm?sk=19363

Stephens, W., Y. Li, V. Lekkas, J. Abraham, C. Calhoun and T. Kimner (1995), "Conventional Home Mortgage Price Index," *Journal of Housing Research* 6:3, 389-418.

Summers, R. (1973), "International Comparisons with Incomplete Data," *Review of Income and Wealth* 29:1, 1-16.

van der Wal, E., D. ter Steege and B. Kroese (2006), "Two Ways to Construct a House Price Index for the Netherlands: The Repeat Sale and the Sale Price Appraisal Ratio," paper presented at the OECD-IMF Workshop on Real Estate Price Indexes held in Paris, November 6-7, 2006.

Verbrugge, R. (2006), "The Puzzling Divergence of Rents and User Costs, 1980-2004," paper presented at the OECD-IMF Workshop on Real Estate Price Indexes held in Paris, November 6-7, 2006.
http://www.oecd.org/dataoecd/42/57/37612870.pdf Published in *Review of Income and Wealth* 54 (4), 671-699.

Walras, L. (1954), *Elements of Pure Economics*, a translation by W. Jaffé of the Edition Définitive (1926) of the *Eléments d'économie pure*, first edition published in 1874, Homewood, Illinois: Richard D. Irwin.

Wenzlick, R. (1952), "As I See the Fluctuations in the Selling Prices of Single Family Residences," *The Real Estate Analyst* 21 (December 24), 541-548.

Woolford, K. (2006), "An Exploration of Alternative Treatments of Owner Occupied Housing in a CPI," paper presented at the Economic Measurement Group Workshop 2006, Coogee Australia, December 13-15. http://www.sam.sdu.dk/parn/EMG%20Workshop%20'06%20program.pdf

Wyngarden, H. (1927), *An Index of Local Real Estate Prices*, Michigan Business Studies Volume 1, Number 2, Ann Arbor: University of Michigan.

Chapter 7

REPORTED PRICES AND RENTS OF HOUSING: REFLECTIONS OF COSTS, AMENITIES OR BOTH?

Alan Heston and Alice O. Nakamura[1]

1.   Introduction

For the official economic statistics of nations, it is important that temporal and spatial variations in the cost of dwelling services are carefully measured.[2] Housing services often account for a quarter or more of reported consumer expenditures. The costs of owner occupied and rental housing services have important roles to play in both the Consumer Price Index (CPI) and the System of National Accounts (SNA).

For official statistics purposes, often an index of market rents does double duty as an index for the user cost of the services of rental occupied housing (ROH) and owner occupied housing (OOH).[3] This treatment of the cost of OOH services is referred to as rental equivalence. On theoretical grounds, the rental equivalence approach is often said to be equivalent to the user cost approach, and both approaches are in use by official statistics agencies.[4] However, this paper raises questions about the presumption that the approaches can be viewed as equivalent in

---

[1] Alan Heston is with the Economics Department at the University of Pennsylvania, and can be reached at aheston@sas.upenn.edu. Alice Nakamura is with the School of Business at the University of Alberta and can be reached at alice.nakamura@ualberta.ca. This paper builds upon previous work of others, many of whom, but probably not all, are cited. In addition the paper has benefited from discussions with and written comments from a number of people including Bettina Aten, Stan Austin, Erwin Diewert, Thesia Garner, Eva Jacobs, Rocky Kochar, Emi Nakamura, Don Paquin, and Harold Watts. Support from NSF Grant SES 0317699 is gratefully acknowledged. This paper draws on experience gained from the Cost of Living Allowance (COLA) program of the Office of Personnel Administration of the U.S. Government. As part of research under the COLA program, Rakesh Kochar of Joel Popkin and Company, in Chapter 3 of their report, evaluated housing based on a 1998 survey of employees.

[2] We recommend two papers as especially helpful for laying out the basic issues. Diewert (2003) provides a theoretical treatment of the user cost of both housing and other durables. He focuses on temporal indexes in a consumer price index context, but his framework is general. And, Sergeev (2004) presents a well argued practical application to spatial estimates of housing services for Europe, with special attention to the .problems that emerged in trying to integrate formerly planned economies into the European Comparison Programme and the International Comparisons Programme (ICP). See also Kravis and Summers (1982) and Summers and Heston (1988). In addition, Diewert (2011), which was first presented at a 2006 OCED workshop, takes up additional issues not covered in his 2003 paper including the treatment of real estate for commercial as well as residential properties, the treatment of the land versus structure components of properties, and ways of using appraisal information for constructing measures of inflation for OOH services. In this paper, Diewert also proposes a new opportunity cost approach to accounting for OOH costs in measures of inflation: an approach developed further in Diewert and Nakamura (2011).

[3] See Eiglsperger (2006) and Christensen, Dupont and Schreyer (2005) for helpful surveys of international practice.

[4] See Diewert (1974, 2003, 2006). See also Katz (2011, appendix A) and Diewert and Nakamura (2011).

Heston, A. and A.O. Nakamura (2011), "Reported Prices and Rents of Housing: Reflections of Costs, Amenities or Both?" chapter 7, pp. 117-124 in
W.E. Diewert, B.M. Balk, D. Fixler, K.J. Fox and A.O. Nakamura (2011),
***PRICE AND PRODUCTIVITY MEASUREMENT: Volume 1 -- Housing.* Trafford Press.**

practice, and more fundamentally about the presumption that shelter in a rented dwelling versus shelter in an otherwise similar owned dwelling are the same product.

The U.S. Bureau of Labor Statistics (BLS) incorporates changes in the cost of owner occupied housing (OOH) into the CPI using the rental equivalence approach. Also, the guidelines for the 1993 and the new 2008 SNA specify that a rental value of the housing stock should be included as part of the aggregates for personal consumption, personal income, income of proprietors and value added for the real estate industry.[5] The U.S. national accounts imputation for OOH services is obtained by applying to the stock of owner occupied housing the ratios of rent to property value (rent-to-value ratios) obtained from *tenant* occupied housing.[6]

The underlying economic theory is clear on how the discounted present value of a stream of rent payments relates to the price of a dwelling given frictionless markets.[7] However, in the real world, are the services that renters and owner occupiers get from otherwise similar dwellings the same, or in some sense sufficiently comparable? The results of the empirical portion of this paper lead us to believe that the answer to the above question is "no." In our view, too little attention has been devoted to the implicit assumption that housing cost information for *either* renters or owner occupiers can be suitably adjusted for use in assessing movements over time and space in the cost of housing for *both* renters and owners.

2.   Evidence of Patterns in Owner and Renter Valuations

The U.S. Bureau of Labor Statistics (BLS) asks owner occupiers the following question in the Consumer Expenditure Survey (CES):

> *"If someone were to rent your home today, how much do you think it would rent for monthly, unfurnished and without utilities?"* [8]

The BLS uses responses to the above question in determining the CPI weight for OOH versus ROH services. Note that in table 1, based on the 2002 CES, owner occupiers are found to devote a lower percentage of household expenditures to shelter than renters, and to have a higher average income.

Table 1. Household Expenditures (Actual and Imputed) for Owners versus Renters, 2002

	Total expenditures ($)	Shelter ($)	Shelter (%)	Average income before tax ($)
Homeowner	46,908	8,458	18.0	59,345
Renter	28,372	6,458	23.2	30,386

Source: Based on CES data.

---

[5] See McBride and Smith (2001), and also Katz (2011), on the rent-to-value ratio approach.

[6] The European Commission (2001, p. 68) recommends: "In the case of privately rented dwellings constituting less than 10 percent of the total dwelling stock by number *and* where there is a large disparity between private and other paid rents (say, by a factor of three), as an alternative objective assessment, the user-cost method may be applied."

[7] Katz (2011, appendix A) and Diewert and Nakamura (2011) provide summaries of this theory.

[8] See BLS, 12/4/2003 at bls.gov/cex/csxann02.

Implicit assumptions commonly made in compiling housing statistics are that renters and owner occupiers value housing services in equivalent ways, *and* that the populations of available rental market and owner occupier housing units span the same quality universe. We can think of five reasons to question these assumptions:

R1. People, in the United States at least, seem to prefer to own their accommodations. Higher income people (e.g., Senator McCain and his wife) can better afford to indulge this preference. This situation could cause the rental market to be increasingly thin, moving up the income distribution, for rental dwelling units that are truly equivalent to those owner occupiers inhabit. Moving up in quality, the people who can afford to own may be increasingly uninterested in rental accommodation. Sometimes, however, higher end homes must be rented. For instance, an executive with a luxury home who is given an overseas assignment expected to last a year or so might choose to rent out their home in their home country while on that assignment as a way of reducing the risk of the home being robbed. Also, luxury homes are sometimes rented for periods of a year or so when there has been a death or a divorce but the division of property is still pending.

R2. The list of characteristics used in classifying homes omits many factors that could affect market values.

R3. Renters and owners may not have the same sorts of information. Homeowners may, on average, make more effort to learn about their homes before buying them than prospective renters make before signing rental agreements. Invoking an asymmetry of information framework, one might expect rentals entering the market to be of lower quality than owner-occupied units for features that cannot be readily measured.

R4. Owners may care more about certain amenities than renters because the average owner moves less often.

R5. We thought that owner pride might be a factor too. For example, we thought that a property owner might place greater value than the market would on, say, a purple bathroom with hot tub that they had designed.

Further study is needed of how owners and renters in different income and wealth groups value and purchase housing services. Here we take a small step toward trying to fill this need. The empirical work reported below is based on a survey of federal government employees conducted as part of a Safe Harbor process regarding the Cost of Living Allowance (COLA) program administered by the United States Office of Personnel Management. This program began in 1948 and pays an allowance above the federal salary schedule in three geographic areas (Alaska, the Caribbean and the Pacific) based on prices in these COLA areas relative to the Washington D.C. housing area. The program came under litigation. As a by-product, research was undertaken to improve the methodology of the comparisons. COLA survey data include a large number of dwelling characteristics, and both renters and owner occupiers were asked the CES question (reproduced at the start of this section) about what they believe their dwellings would rent for.[9] In compiling the CPI, the BLS only uses the CES information for renters and for

---

[9] This program is directed at comparing the costs of living for federal employees in the non-continental United States to Washington D.C. area. Housing is one of the most important and most difficult of the comparisons required under this program. The COLA areas include Alaska, Guam, Hawaii, Puerto Rico, and the U.S. Virgin Islands: a very diverse range of climates and housing needs.

owner occupiers for determining the expenditure share weights for the rental and OOH index CPI components. However, this information can also be used to examine issues such as rent-to-value patterns, as we do in this study.

In the COLA sample, 82 percent of the respondents were homeowners, which is well above the 66 percent average for the United States as a whole.[10] Sample characteristics, including the average for rent as a percentage of the price of a dwelling, are given in table 2.

Table 2. COLA Program Results

	Number	Monthly Rent ($)	CV of Rent	Floor Area	Rent/Price (%)
Owners	3564	1308	0.38	1763	6.61
Renters	748	918	0.44	1295	5.97

A semi log regression was estimated using observations on both rented and owner occupied dwellings in the three COLA regions and the Washington D.C. housing area.[11] In table 3, the coefficients in rows a and b have been converted to index form, with the average rent of owner occupiers in the Washington D.C. area set equal to 100.[12] For the Caribbean, for example, the entry of 75.4 in row b means that, controlling for the other included factors (see appendix A), OOH rent equivalents are estimated at 75.4 percent of the Washington D.C. area level.[13]

Table 3. Rent Indexes for Owners and Renters
(with the average for Washington D.C. area homeowners is set equal to 100)

COLA AREA	Alaska	Washington	Caribbean	Hawaii-Pacific
a. Renters	98.4	86.2	68.5	113.2
b. Homeowners	117.9	100.0	75.4	109.9
c. Owner premium [(b/a)-1]*100	19.9	15.9	10.1	3.0

Note: The table entries are based on the relevant coefficient values from the pooled regression for which results are shown in appendix A.

The estimated percentage premiums for homeowners versus renters are shown in row c.[14] The premium is only 3 percent for the Hawaii-Pacific area, but is roughly 10 to 20 percent for the other areas. The implications of the owner premium figures in table 3 differ depending on the cause. The values are large enough to merit concern and further investigation.

Though the results do not seem to be widely known outside of official statistics circles, other analysts have reported declines in the rent-to-value ratio as the average house price

[10] For the CES data, homeowners exhibited a larger standard deviation ($500 compared to $404 for renters).

[11] See appendix A for the list of included explanatory variables and the full regression estimation results.

[12] Goldberger's (1968) adjustment was used, adding half the standard error to a coefficient before exponentiating it.

[13] The D.C. housing area includes the District of Columbia and adjacent areas of Maryland and Virginia.

[14] As a further test of the direction of the premium, three pairwise regressions of the COLA areas with Washington were also estimated, all using the same specification as the pooled regression in the appendix.

increases (e.g., Garner and Short, 2001 and McBride and Smith, 2001). The rent-to-value ratios reported are about 17 percent for dwellings under $20,000 and 6 percent for dwellings in the $200,000-300,000 class in the early 1990s. Indeed, this is why the BEA now calculates rent-to-value ratios for dwellings grouped by value class.[15]

This effect can be explored with the COLA data because both owner occupiers and renters were asked to estimate the market values of their dwellings. The simple group averages display the same basic pattern found by others. To further investigate home value related, and also possible owner versus renter, differences in rent-to-value ratios, the following semi log regression was run using COLA data:

(1) $\text{Log}(\text{Rent}/\text{Value}) = \alpha \text{Value} + \beta_i O_i + \lambda_i R_i,$

where $i = 1,\ldots,4$ represents Alaska, the Caribbean, the Pacific and Washington, respectively; O is a dummy variable set equal to 1 for owners and equal to 0 otherwise; and R is a dummy variable set equal to 1 for renters and equal to 0 otherwise. (The omitted variable is for owners in the D.C. housing area.) Table 4 shows the predicted rent-to-value ratios in percentage terms, obtained using estimated equation (1), for four selected dwelling values and each of the COLA areas and the D.C. housing area, for renters (columns 1-4) and for owners (columns 5-8).[16]

Table 4. Estimated Rent-to-value Ratios (as Percentages)

	Renter				Owner			
	Alaska	Wash D.C.	Carib	Hawaii-Pacific	Alaska	Wash D.C.	Carib	Hawaii-Pacific
Value($)	(1)	(2)	(3)	(4)	(5)	(6)	(7)	(8)
50,000	13.0	8.9	6.3	6.9	10.1	8.8	7.6	7.3
100,000	12.0	8.2	5.8	6.4	9.3	8.1	7.0	6.8
200,000	10.2	6.9	4.9	5.4	7.9	6.9	6.0	5.7
500,000	6.2	4.3	3.0	3.3	4.8	4.2	3.7	3.5

We see from table 4 that the rent-to-value estimates from the estimated equation (1) decline by more than 50 percent moving down the columns from a $50,000 to a $500,000 dwelling. Thus, we find that the rents that properties can command on the market decline

---

[15] The BEA derives its estimate of the flow of rental services for OOH from the Census of Population and Housing and the Rental and Vacant Property Questionnaire of the Residential Finance Survey (RFS). For the RFS, property owners or their agents provide gross rental receipts from their units, excluding any extra services and estimate the selling price of the property. From these data, a table is produced of rent-to-value ratios by 15 value classes that BEA collapses to 11 classes. The total value of housing in each class is then derived from the American Housing Survey (AHS) that in turn depends on the estimate of the sale value of houses from those surveyed, about 50 to 60,000 units every two years. Total rental services are the product of value ratios in a benchmark year times the number of sample units in each value class. The average value over all value classes provides an average rent estimate in a benchmark year, which can be applied to the total of OOH. Between census years, this average rent must be updated taking into account improvements in quality of owned dwellings and any inflation in rents. The quality of the benchmark estimates depends on the stability of the rent-to-value ratio over time and across space.

[16] The equation statistics are $\text{adjR}^2 = .528$ with an F ratio of 494.6, with most of the explanatory power attributable to the value of the property. The coefficient on value was -.1629 per 100,000 value with a standard error of .0042.

dramatically as a percent of the dwelling values. These results seem most compatible with a market-driven cause like R1 above.

The answers that renters and owner occupiers provide for the CES question quoted at the start of this section are used by the BLS in estimating the expenditures of renter and owner occupier households on different categories of goods and services. A decline in rent-to-value ratios as property values rise will not necessarily lead to a bias in the CPI (because the rates of growth could still be the same). However, the documented decline could make the weighting factor for OOH too low, which could contribute to an underestimation of the level of OOH housing services and the level of total consumption. This effect also flows from an opportunity or user cost framework where elements in the calculation, like the cost of fund or expected return, are systematically related to income (see Diewert 2003 and Katz 2011).

How do our COLA estimates compare with other sources? In 2003, a report was prepared comparing estimates of the components of consumer expenditure based on the BLS Consumer Expenditure Survey and on the BEA consumer expenditure (CE) headings. Using additional information from the CES, Garner, Janini, Passero, Paszkiewicz, and Vendemia (2006) replicate the BEA rent-to-value ratio results. More specifically, they find that the rent-to-value ratio is 13.2 percent for a $50,000 home and 6 to 7 percent for a $200,000 home: roughly the same gradient we obtained using COLA data (table 4).

3.   Concluding Remarks

Controlling just for the physical features of owner occupied and rental dwellings, homeowners are found to put a premium on the housing services provided by their dwellings versus what renters would pay. However, the rent-to-value ratios are found to also differ by location and by the value of the property. We find, moreover, that when we allow for location and especially for home value, there no longer is evidence of a systematic premium for how owners value the housing services of their dwellings compared with renters.

For both owner occupiers and renters, we show that rent-to-value ratios fall moving from relatively low to relatively high value homes. This result is obtained for multiple locations, and using large sized data samples for different years.

For a nation like the United States, the services of owner occupied housing are measured to be more than a quarter of consumer expenditures, so it is very important that temporal and spatial variations in OOH costs are carefully measured. It does not seem to us that statistical authorities devote the proportion of resources to housing as to other categories of expenditure based on relative importance in the consumer budget. We feel this situation reflects, in part, a failure on the part of those controlling the budget allocations for the official statistics agencies to recognize the need for providing funding so that the statistics agencies can afford to improve their housing sector measures of inflation.

Appendix A. Hedonic Regression Results

Pooled Regression of Ln Rent on Rent Determining Variables, GLM Procedure, Homeowners and Renters Distinguished

Variable	Coefficient estimate	Standard error	t value	Pr> |t|
Intercept	6.220476	0.05531	112.47	<.0001
Renter in Alaska	-0.03601	0.038923	-0.93	0.3549
Renter in Caribbean	-0.39842	0.039631	-10.05	<.0001
Renter in Hawaii	0.07808	0.03247	2.4	0.0162
Renter in Washington	-0.17505	0.054213	-3.23	0.0013
Owner in Alaska	0.15516	0.019234	8.07	<.0001
Owner in Caribbean	-0.29388	0.02336	-12.58	<.0001
Owner in Hawaii	0.11526	0.018133	6.36	<.0001
Owner in Washington	0			
Number of bathrooms	0.118175	0.008976	13.17	<.0001
Number of bedrooms	0.02459	0.007363	3.34	0.0008
Number of other rooms	0.021024	0.006099	3.45	0.0006
Above average condition	0.0619482	0.011052	5.61	<.0001
Close to school	-0.04191	0.013467	-3.11	0.0019
Close to park	0.03844	0.013427	2.86	0.0042
Traffic or crime problem	-0.10042	0.03213	-3.13	0.0018
Parking available	0.05048	0.019688	2.56	0.0104
Cable available	0.05236	0.012741	4.11	<.0001
Deck	0.059659	0.011099	5.38	<.0001
Room air conditioning	0.055859	0.013413	4.16	<.0001
Age*Own 0	-0.002	0.001018	-1.96	0.05
Age*Own 1	0.000715	0.000397	1.8	0.0714
Area squared	-3.4E-08	1E-08	-3.17	0.0015
Area in sq. feet	0.000247	4.08E-05	6.07	<.0001

Notes: The omitted dummy variable is for owners in the D.C. housing area. The equation was run with separate coefficients for the age of the house of owners and age of house of renters to illustrate the differential effect. 4,312 observations were read; 4276 observations were used. The R-Square for the estimated equation is .4294, with a coefficient of variation of 4.666 and a Root MSE of .328384. The F Value for the equation as a whole is 145.48, with 22 degrees of freedom in the numerator and 4253 degrees of freedom in the denominator.

References

Aten, B. (1996), "Some Poverty Lines are More Equal than Others," Discussion Paper 95-6, *Center for International Comparisons at the University of Pennsylvania*, February. Pwt.econ.upenn.edu/papers/

Christensen, A.-K., J. Dupont and P. Schreyer (2005), "International Comparability of the Consumer Price Index: Owner-Occupied Housing," presented at the OECD Seminar, "Inflation Measures: Too High -- Too Low -- Internationally Comparable? Paris, 21-22 June.

Crone, T.M., L.I. Nakamura and R.P. Voith (2011), "Hedonic Estimates of the Cost of Housing Services: Rental and Owner Occupied Units," chapter 4 in W.E. Diewert, B.M. Balk, D. Fixler, K.J. Fox and A.O. Nakamura (eds.), *Price and Productivity Measurement, Volume 1: Housing* Trafford Press.

Diewert, W.E. (1974), "Intertemporal Consumer Theory and the Demand for Durables," *Econometrica* 53, 497–516.

Diewert, W.E. (2003), "The Treatment of Owner Occupied Housing and Other Durables in a Consumer Price Index" Discussion Paper 03-08, Department of Economics, University of British Columbia, Vancouver, Canada, available at http://www.econ.ubc.ca/discpapers/dp0308.pdf. This paper is forthcoming in W.E. Diewert, J. Greenless and C. Hulten (eds.), *Price Index Concepts and Measurement,* NBER Studies in Income and Wealth, forthcoming U. of Chicago Press.

Diewert, W.E., (2006), The Paris OECD-IMF Workshop on Real Estate Price Indexes: Conclusions and future Directions. Paper presented at the OECD-IMF Workshop on Real Estate Price Indexes, Paris, 6-7 November 2006. http://www.econ.ubc.ca/diewert/dp0701.pdf Published as chapter 6, pp. 87-116 in Diewert, W.E., B.M. Balk, D. Fixler, K.J. Fox and A.O. Nakamura (2011), *PRICE AND PRODUCTIVITY MEASUREMENT: Volume 1 -- Housing*. Trafford Press.

Diewert, W.E. and A.O. Nakamura (2011), "Accounting for Housing in a CPI," chapter 2, pp. 7-32 in Diewert, W.E., B.M. Balk, D. Fixler, K.J. Fox and A.O. Nakamura (2011), *PRICE AND PRODUCTIVITY MEASUREMENT: Volume 1 -- Housing*. Trafford Press.

Eiglsperger, M. (2006), "The Treatment of Owner-Occupied Housing in the Harmonised Index of Consumer Prices," presented at the workshop on "CPI Measurement: Central Banks Views and Concerns," Bank for International Settlements in Basel, Switzerland.

European Commission (2001), Eurostat Projects on Non-financial National Accounts With the Candidate Countries, 1998-2000, Luxembourg: Office for Official Publications of the European Communities.

Garner, T.I. ,G. Janini, W. Passero, L. Paszkiewicz, and M. Vendemia (2006), "The Consumer Expenditure Survey in Comparison:Focus with Personal Consumption Expenditures," Monthly Labor Review 129 (9) September, 20-46.

Garner, T.I. and P. Rozalakis (2001). "Owner Occupied Housing: An Input for Experimental Poverty Thresholds," SGE-ASSA Annual Meeting, New Orleans, Poverty Measurement Working Paper, Census Bureau website.

Garner, T.I. and K. Short (2001), "Owner-Occupied Shelter in Experimental Poverty Measurement with a 'Look' at Inequality and Poverty Rates," paper presented at the Annual Meeting of the Southern Economics Association, Tampa, Florida, November.

Garner, T.I. and R. Verbrugge (2011), "The Puzzling Divergence of Rents and User Costs, 1980-2004: Summary and Extensions," chapter 8, pp. 125-146 in Diewert, W.E., B.M. Balk, D. Fixler, K.J. Fox and A.O. Nakamura (2011), *PRICE AND PRODUCTIVITY MEASUREMENT: Volume 1 -- Housing*. Trafford Press.

Gerking, S.D. and W.N. Weirick (1983), "Compensating Differences and Interregional Wage Differentials, *Review of Economics and Statistics* 55 (3) August, 483-487.

Goldberger, A.A. (1968), The Interpretation and Estimation of Cobb-Douglas Functions, *Econometrica* 35, 464-472.

Joel Popkin and Company (1999), "Appendix A: JOEL POPKIN AND COMPANY RESEARCH SUMMARY," Company; this report is on the OPM website under COLA program.

Katz, A.J. (2011), "Estimating Dwelling Services in the Candidate Countries: Theoretical and Practical Considerations in Developing Methodologies Based on a User Cost of Capital Measure," chapter 3, pp. 33-50 in Diewert, W.E., B.M. Balk, D. Fixler, K.J. Fox and A.O. Nakamura (2011), *PRICE AND PRODUCTIVITY MEASUREMENT: Volume 1 -- Housing*. Trafford Press.

Kravis, I, A. Heston and R. Summers (1982), *World Product and Income*, Johns Hopkins University Press.

Malpezzi, S. (1998), "Remarks on Geographic Variation in Housing Prices and the Measurement of Poverty, U.S. Bureau of the Census, Poverty Working Papers, August 10th Revision.

McBride, D. and G. Smith (2001), "Rental Income of Persons, Gross Nonfarm Housing Product, Households and Institutions Compensation and Related Measures of the National Income and Product Accounts," Bureau of Economic Analysis, Income Branch.

National Academy of Science (1995), *New Method Proposed For Measuring U.S. Poverty,* Report of the Panel of the National Research Council's Committee on National Statistics.

Roback, J. (1982), "Wages, Rents, and the Quality of Life," *Journal of Political Economy*, 90 (6).

Sergeev, S. (2004), "International Comparisons of Housing (experience from the European Comparison Program)", document circulated at the Washington Technical Advisory Group meeting for the ICP, Jan. 21-23, 2004. http://siteresources.worldbank.org/ICPINT/Resources/Housing_ECP_Exper_Dec03SS.DOC

Summers, R. and A. Heston (1988), "A New Set of International Comparisons of Real Product and Price Level Estimates for 130 Countries," *Review of Income and Wealth*, 34, 1-25.

Verbrugge, R. (2008), "The Puzzling Divergence of Rents and User Costs, 1980-2004," *Review of Income and Wealth* 54 (4), 671-699.

Chapter 8

THE PUZZLING DIVERGENCE OF U.S. RENTS AND USER COSTS, 1980-2004: SUMMARY AND EXTENSIONS

Thesia I. Garner and Randal Verbrugge[1]

1.   Introduction

This paper constructs, for the five largest cities in the United States, user costs and rents *for the same structure, in levels* (i.e., measured in dollars). The levels formulation has the advantage that one can answer questions like "Is it cheaper to rent or to own?" or "Are houses overvalued?" These new measures are constructed using Consumer Expenditure Survey (CE) Interview data from 1982 to 2002, along with house price appreciation forecasts from Verbrugge (2008). The data are used to construct both a price/rent ratio and a user cost estimate for a hypothetical median-valued structure over time in each of the five cities. We find that, for the median structure in each city, the estimated user costs and rents diverge to a surprising degree, in keeping with the previously noted findings of Verbrugge (2008). Moreover, it is not always cheaper to own: the estimated user costs sometimes lie well above rents.

2.   Motivation and Summary

Accurate measurement of the value and costs of homeownership is crucial for estimating inflation dynamics, as well as for generating consumption measures, since shelter occupies such a large fraction of total consumption. Mismeasurement could alter both the level and dynamic properties of key macroeconomic aggregates. In many simple models, an appropriate measure of homeowner costs is given by an *ex ante* "user cost" measure consisting of the expected financing, maintenance and depreciation costs minus the present value of its expected resale price.

[1] Thesia Garner and Randal Verbrugge are with the U.S. Bureau of Labor Statistics (BLS). They can be reached at garner.thesia@bls.gov and verbrugge.randal@bls.gov, respectively. Thanks to Uri Kogan, who provided outstanding research assistance, and to Chris Cope, who answered detailed questions about the Consumer Expenditure Survey (CE) data. In that this paper summarizes Verbrugge (2008), thanks for comments are also due to Richard Ashley, Susanto Basu, Mark Bils, Erwin Diewert, Paul Emrath, Tim Erickson, Josh Gallin, Bob Gordon, John Greenlees, John Haltiwanger, Jonathan Heathcote, David Johnson, Greg Kurtzon, Steve Landefeld, Maria Luengo-Prado, Elaine Maag, Alice Nakamura, Leonard Nakamura, Marc Prud'homme, Marshall Reinsdorf, Matthew Shapiro, Robert Van Order, Christina Wang, Elliot Williams, Anthony Yezer, and Peter Zadrozny, and participants at the 2004 SSHRC and 2004 IARIW conferences. However, none is responsible for remaining errors. All views expressed in this paper are those of the authors and do not reflect the views or policies of the Bureau of Labor Statistics or the views of other BLS staff members.

Garner, T.I. and R. Verbrugge (2011), "The Puzzling Divergence of Rents and User Costs, 1980-2004: Summary and Extensions," chapter 8, pp. 125-146 in
Diewert, W.E., B.M. Balk, D. Fixler, K.J. Fox and A.O. Nakamura (2011),
PRICE AND PRODUCTIVITY MEASUREMENT: Volume 1 -- Housing. Trafford Press.

Simple frictionless theory models imply that a house's rental price will equal its user cost. However, Verbrugge (2008) showed that in the case of U.S. housing data, standard (frictionless) *ex ante* user costs and rents diverge markedly, for extended periods of time, and yield different implications regarding the rental versus ownership choices that would maximize the incomes of the individuals involved over time: a seeming failure of arbitrage[2] and a puzzle from the perspective of standard capital theory. It is well known that *ex post* user cost measures are typically *much* more volatile than the corresponding rent measures (see, e.g., Gillingham 1983). But *ex ante* user cost measures are of greater interest; theory suggests that rents should equal *ex ante* user costs, and *ex ante* user costs form the basis on which economic decisions are made. Prior to Verbrugge's paper, one might have expected a tighter empirical linkage between rents and *ex ante* user cost measures, since these measures involve expected rather than actual home price appreciation. Such considerations have led Diewert (2003) and others to suggest that, for official statistics purposes, *ex ante* user cost measures are superior to *ex post* measures.

Verbrugge (2008) constructed several estimates of *ex ante* user costs for U.S. homeowners and compared these to rents. That study had four novel findings, which are reviewed in more detail in section 5. To summarize: first, even if appropriately smoothed, *ex ante* user costs are far more volatile than rents. Indeed, their extreme volatility probably rules out the use of *ex ante* user costs as a measure of the costs of homeownership in consumer price indexes.[3] Second, rents and user costs diverge not only in the short run, but gaps persist over extended periods of time, contradicting the hypothesis that user costs and rents are roughly equivalent measures of the cost of housing services in the medium run. Furthermore, rents do not appear to respond very quickly to their presumed theoretical determinants (see Verbrugge 2007b).[4] These findings constitute a puzzle to the standard theory, and cast grave doubt on the usefulness of currently available user cost measures for monitoring inflation. Third, despite these divergences, and despite the large size of the detached unit rental market, this earlier research suggests that there were no unexploited profit opportunities, due to the large transactions costs typifying real estate transactions. It seems clear that transactions costs must be incorporated into a user cost treatment of owned housing as Diewert (2007), Diewert and Nakamura (2011) and others suggest. What is less clear is the ultimate form that the resulting user cost measures will take; theory is only beginning to grapple with these issues (see, e.g., Martin 2004, Díaz and Luengo-Prado 2008, and Luengo-Prado et al. 2008). Finally, the use of theoretically-inferior expected appreciation measures (such as expected CPI inflation) yield user cost measures which feature less divergence; this suggests that rent inflation stickiness may play a key role in explaining the observed rent-user cost divergence.

---

[2] Himmelberg, Mayer and Sinai (2005) focus on explaining house price dynamics, and ask whether these have been driven by bubbles or fundamentals. However, that study did not directly address the issue of rents versus user costs, since its measure of expected appreciation was a one-sided fifteen-year moving average. Such a measure cannot possibly reflect the covariance between interest rates and expected appreciation at higher frequencies, which is crucial for exploring the relationship between rents and *ex ante* user costs.

[3] Statistics Iceland uses an estimate of user costs to compute shelter costs (Diewert, 2003; Guðnason and Jónsdóttir, 2006, 2011). In Iceland's user cost measure, CPI inflation is used in place of expected house price appreciation; real capital gains are thus ignored, with this choice being made on grounds of being outside the scope of the CPI. Of course, expected inflation will not generally equal expected house price appreciation. We also note that interest rate smoothing has recently been deemed necessary.

[4] This accords with earlier work by Follain, Leavens and Velz (1993), DiPasquale and Wheaton (1992) and Blackley and Follain (1996). In contrast, Green and Malpezzi (2003) find a stronger relationship between rents and user costs.

As already noted, this paper extends Verbrugge (2008) by constructing, for the five largest cities in the United States, user costs and rents *for the same structure, in levels* (i.e., measured in dollars). The levels formulation is an advantage, since – as stressed by Smith and Smith (2006) – one cannot easily use the movements of indexes to answer questions like, "Is it cheaper to rent or to own?" or "Are houses overvalued?" One must have data on the value of a particular house *and* its associated rent level in order to directly compare that home's user cost to its rent.

These new measures are constructed using Consumer Expenditure Survey (CE) Interview data from 1982 to 2002, along with house price appreciation forecasts from Verbrugge (2008). The CE asks owner-occupants to report the characteristics, current market value, and rental equivalence of their homes. We constructed a regression model for each city that relates the log of reported monthly rental equivalence to reported market value and housing characteristics. These estimates were used to predict the rent associated with a structure with median characteristics in each city. The property value of this median house was used to construct a user cost measure for this structure. We find that, for the median structure in each city, estimated user costs and rents diverge to a surprising degree, in keeping with the previously noted findings. It is not always cheaper to own: user costs, even after adjusting for the tax advantages to ownership, sometimes lie well above rents. Finally, the dynamics of the estimated price-to-rent ratio are generally similar to those found in conventional estimates based upon indexes, suggesting that the present study might be useful for scaling other estimates.

The outline of the study is as follows. Section 3 describes the data. Section 4 discusses the construction of the user cost measures. Section 5 presents the findings of Verbrugge (2008), and section 6 presents new findings based upon CE data. Section 7 offers some conclusions.

3. Data Description

Several sources of data are used for this study and Verbrugge (2008). Data used include the internal U.S. Bureau of Labor Statistics (BLS) rental housing data, Consumer Expenditure (CE) Interview data, the Freddie Mac Conventional Mortgage Home Price Indexes (CMHPIs) for the United States and for 10 U.S. metropolitan areas, the U.S. Census Bureau's new home price index, the average contract rate on commitments for 30-year conventional fixed rate first mortgages in the United States, and CPI rent indexes for all-U.S. and for 10 metropolitan areas.

3.1 Consumer Expenditure Survey (CE) Data

CE Interview data collected between 1982 and 2002[5] from five of the largest cities in the United States were used as the basis for estimating user costs and rents for the same structure. CE Interview survey data have been collected on a continuing basis since 1980. On behalf of the

---

[5] Data for more recent years are not considered since the character of the data changed markedly in 2003; improvements to the data collection instrument resulted in higher responses to the rental equivalence question.

BLS, the U.S. Census Bureau collects data from consumer units[6] using personal interviews for this survey. The CE Interview is designed so that each consumer unit in the sample is interviewed over five consecutive quarters, once every three months. The first interview is used to bound expenditure estimates using one-month recall, and to collect other basic data such as housing unit characteristics (e.g., number of rooms). Interviews two through five are used to collect detailed expenditures and related information from the three months prior to each interview, and for the current month in some cases (e.g., rental equivalence).

Among the data collected in the CE Interview are estimated current market values and "rental equivalences" or rental values for owner-occupied and vacation homes. Current market value is asked only in the first interview (if the property was currently owned), and is subsequently inventoried to the following interviews.[7] Since July 1993, the rental values for owner-occupants have been collected each quarter, rather than only once as was the case earlier. Consumer units are asked, "About how much do you think this property would sell for on today's market?" and "If someone were to rent your home today, how much do you think it would rent for monthly, unfurnished and without utilities?"

For this study, a number of restrictions were placed upon the data. Only owner-occupied housing was considered. None of the costs of this housing could have been paid for by Federal, State, or local government. Only second interview data were used; this ensured that market values and rental equivalences referred to the same time period (pre-July1993 data) or to quarters that were adjacent (post-June 1993 data). The only exception would be for newly acquired properties. If the property value, rental equivalence, or number of rooms in the housing unit was missing or imputed, the observation was dropped from the sample. This reduced the sample significantly. In addition, since regression analysis was to be used to estimate the predicted rental values of property types, we wanted to reduce the effect of overly influential observations. Observations were dropped from the sample if the ratio of property value to rental equivalence was plus or minus 2.5 times the standard deviation of the mean of the ratios. This resulted in only 45 observations being dropped. Additional outlier treatment is discussed in section 6.

As noted above, we restricted our attention to five of the largest cities in the United States, to facilitate comparisons of results from this study with those of Verbrugge (2008). In particular, homeowners living in the following primary sampling units (the geographic area designation used for sample selection) were included in the study sample: New York City and New York-Connecticut suburbs; Philadelphia-Wilmington-Atlantic City, PA-NJ-DE-MD; Chicago-Gary-Kenosha, IL-IN-WI; Houston-Galveston-Brazoria, TX; and Los Angeles County and Los

---

[6] A consumer unit is defined as: (1) all members of a particular housing unit who are related by blood, marriage, adoption, or some other legal arrangement, such as foster children; (2) a person living alone or sharing a household with others, or living as a roomer in a private home, lodging house, or in permanent living quarters in a hotel or motel, but who is financially independent; or (3) two or more unrelated people living together who share certain major expenditures. Financial independence is determined by the three major expense categories: housing, food, and other living expenses. To be considered financially independent, at least two of the three major expense categories are to be provided entirely, or in part, by the respondent. Students living in university sponsored housing are included in the sample as separate consumer units. (See http://stats.bls.gov/CE/csxgloss.htm)

[7] If a property is owned when the first interview takes place, the interview respondent is asked to estimate the current market value of the property as of the date of the interview. If a property is acquired in a later interview, the current market value of the property is collected as of the time of the first interview after acquisition of the property. Beginning in April 2007, the market value of owner-occupied housing and vacation homes has been asked each quarter, rather than only once.

Angeles suburbs, CA. The regression model was run for each year for each of the five geographic areas.

The total number of second interview reports from owner-occupants whose housing was not paid for by the government is 9,243 for the 1982-2002 time period. Our restrictions regarding missing and imputed data and outliers further reduced the sample size to 4,952; this is about 54 percent of the base sample of owners.

3.2   House Price Indexes

The CMHPI indexes, like the more widely known Office of Federal Housing Enterprise Oversight (OFHEO) indexes, are quarterly house price indexes constructed using a weighted repeat sales method (see Case and Shiller, 1987, 1989) based upon Freddie Mac/Fannie Mae repeat mortgage transactions data; the CMHPI construction is described in Stephens et al. (1995). The Census new home price index is an index which uses hedonic regression techniques to estimate a price index for constant quality *newly constructed* homes over time; independent variables include numbers of bedrooms and bathrooms, air conditioning, and so on. Verbrugge (2008) discusses potential benefits and weaknesses in these indexes. As will be noted below, however, the major conclusions do not depend upon whether the CMHPI, Census, or CE-based house price indexes are used.

3.3   Interest Rate and Marginal vs. Average User Cost

A key component in a user cost series is the interest rate. The choice of the interest rate is contentious. In one view, the interest rate used in a particular agent's user cost should correspond to their idiosyncratic opportunity cost of capital – the rate at which future nominal returns are discounted. However, the work of Wang, Basu and Fernald (2005) implies that the appropriate interest rate is rather the rate which corresponds to the risk associated with housing investment – and should thus include both a risk premium and a default premium. These considerations suggest the use of the current mortgage interest rate, which contains both a risk premium and a default premium. Further lending support to this view is the fact that actual debt in the house must be financed at a mortgage interest rate. (This choice is also convenient in that it leads to a simpler user cost expression.) However, as in the case of the house price index, the basic character of our results is not affected if the T-bill interest rate – a rate that contains neither a risk nor a default premium – is used in place of the mortgage interest rate.

A second issue related to the interest rate is that of marginal versus average user cost. A quarterly user cost measure will most naturally be a *current* user cost, i.e., it will incorporate the current period home price and the current period interest rate. However, rent indexes generally do *not* share this temporal feature. Instead, these indexes are averages constructed from a sample of all existing rent contracts, rather than from a sample of *new* contracts each period; thus, these indexes are implicitly temporally aggregated, being averages of contracts that were renewed this month, renewed last month, and so on. Additionally, in the case of BLS rent indexes in particular, there is an *explicit* temporal aggregation, which is briefly discussed below; see Ptacek and Baskin (1996) for details on the construction of the BLS rent indexes.

Fortunately, one could transform the marginal user cost series into a temporally aggregated series which approximately matches this temporal structure of the rent indexes. Most rent contracts are renewed annually; if one assumes that all rental contracts are renewed on an annual basis, and that renewal dates (and new contract dates) are distributed uniformly across all quarters, the user cost series can be put on the same temporal basis by replacing the current user cost with its average over the current and previous three quarters (i.e., a one-sided 4-quarter moving average). This transformation will clearly impact the volatility of the user cost series, but will *not* influence its lower frequency dynamics.

3.4 Comparability of Rent Measure to User Cost Measure

If the goal is to compare estimated user costs to rents, one would ideally want to construct a measure of user costs that is as comparable as possible to the rental data. Both CPI and CMHPI indexes are constructed on the basis of price *changes* of units in the sample, a procedure which implicitly controls for unit-specific characteristics. But their underlying data sources are not completely comparable. The CPI rent sample includes some rent-regulated units; only about one-quarter of this sample consists of detached housing; and the CPI performs a quality-adjustment whenever there are major structural changes (such as the addition of air-conditioning).[8] The CMHPI sample consists mostly of detached housing units, and there is no adjustment for major structural changes. This comparability issue was partly addressed in Verbrugge (2008) via the construction of a detached rent index based upon CPI microdata. Here we address this issue by using, for each included dwelling, the CE rent and house price measures derived *from the same structure.*

4. User Costs

In principle, the *ex ante* user cost is the *expected* annual cost associated with purchasing a house, using it for one year, and selling it at the end of the year.[9] In this paper, in keeping with most of the literature, transactions costs and financing constraints (such as minimum down payments) are ignored. (Other authors, such as Diewert (2003), McCarthy, Peach and McKay (2004), and Diewert and Nakamura (2011), define user cost measures which incorporate transactions costs. But transactions costs fundamentally alter the dynamic decision problem

---

[8] The rents used to construct Rent indexes are the current dollar rent, plus any other payments or payments-in-kind paid by the tenant in the form of subsidies or work reductions. OER indexes are constructed using different aggregation weights (for example, rent-regulated units are removed), and the rents receive a utilities adjustment; see Verbrugge (2007a) and Poole and Verbrugge (2008). All rents receive an aging-bias adjustment; see Gallin and Verbrugge (2007).

[9] The standard frictionless theory, which builds upon Hall and Jorgenson (1967), implies that rents equal user costs, and is exposited in Gillingham (1980, 1983) and Dougherty and Van Order (1982); see also Diewert (2007) and Diewert and Nakamura (2011). Wedges resulting from taxes and transactions costs were considered in Verbrugge (2008).

facing households, leading to complex and idiosyncratic user cost expressions that appear to pose difficult measurement problems; see Martin (2004), Díaz and Luengo-Prado (2008), and Luengo-Prado et al. (2008).) Here we assume that the user cost should equal the market rent for an identical home when landlords are risk neutral and there is perfect frictionless competition with no transactions costs.

In Verbrugge (2008), three different (one year) user cost formulas were employed, all of which are standard.[10] Since results were not affected, here we focus on the simplest measure, which ignores the preferential tax treatment given to homeowners:

$$(8-1) \qquad \text{user cost}_t = P_t^h (i_t + \gamma - E\pi_t^h)$$
$$= P_t^h \psi_t$$

In (8-1), P_t^h is the price of the home, i_t is a nominal interest rate,[11] γ is the sum of depreciation, maintenance and repair, insurance, and property tax rates (and potentially a risk premium, if this is not in i) – all assumed constant,[12] π_t^h is the 4-quarter (constant quality) home price appreciation between now and 1 year from now, and E represents the expectation operator (so that the final term is expected annual constant quality home price appreciation). As Diewert (2003) points out, one may interpret $(i_t - E\pi_t^h)$ as a period t real interest rate.[13] For house price data that are quarterly, this gives rise to a quarterly user cost series. (Note that some authors refer to ψ_t as the user cost.)

Though it is common to use a crude proxy for $E\pi^h$, Verbrugge (2008) constructed a *forecast* for $E\pi^h$, as described below. This choice is crucial, for three reasons. First, expected home price appreciation is extremely volatile; setting this term to a constant is strongly at odds with the data, and moreover its level of volatility, and its correlation with i_t, is of central importance to the dynamics of user costs. Second, this term varies considerably across cities, and its temporal dynamics might well vary across cities as well. Finally, the recent surge in $E\pi^h$ is well above its 15-year average, and implies that the user cost/rent ratio has fallen dramatically. A *single* year appreciation rate was used since the study considered the *one year* user cost, in order to remain comparable to the typical rental contract.

Note that the user cost consists of two terms which are multiplied together: property value P_t^h, and the parenthetical expression ψ_t. Movements in ψ are dominated by changes in the

---

[10] See, e.g., Katz (1983), Diewert (2003), Green and Malpezzi (2003), Glaeser and Shapiro (2003), and Katz (2011). The measures here are end-of-period user costs, easily transformed into beginning-of-period user costs by dividing by $(1+ i_t)$, or to middle-of-period user costs by dividing by the square root of this term (Katz 2011). For the present purposes, this choice turns out to be inconsequential.

[11] See section 3.3 on the choice of the appropriate interest rate.

[12] BEA estimates of the depreciation rate indicate minimal variation; it remains in the range of 0.015-0.016. Census estimates of maintenance and repairs imply only modest variation once a strong seasonal component is removed. Although it would be preferable to use actual property tax rates, in fact these rates often diverge significantly from official property tax rates, since tax requirements can be based upon out-of-date official appraisal data.

[13] Many other authors base their user cost measures upon an expression such as $(r+\gamma-E\pi^h)$, where r is a *real* interest rate. This is erroneous, as can be understood by comparing two riskless economies which differ only in their rate of inflation.

"gap" between interest rates and expected home price appreciation. We would not expect ψ to exceed 20%, nor to drop to 0%; thus, over long periods of time, user costs must track home prices. However, variations in ψ will be *strongly* amplified, since the term is multiplied by the home price. Put differently, unless interest rates and home price appreciation move almost perfectly in sync with each other – implying that expected home price appreciation is driven only by interest rates – we should expect user costs to be highly volatile. The larger is γ, the less volatile are user costs. Furthermore, as Himmelberg, Mayer and Sinai (2005) point out, the smaller is ψ, the more it will move when i moves.

As noted, to construct regional user cost measures, one must forecast four-quarter-ahead regional home price appreciation, π_t^h. The forecasting approach used in Verbrugge (2008) combined three forecasts, and this produced a reasonable fit to the data (in contrast to the traditional 15-year average). Home price appreciation has a significant forecastable component; periods of home price appreciation tend to be followed immediately by periods of additional home price appreciation. In keeping with this, both anecdotal and survey evidence (e.g., Case, Quigley and Shiller, 2003) suggest that homebuyers' appreciation expectations appear to be simple extrapolations of recent appreciation rates. For some cities and time periods, to ensure that the user cost expression remained sensibly bounded below, an alternative "censored" forecast was used. This censored forecast equaled $\hat{\pi}_{t+4}^h$ except when the inequality $(i_t + \gamma - \hat{\pi}_{t+4}^h) < 0.005$ held, in which case the forecast was set to $\hat{\pi}_{t+4}^h = i_t + \gamma - 0.005$. Two final notes regarding Verbrugge (2008): first, the forecast series were *not* appreciably smoother than the actual home price appreciation series; this plays a key role in the volatility present in *ex ante* user costs, since it turns out that – at least over the more recent period – mortgage interest rates are not perfectly correlated with expected house price appreciation, leading to substantial volatility in ψ_t. Second, the divergence between rents and user costs does not appear to hinge crucially upon the forecasting method used (see Verbrugge, 2008).

In our view, though commonly practiced or suggested, it is inappropriate to smooth appreciation forecasts: if expectations about future house price inflation are volatile, then this should be reflected in *ex ante* user costs. Smoothing forecasts using two-sided filters is especially inappropriate, since this implicitly grants the forecaster with information from the future, and distorts parameter estimates (see Ashley and Verbrugge, 2007). The only smoothing which might be justified in this context is the smoothing outlined in section 3.3, a procedure which transforms a marginal user cost series into a (temporally) "averaged" user cost series, in order to mimic the temporal structure of the BLS rent indexes.

5.   Review of Results in Verbrugge (2008)

Over the period January 1980 (1980:1) through January 2005 (2005:1), nominal aggregate home prices (measured by the CMHPI) rose by 125%[14] (or, as measured by the

---

[14] Individual cities, of course, had different experiences: Boston's prices rose by 206%; Houston's, only 64%.

Census price index, by 92%), nominal aggregate CPI rents rose by 100%, and the CPI[15] rose by 82%. But we would not necessarily expect these measures to rise by exactly the same amount: not only are underlying structural characteristics different, but more fundamentally, theory tells us that rents should coincide with *user costs*, not house prices.

Figure 1 compares the movement in two aggregate rental series and two aggregate user cost series. The rental series are the official CPI rent index,[16] and a research series constructed in Verbrugge (2008) which tracks rental inflation in detached rental units. The user cost series are constructed as in (8-1), using either CMHPI (and CMHPI-based appreciation forecasts) or the Census index (and Census index-based appreciation forecasts). Each series is logged, and user costs are smoothed using a one-sided 4-quarter moving-average to mimic the implicit smoothing in BLS rent series. Then the log user cost series and the log CPI rent series are shifted by a constant so that each has an average value of 1.0 over the time period 1980 through 2005 quarter one. Finally, the log detached rental series is shifted by a constant so that its value in January 1988 equals that of the CPI rent series.

Figure 1. Log User Cost versus Log Rent Based on Indexes for All U.S.

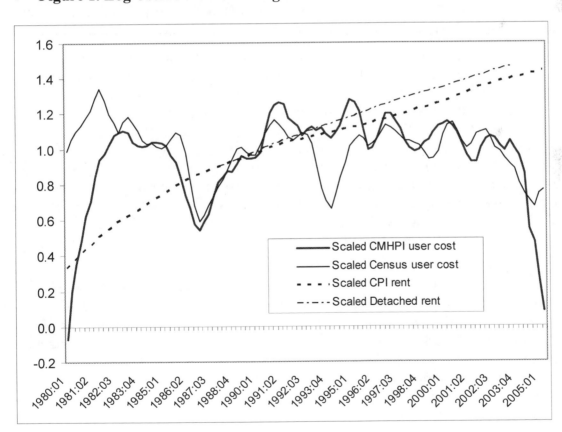

This graph provides little evidence in favor of the hypothesis that user costs and rents are equivalent measures of the cost of housing services – reinforcing the theoretical arguments in Díaz and Luengo-Prado (2008). This is true regardless of which measures of rents or of house prices are used. Rents steadily and smoothly increase over the period. User costs, in contrast, are anything but smooth, and do not even appear to share the trend in rents. In the case of the user cost series constructed using the CMHPI, this series jumps up dramatically at the beginning of the period, and is subsequently more or less trendless, before ending with a significant dip. In the case of the user cost series constructed using the Census index, this series appears to have a slight downward trend over the entire period. Housing *prices* increased steadily over this period; the reduction in the differential between mortgage interest rates and expected home price appreciation over this period is responsible for the failure of user costs to track the rise in home prices. In other words, the deviation between rents and user costs is largely explained by the movements in ψ_t: seemingly small changes in interest rates or expected appreciation can have very large effects on user costs, since these often represent large *percentage* changes in ψ_t.[17] (To give a sense of the importance of these terms in ψ_t, note that toward the end of this period, expected appreciation in housing prices caused user costs to plummet. If one counterfactually imposed a "pessimistic" expected appreciation of 0% in the final period, the scaled CMHPI user cost index would have risen to a level 26% *above* the scaled rent index.)

Noteworthy are the lengthy periods of divergence. Similar divergence is visible, to a greater or lesser extent, in each of the ten cities that were examined, and across the four Census regions; see Verbrugge (2008). After 1980, following a period of very low user costs, CMHPI-user costs rose rapidly, driven by rising interest rates and falling expected appreciation rates. The rise in user cost between 1987 and 1990 resulted primarily from a decline in expected home price appreciation. Since 1981, despite rising home prices, user costs – while volatile – have displayed no upward trend at all: the steady upward trend in home prices has been effectively "cancelled out" by a reduction (over this period) in the gap between the mortgage interest rate and the expected home price appreciation. In contrast, rental prices *have* risen steadily over this period. Thus, the relative price of homeownership to renting has fallen substantially over the period. The decline in the relative price of homeownership is consistent with the concurrent uptick in homeownership rates.[18]

We turn next to the second finding, related to volatility. The growth-rate comparison is crucial for statistical agencies which are responsible for producing inflation statistics: measuring inflation in homeowner shelter costs via the rental equivalence method means using rent *inflation* in neighboring rental markets – adjusted for the costs of utilities and so on – as the measure of *inflation* in homeowner shelter costs. Thus, for such agencies, the growth rate comparison is more important. The contrast is stark. Not only are the respective *means* of the rent index growth and user cost index growth series different (rent inflation being, on average, well above user cost inflation over this period), their *volatility* is also strikingly different. In particular, the volatility in the inflation rate of smoothed aggregate user costs is over 10 times larger than that in aggregate

---

[17] Recall that $d \ln(\text{user cost}_t) = d \ln P_t^h + d \ln \psi_t$.

[18] Chambers, Garriga and Schlagenhauf (2008) attribute much of this uptick to mortgage market innovations such as interest only mortgages. These explanations could be complementary.

rents.[19] The divergence would be even greater on a monthly basis. As owner-occupied housing typically possesses a large weight in consumer price index formulas, this level of volatility would essentially render such indexes useless – such volatile movements in housing costs would drive the entire index on a month-to-month basis, likely drowning out the signal in noise.

The apparent divergence between rents and user costs highlighted above is confirmed via regression analysis in Verbrugge (2007b): there is only weak evidence that rents respond to the determinants of user costs. In other words, regression analysis confirms the conclusions above: rents and user costs are not related in the expected manner. (Indeed, even cointegration between rents and user costs can be rejected in the aggregate, and in most of the cities as well.)

The third novel finding relates to the issue of arbitrage. The massive divergences suggest the presence of unexploited profit opportunities, particularly since about one-quarter of all rental housing consists of detached units, which are readily moved between owner and renter markets (so that the capital specificity issue highlighted by Ramey and Shapiro (2001) should not play a big role). However, Verbrugge (2008) found that the large costs associated with real estate transactions would have prevented risk neutral investors from earning expected profits by using the transaction sequence *buy-earn rent on the property-sell*, and would have prevented risk neutral homeowners from earning expected profits by using the transaction sequence *sell-rent from someone else for one year-repurchase*.

The fourth novel finding hints at a possible resolution to the divergence puzzle. As long as one uses a reasonably accurate forecast of annual appreciation in the user cost formula, one finds large divergence. But if one instead replaces expected annual appreciation with expected CPI inflation (which corresponds to an assumption of no real capital gains even in the short run) or alternatively with an annualized longer-horizon forecast, the resultant user cost measures feature appreciably less divergence from rents. Thus, a rationalization for rent inflation stickiness might provide the basis of an explanation for the divergence puzzle.

6. Extensions: Dollar User Costs and Rents for Median Structures in Five Cities

The research conducted by Verbrugge (2008) is based on rent and house price data that are in the form of indexes (i.e., the CPI, CMHPI and the Census new home price index); thus, one could not directly compare dollar rents with dollar user costs. Moreover, the indexes used by Verbrugge are not completely comparable; see section 3.4. However, Consumer Expenditure Survey (CE) Interview data include both property value and characteristics data, *and* rental equivalence data, in dollars, *for the same property* – which does allow the comparison of dollar rents and dollar user costs for a given property (once an appropriate measure of expected appreciation is constructed).[20] It further allows one to compute the house price/rent ratio for a property with given characteristics.

---

[19] As noted earlier, similar temporal and volatility divergences were observed between rents and the two CPI-U experimental *ex post* user cost indexes, which were constructed in 1979 (with a start date of 1967) and published through 1983. Both of these measures used 5-year appreciation rates. See BLS (1980). The large rent-to-price volatility noted by Phillips (1988a,b) is only about one-fifth as large.

[20] It is reasonable to assume that property owners have ready access to measures of recent house price appreciation, since these are both important inputs into housing decisions and are frequently reported upon by the popular press.

Consumer Expenditure Interview data collected from January 1982 through December 2002 were used to obtain cross sections (over time) of reported rental equivalence, property value, and number of rooms for owner-occupied structures, for five cities. On an annual basis for each city, the CE data were used to estimate the log rent level based upon the property value and number of rooms of the structure, using the simple regression model specification in (8-2):

$$(8\text{-}2) \quad \ln(\text{rent}_{i,t}) = a + b_1(p_{i,t}^h) + b_2(p_{i,t}^h)^2 + d(\text{rooms}_{i,t}) + gI_{\text{Jan}-\text{Jun}} + e_{i,t}$$

where $I_{\text{Jan}-\text{Jun}}$ is an indicator variable which takes the value 1 if the CE interview takes place in the first half of the year. The indicator variable is included since rents on average rise over time and because we wanted to produce semi-annual indexes rather than annual indexes. The model was estimated separately for each of the five cities under consideration: New York, Philadelphia, Chicago, Houston, and Los Angeles. To prevent the influence of non-representative observations, we dropped each sample observation which, after an initial fit of the model (8-2), possessed an externally studentized residual greater than 2.5. Regression sample sizes ranged from a low of 16 for Houston (in 1984) and Philadelphia (in 1995) to a high of 135 for Los Angeles (in 2000). Regressions were run without weights. The average adjusted R^2 was 0.66, with a minimum of 0.33.

Using coefficient estimates derived from (8-2), after applying the requisite log bias adjustment, one can form an estimate of the expected rent for any hypothetical property with particular characteristics. The characteristic values that we selected are those at the median, i.e., the median number of rooms and the median property value, within each city. (Hereafter we refer to this hypothetical structure as the median structure.) For each city, taking these estimated rents as true market rental prices, we constructed semi-annual measures of rents for this median structure. We constructed semi-annual measures of user costs using the house price appreciation forecasts from Verbrugge (2008), along with the median structure price or house value. We then constructed the price/rent ratio for each city, and plotted these in figure 2. The price was the median house value and the rent was the estimated market rent for the median structure. User costs and rents for each city are plotted in figures 3a-3e.

The price/rent ratio has received much attention lately, because several studies (e.g., Leamer 2002, Krainer 2003, Hatzius 2004) have suggested (on the basis of "P/E ratio" logic) that since house price indexes have risen faster than rent indexes, house prices are likely overvalued. (As noted previously, one cannot use indexes to adequately address this question; instead, as in this study, one must have *level* data on rents and house prices, since this question is fundamentally about levels.) Smith and Smith (2006) remind us that, although the fundamental value of a house does depend upon rents, we should not expect the price/rent ratio to be constant. This is because the price/rent ratio depends upon many variables: not only interest rates, tax laws, risk premia, and the like, but also anticipated *future* values of rents, interest rates, and so on. Still, as Krainer (2003) points out, if houses were indeed overvalued, we might expect to see signs of it in the historical price/rent ratio.

Figure 2: Price/Rent Ratio for Median Structure, 1982-2002

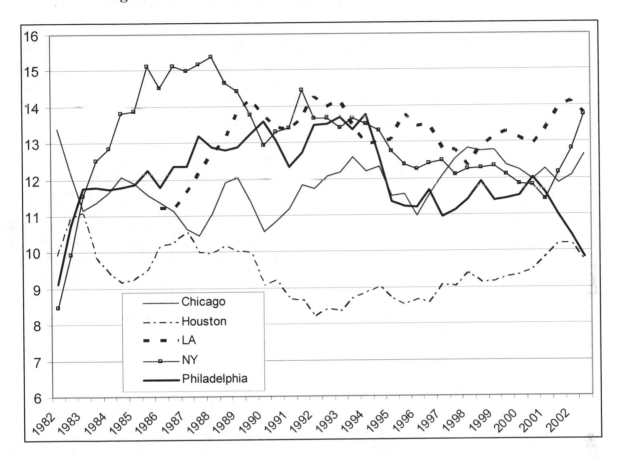

In figure 2, we plot price/rent ratios for the hypothetical median structure in our CE sample, which are smoothed using a 3-period moving average since there is substantial variation. Over this time period, we observe the following lower frequency movements of these ratios. 1) The price/rent ratio in Chicago displays no discernible trend, with an average of 11.7. 2) The price/rent ratio in Houston is generally low, and displays a decline followed by a slight rebound starting at about 1992. 3) Between 1986 and 1990, the price/rent ratio in Los Angeles climbs rapidly and flattens out, then starts in 1992 to gradually decline to a low of 12 (in early 1998) before rebounding up to 14. 4) The price/rent ratio in New York starts at a very low level and displays rapid growth until 1988 (peaking above 15), followed by a decline until early 2001, and then climbs rapidly up to 14. 5). The price/rent ratio in Philadelphia starts at a very low level, grows until 1990 and then falls starting in 1994, ending where it began, with a price/rent ratio of only 10.

How do these dynamics compare to those in the ratio of the CMHPI index to the BLS rent index? There are broad similarities, but some key differences as well. The ratio of indexes is much smoother. The comparison is closest for New York, Los Angeles, and Houston, where both the general character and the turning points are very similar to those based upon CE data. Most of the differences relate to behavior toward the end of the period. In particular, the index ratio starts to climb in *every* city somewhere in the 1996-1999 period, eventually rising to meet or exceed the level of its previous peak in all cities except Houston. This is not true of the CE-based ratios, and indeed, in Philadelphia the CE-based ratio *falls* at the end. And as for Chicago, the

CMHPI/BLS rent ratio rises modestly until 1990 (in contrast to the CE-based ratio, which falls), plateaus, and then rises again starting in 1999. It is difficult to discern these dynamics in the CE-based ratio.

What explains the divergences between these measures? Turning points are likely influenced by sampling variation, and such variation can also conceal broad trends. Price/rent ratios vary by price level. This can exacerbate the effect of sample size if the data are dissimilar; and it implies that the estimated ratio is sensitive to the dynamics of the sample median.[21] And the low frequency divergences, particularly toward the end of the sample, may partly reflect the greater house price inflation suggested by CMHPI indexes than by other indexes, such as the Census home price index. Similarly, the CMHPI index for Philadelphia displays about 5% greater growth between 1990 and 2002 than does Gillen's hedonic Philadelphia House Price Index (Gillen, 2005).[22]

Overall, the behavior of our CE-based measures are not too dissimilar from index-based measures, which is reassuring and perhaps suggests that it might be useful to scale or normalize conventional measures to match the estimates here. Some may question the use of reported rental equivalence as an accurate measure of rents. But, previous research finds these to be similar for similar renter and owner structures. Francois (1989) analyzed CPI housing survey data which were collected from renters and owners to compare owners' reported rental equivalence with imputed rents based on renters' rents for structures with the same characteristics. After accounting for renter length-of-residency discounts and rent-control in his regression-based analysis, Francois found that imputed rents and reported rental equivalence on average were not statistically significantly different. Francois noted that this is in contrast to the findings of others who reported rental equivalence estimates to be substantially higher than imputed rents.

Figures 3a-3e demonstrate that there are large divergences between rents and user costs in these five cities. For these graphs, we use the following user cost formula, which captures the tax advantages to homeownership:

$$(8\text{-}3) \quad \text{user cost}_t = P_t^h [i_t (1 - \tau_t^{Fed}) + \tau_t^{prop} (1 - \tau_t^{Fed}) + \breve{\gamma} - E\pi_t^h]$$

In (8-3), τ_t^{prop} is the property tax rate (assumed fixed at 2%), τ_t^{Fed} is the marginal federal income tax rate facing a family of four with twice the median income,[23] $\breve{g}$ (which, unlike in (8-1), does not include the property tax rate) equals 5%, and $E\pi_t^h$ is censored as above. We also plot both the predicted gross rent (i.e., the estimated rent on the hypothetical structure) and the predicted after-tax net rent (i.e., $(1 - \tau_t^{Fed})$*rent). As consumers, potential homeowners compare gross rents to after-tax user costs. But we might not expect after-tax user costs to track gross rents; instead, we might expect market forces to equilibrate *after-tax* net rent to *landlord* user costs. Landlord user costs mainly differ from (8-3) in that, for landlords, appreciation is taxable income but

---

[21] For this reason, we actually use a smoothed time estimate of the median, rather than the sample median.

[22] Philadelphia is an interesting case for other reasons: for example, in 1999, 60% of the housing units in Philadelphia were priced at less than 90% of construction costs (Glaeser and Gyourko 2002, based upon American Housing Survey Data), and house prices in that year were roughly where they were in 1990. The CE data for Philadelphia are also unusual; for example, the median property value displays quite large swings over time.

[23] These tax rates were constructed in Maag (2003). The use of a 2% property tax rate, and the marginal federal income tax rate facing a family of four with twice the median income, are fairly typical practices in the literature. This family type is selected as being representative of homeowners.

maintenance and insurance expenses are tax-deductible. Still, landlord user costs are reasonably-well approximated by (8-3); they usually exceed (8-3) modestly, but are occasionally smaller.[24]

Figure 3a: Net and Gross Rent and User Cost for Median Structure, Chicago

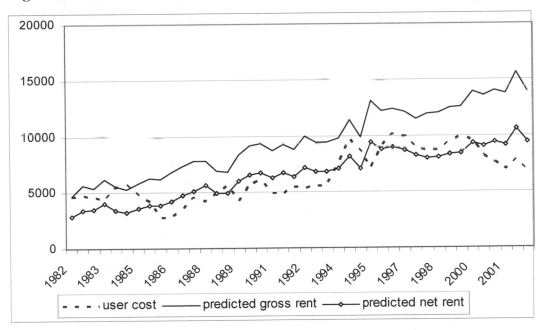

Figure 3b: Net and Gross Rent and User Cost for Median Structure, Houston

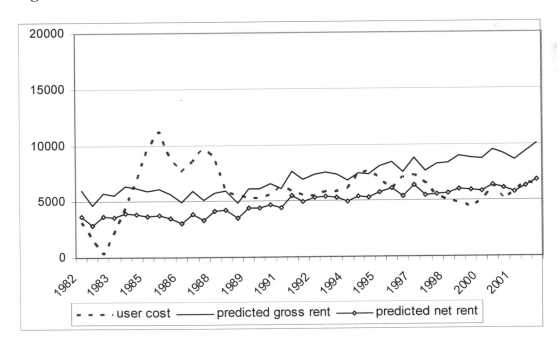

---

[24] Strictly speaking, one should compare after-tax user costs (which incorporate both local property taxes and federal deductions) to after-federal-tax rents, adjusted for the vacancy rate, in order to make this comparison precise. See Garner and Verbrugge (2011), who locate a closer link between user costs and rents upon making these adjustments *and* applying the popular (but ad-hoc) appreciation measure, expected CPI inflation.

Figure 3c: Net and Gross Rent and User Cost for Median Structure, New York City

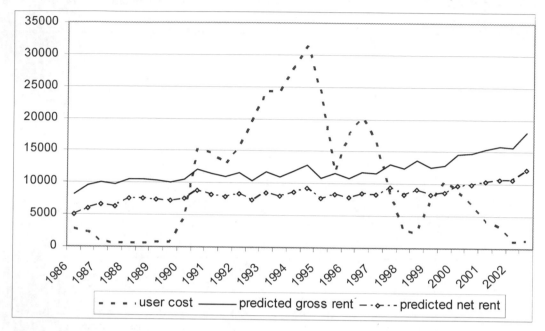

Figure 3d: Net and Gross Rent and User Cost for Median Structure, Los Angeles

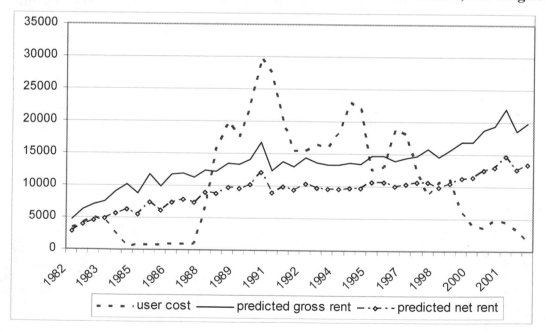

Figure 3e: Net and Gross Rent and User Cost for Median Structure, Philadelphia

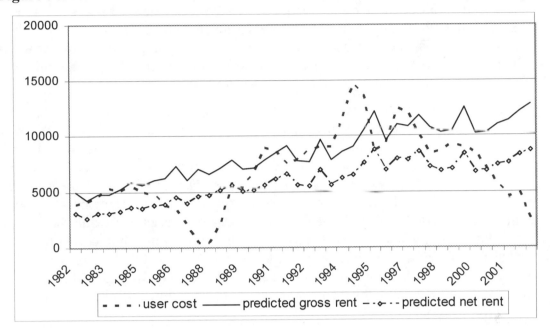

For each city, there is at least one episode during which we observe a significant and lengthy divergence between rents and user costs. User costs are much more volatile than rents. Low frequency movements appear to be only loosely related. Indeed, in New York and Los Angeles, the two series appear almost unrelated. It is not surprising that researchers have difficulty detecting a relationship between rents and user costs over extended periods of time.

Since these series are in levels, we may directly compare user costs and rents in dollars at each point in time. The most surprising conclusion is that, even taking account the tax advantages of homeownership, user costs sometimes are *well above* rents. It is not always cheaper to own than rent (when comparing the same structure). However, in the latter part of the period, user costs were well *below* gross rents in every city (and even below net rents, except for in Houston), contrary to what popular press accounts had suggested.

These results are very similar to those in Verbrugge (2008) in which different rent and house price measures are used. This leads to two conclusions. First, different rent and house price measures (and different tax adjustments) will lead to different low frequency dynamics; but the differential between the interest rate and expected appreciation, which is likely the key driver of user costs, appears to dominate even the medium frequency dynamics. Second, since these CE-based measures also display the large divergences observed between CMHPI based user costs and BLS rents, this suggests that these divergences do not stem from index construction errors.

7.   Conclusions

Verbrugge (2008) demonstrated that appropriately smoothed *ex ante* user costs diverge markedly from rents, an apparent puzzle from the perspective of standard capital theory. In particular, these measures diverge markedly both in growth rates – user costs are substantially more volatile – and in levels – user costs diverge from rents over extended periods of time. These divergences hold at both aggregate and disaggregate levels. These findings are of substantial importance to statistical agencies, since housing services form a large proportion of the typical household's total consumption, so that the choice of the homeowner inflation measure is crucial for inflation measurement. We offer our conclusions below.

In this paper, we extend Verbrugge (2008) by comparing, for five cities, user costs and rents for the same median structure, in levels (i.e., measured in dollars). These measures are constructed using Consumer Expenditure Interview Survey data, combined with house price appreciation forecasts. The overall picture that emerges is similar: our estimated user costs and rents diverge to a surprising degree. It is sometimes far cheaper to rent. (However, for most home owners, it would not have been profitable to become a renter temporarily: Verbrugge (2008) found that the large costs associated with real estate transactions would have prevented risk neutral agents from making profits in expectation by selling one's home, renting for a year, then repurchasing the house.) Arbitrage is evidently rather slow, likely compounded by the search process that plays a key role in real estate transactions. We also found that the dynamics of the estimated price/rent ratio are broadly similar to the dynamics of conventional price/rent ratio measures for housing.

Do any other factors contribute to the measured divergence? Verbrugge (2008) used indexes from multiple sources, leaving open the possibility that errors in the construction of these indexes might have been responsible for some or all of the divergence. But our finding of divergence in CE-based measures suggests that the explanation lies elsewhere. It is possible that the expected house price appreciation measure could be improved upon; but evidence in Verbrugge (2008) suggests that results are not sensitive to details in how this is constructed. Our understanding of user costs is almost certainly deficient; but Verbrugge (2008) argues that even using current generation user cost approximations (e.g., Díaz and Luengo-Prado 2008, Martin 2004) would not result in an elimination of the puzzling divergence.

In our view, the findings of this study suggest that statistical agencies responsible for compiling price statistics should use rental equivalence as their measure of homeowner user costs, rather than current-generation user cost measures, when this is feasible. First, until the divergence between rents and user costs is explained, it is more conservative to continue to use rental equivalence. Second, there are theoretical justifications for using rental equivalence, outlined in detail in Poole, Ptacek and Verbrugge (2005). Residential real estate is typically a composite good: the structure, a depreciating capital good which delivers a flow of consumption services over a long period of time; and land, an appreciating asset. But financial assets are considered out-of-scope for most price indexes – consumer price indexes seek to track inflation in *current* consumption costs – which suggests that the financial aspects of homeownership are also out-of-scope. A focus on pricing the flow of services, but separating out the financial aspects, leads rather immediately to the idea of estimating the value of those services using the prices of market analogues. The fact that user costs diverge from rents merely reflects, in this view, out-of-scope financial asset movements and transactions costs. Reinforcing this conclusion is the perplexing nature of asset price dynamics. To the extent that these dynamics are poorly understood by current theory, it is difficult to convincingly defend the use of one appreciation imputation over against another.[25] Finally, standard measures of *ex ante* user costs are highly volatile, even if they are smoothed to mimic the implicit smoothing in the CPI rent series; this volatility alone probably renders them unsuitable in a price index. Longer horizon forecasts ameliorate this problem (see Verbrugge 2008 and Garner and Verbrugge 2011), but do not completely resolve it.

Of course, in some countries the rental equivalence method may not be practicable. To price the service flow from an owned dwelling, then, a user cost approach is necessary. In that case, Verbrugge (2008) suggests using a very long horizon appreciation forecast (such as a long moving average), or an inflation forecast, in the user cost formula.

References

Ashley, R. and R. Verbrugge (2007), "To difference or not to difference: a Monte Carlo investigation of spurious regression in Vector Autoregressive models," *International Journal of Data Analysis and Techniques and Strategies*, forthcoming.

Baker, D. (2004), "Too Much Bubbly at the Fed? The New York Federal Reserve Board's Analysis of the Run-Up in Home Prices," Center for Economic and Policy Research.

Blackley, D.M. and J.R. Follain (1996), "In Search of Empirical Evidence that Links Rent and User Cost," *Regional Science and Urban Economics* 26, 409-431.

Brookings Institution (2003), "CPI Housing: Summary," Summary of Workshop: *Two Topics in Services: CPI Housing and Computer Software*, May 23, 2003, Brookings Institution.

Bureau of Labor Statistics (1980), "CPI Issues," Bureau of Labor Statistics Report 593, February.

Calhoun, C, (1996), "OFHEO House Price Indices: HPI Technical Description," manuscript, OFHEO.

Case, B, H.O. Pollakowski and S.M. Wachter (1997), "Frequency of transaction and house price modeling." *Journal of Real Estate Economics* 14, 173-187.

Case, K. and R. Shiller (1987), "Prices of Single-Family Homes since 1970: New Indices for Four Cities." *New England Economic Review* (September/October), 45-56.

Case, K. and R. Shiller (1989), "The efficiency of the market for single-family homes," *American Economic Review* 79, 125-137.

Case, K., J.M. Quigley and R. Shiller (2003), "Home-Buyers, Housing and the Macroeconomy," in A. Richards and T. Robinson (eds.), *Asset Prices and Monetary Policy*, Reserve Bank of Australia, 149-188.

Chambers, M., C. Garriga, and D.E. Schlagenhauf (2008), "Accounting for Changes in the Homeownership Rate," *International Economics Review*, forthcoming.

Crone, T., L.I. Nakamura and R. Voith (2000), "Measuring Housing Services Inflation," *Journal of Economic and Social Measurement* 26, 153-171.

Crone, T., L.I. Nakamura and R. Voith (2006) "The CPI for Rents: A Case of Understated Inflation," Working Paper 06-7, January 2006, Federal Reserve Bank of Philadelphia.

Davis, M. and J. Heathcote (2005), "The price and quantity of residential land in the United States," Georgetown University.

---

[25] Imposing the equality of rents and user costs and solving for expected appreciation as a residual results in an implied expected appreciation series which diverges markedly from actual appreciation. The correct expected appreciation measure derives from applying the correct model to the data; in other words, "fundamentalist" forecasts are required. However, we do not fully understand house price dynamics; over this period, there was controversy over whether there was a bubble, for example. Martin (2006) provides a structural model of house price dynamics with surprising implications.

Díaz, A. and M.J. Luengo-Prado. (2008), "On the User Cost and Home Ownership," *Review of Economic Dynamics*, 11 (3), 584-613.

Diewert, W.E. (2007), "Durables and Owner Occupied Housing in a Consumer Price Index," Discussion Paper 03-08, Department of Economics, University of British Columbia, Vancouver, Canada, available at http://www.econ.ubc.ca/discpapers/dp0308.pdf; forthcoming in W.E. Diewert, J. Greenlees and C. Hulten (eds.), *Price Index Concepts and Measurement*, NBER Studies in Income and Wealth, U. of Chicago Press.

Diewert, W.E. and A.O. Nakamura (2011), "Accounting for Housing in a CPI," chapter 2, pp. 7-32 in Diewert, W.E., B.M. Balk, D. Fixler, K.J. Fox and A.O. Nakamura (2011), *PRICE AND PRODUCTIVITY MEASUREMENT: Volume 1 -- Housing*. Trafford Press.

DiPasquale, D. and W.C. Wheaton (1992), "The Costs of Capital, Tax Reform, and the Future of the Rental Housing Market," *Journal of Urban Economics* 31, 337-359.

Dougherty, A. and R. Van Order (1982), "Inflation, Housing Costs, and the Consumer Price Index," *American Economic Review* 72 (1), March, 154-164.

Dreiman, M.H. and A. Pennington-Cross (2004), "Alternative Methods of Increasing the Precision of Weighted Repeat Sales House Price Indices," *Journal of Real Estate Finance and Economics* 28(4), 299-317.

Follain, J.R., D.R. Leavens, and O.T. Velz (1993), "Identifying the Effects of Tax Reform on Multifamily Rental Housing," *Journal of Urban Economics* 24, 275–98.

Francois, J. (1989), "Estimating Homeownership Costs: Owners' Estimates of Implicit Rents and the Relative Importance of Rental Equivalence in the Consumer Price Index," *American Real Estate Economics Association Journal* 17, 87-99.

Fratantoni, M. and S. Schuh (2003), "Monetary Policy, Housing Investment, and Heterogeneous Regional Markets," *Journal of Money, Credit and Banking* 35 (4), 557-590.

Gallin, J. (2003), "The Long-Run Relationship between House Prices and Income: Evidence from Local Housing Markets," Federal Reserve Board.

Gallin, J. (2004), "The Long-Run Relationship between House Prices and Rents," Federal Reserve Board.

Gallin, J., and R. Verbrugge (2007), "Improving the CPI's Age-Bias Adjustment: Leverage, Disaggregation and Model-Averaging," Bureau of Labor Statistics (BLS) Working Paper #411.

Garner, T.I., and R. Verbrugge (2011), "Reconciling User Costs and Rental Equivalence: Evidence from the U.S. Consumer Expenditure Survey." submitted for publication in the Bureau of Labor Statistics (BLS) Working Paper Series.

Gatzlaff, D.H., and D.R. Haurin (1997), "Sample-selection bias and repeat-sales index estimates." *Journal of Real Estate Economics* 14, 33-50.

Gillen, K.C. (2005), "Philadelphia House Price Indices: Technical FAQ and Documentation," Wharton School, University of Pennsylvania.

Gillingham, R. (1980), "Estimating the User Cost of Owner-Occupied Housing," *Monthly Labor Review* 103 (2), 31-35.

Gillingham, R. (1983), "Measuring the Cost of Shelter for Homeowners: Theoretical and Empirical Considerations." *Review of Economics and Statistics* 65 (2), 254-265.

Glaeser, E. and Y. Gyourko (2002), "Zoning's Steep Price." *Regulation* 25.3, 24-30.

Glaeser, E. and J. Shapiro (2003), "The Benefits of the Home Mortgage Interest Deduction," *Tax Policy and the Economy* 17, 37-82.

Goodman, J. and E. Belsky (1996), "Explaining the Vacancy Rate-Rent Paradox of the 1980s," *Journal of Real Estate Research* 11.3, 309-323.

Green, R. and S. Malpezzi (2003), *A Primer on U.S. Housing Markets and Housing Policy*, Urban Institute Press.

Greenlees, J.S. (1982a), "An Empirical Evaluation of the CPI Home Purchase Index, 1973-1978," *American Real Estate and Urban Economics Journal* 10 (1) Spring, 1-24.

Greenlees, J.S. (1982b), "Sample Truncation in FHA Data: Implications for Home Purchase Indexes," *Southern Economic Journal* 48 (4), 917-931.

Guðnason, R. and G. Jónsdóttir (2006), "The House Price Index, Market Prices and Flow of Services Methods," presented at the OECD-IMF Workshop on Real Estate Price Indexes held in Paris, November 6-7, 2006. http://www.oecd.org/dataoecd/2/42/37583740.pdf.

Guðnason, R. and G.R. Jónsdóttir (2011), "Owner Occupied Housing in the Icelandic CPI," chapter 9, pp. 147-150 in Diewert, W.E., B.M. Balk, D. Fixler, K.J. Fox and A.O. Nakamura (2011), *PRICE AND PRODUCTIVITY MEASUREMENT: Volume 1 -- Housing*. Trafford Press.

Hall, R.E. and D.W. Jorgenson. (1967), "Tax Policy and Investment Behavior," *American Economic Review* 57 (3) June, 391-414.

Hatzius, J. (2004), "Housing and the U.S. Consumer: Mortgaging the Economy's Future," *Goldman Sachs Global Economics Paper* 83.

Haurin, D., P. Hendershott and D. Kim (1991), "Local House Price Indexes: 1982-1991," *Journal of the American Real Estate and Urban Economics Association*, 451-472.

Himmelberg, C., C. Mayer and T. Sinai (2005), "Assessing High House Prices: Bubbles, Fundamentals, and Misperceptions," *Journal of Economic Perspectives* 19 (4), 67-92.

Hinich, M.J. (1982), "Testing for Gaussianity and Linearity of a Stationary Time Series," *Journal of Time Series Analysis* 3 (3), 169-176.

Hinich, M.J. (1996), "Testing for Dependence in the Input to a Linear Time Series Model," *Nonparametric Statistics* 6, 205-221.

Katz, A.J. (1983), "Valuing the Services of Consumer Durables," *Review of Income and Wealth* 29, 405-427.

Katz, A.J. (2011), "Estimating Dwelling Services in the Candidate Countries: Theoretical and Practical Considerations in Developing Methodologies Based on a User Cost of Capital Measure," chapter 3, pp. 33-50 in Diewert, W.E., B.M. Balk, D. Fixler, K.J. Fox and A.O. Nakamura (2011), *PRICE AND PRODUCTIVITY MEASUREMENT: Volume 1 -- Housing*. Trafford Press.

Krainer, J. (2003), "House Price Bubbles," *Federal Reserve Bank of San Francisco Economic Letter* 2003-6.

Landefeld, J.S. and S.H. McCulla (2000), "Accounting for Nonmarket Household Production within a National Accounts Framework," *Review of Income and Wealth* 46 (3), 289-307.

Leamer, E.E. (2002), "Bubble Trouble? Your House has a P/E Ratio Too," UCLA Anderson Forecast.

Luengo-Prado, M., P. Sullivan, R. Verbrugge and K. Vetechova (2008) "The Dynamics of User Costs and Rents," manuscript in progress, Bureau of Labor Statistics.

Maag, E. (2003), "A Brief History of Marginal Tax Rates," *Urban Institute* (www.urban.org).

Martin, R. (2004), "Paper on User Costs and Rents," manuscript in progress, Board of Governors of the Federal Reserve System.

Martin, R. (2006), "The Baby Boom: Predictability in House Prices and Interest Rates," Board of Governors of the Federal Reserve System.

Max, S. (2004), "For Rent, Cheap," *CNN Money*, February 11.

McCarthy, J., R.W. Peach, and A. McKay (2004), "Housing Trends in the 1990s: The Effects on Rent Inflation and Its Measurement in the CPI," manuscript, Federal Reserve Bank of New York.

McCarthy, J. and R.W. Peach (2004), "Are Home Prices the Next "Bubble"? *FRBNY Economic Policy Review*, December.

Phillips, R. (1988a), "Residential Capitalization Rate: Explaining Inter-Metropolitan Variation, 1974-1979," *Journal of Urban Economics* 23, 278-290.

Phillips, R. (1988b), "Unraveling the Residential Rent-Value Puzzle: An Empirical Investigation," *Urban Studies* 25 (6), 487-496.

Poole, R., F. Ptacek, and R. Verbrugge (2005), "Treatment of Owner-Occupied Housing in the CPI," manuscript prepared for FESAC, Bureau of Labor Statistics, submitted for publication in the Bureau of Labor Statistics (BLS) Working Paper Series.

Poole, R., and R. Verbrugge (2008), ""Explaining the Rent-OER Inflation Divergence, 1999-2006," Bureau of Labor Statistics (BLS) Working Paper #410.

Ptacek, F. and R.M. Baskin (1996), "Revision of the CPI Housing Sample and Estimators," *Monthly Labor Review* (December), 31-9.

Ramey, V. and M. Shapiro (2001), "Displaced Capital: A Study of Aerospace Plant Closings." *Journal of Political Economy* 109 (5), 958-992.

Sims, C. (1988), "Bayesian Skepticism on Unit Root Econometrics," *Journal of Economic Dynamics and Control* 12, 463-474.

Stephens, W., Y. Li, V. Lekkas, J. Abraham, C. Calhoun, and T. Kimner (1995), "Conventional Mortgage Home Price Index," *Journal of Housing Research*, 6(3), 389-418.

Stewart, K., and S. Reed (1999), "CPI research series using current methods, 1978-98," *Monthly Labor Review*, 122(6), 29-38.

Stock, James H. and Mark Watson (1999), "A Comparison of Linear and Nonlinear Univariate Models for Forecasting Macroeconomic Time Series," in R.F. Engle and H. White (eds.), *Cointegration, Causality, and Forecasting : A Festschrift in Honour of Clive Granger*, Oxford University Press, 1-44.

Smith, L.B., K.T. Rosen, and G. Fallis (1988), "Recent Developments in Economic Models of Housing Markets," *Journal of Economic Literature* 26, 29-64.

Smith, M.H., and G. Smith (2006), "Bubble, Bubble, Where's the Housing Bubble?" Pomona College.

Verbrugge, R. (2007a), "Do the CPI's Utilities Adjustments for OER Distort Inflation Measurement?," submitted for publication in the Bureau of Labor Statistics (BLS) Working Paper Series.

Verbrugge, R. (2007b), "Investigating the Rent-User Cost Paradox," manuscript in progress, Bureau of Labor Statistics.

Verbrugge, R. (2008), "The Puzzling Divergence of Rents and User Costs, 1980-2004," *Review of Income and Wealth* 54 (4), 671-699.

Wang, C., S. Basu and J. Fernald (2005), "A General-Equilibrium Asset-Pricing Approach to the Measurement of Nominal and Real Bank Output,"http://www.ipeer.ca/papers/Wang_Basu_Fernald_Oct_15_2004.pdf. ; forthcoming in W.E. Diewert, J. Greenlees and C. Hulten (eds.), *Price Index Concepts and Measurement*, NBER Studies in Income and Wealth, U. of Chicago Press.

Chapter 9
OWNER OCCUPIED HOUSING IN THE ICELANDIC CPI

Rósmundur Guðnason and Guðrún R. Jónsdóttir[1]

1.   The Icelandic CPI House Price Index

The house price index used in the Icelandic CPI is based on actual property transaction prices: sales contracts from the Land Registry. Almost every concluded real estate agreement is obtained. It is not only in the interest of buyers that a contract is registered but also a condition for credit services from the Housing Financing Fund and the commercial banks. About 8,000-10,000 real estate sales contracts are closed annually, which represents about 8-10 percent of all the housing in the country. Every sales contract contains standardized information on the property, its owner(s) and the sales price.

A sales contract also includes payment arrangement details; this information is then used for computing the present value of the sales contract. The basic reason for applying the present value is the fact that the value of money paid today is different from the value of money paid in the future. The Icelandic housing price index is computed from changes in the present value of real estate sales and the price changes for real estate are calculated as a three-month moving average, with a one-month delay. For example, the index result in May is based on prices collected in the period of February through April. A stratification method is used in the compilation. The classifications used for this stratification are size, property type and location. The estimator used in the calculation is geometric and the index is calculated superlatively (using the Fisher index, in this case).

2.   Simple User Cost Method for Dealing with Owner Occupied Housing in a CPI

According to the household expenditures survey, about 80 percent of Icelanders live in owner occupied housing (OOH). The rental equivalence approach cannot be used to estimate changes in the cost of OOH because of the small size of the rental market. Instead, the imputed rent is computed as an annuity based on the average house value collected in the Household Expenditure Survey (HES), real interest rates and depreciation.

---

[1] The authors are both with Statistics Iceland. They can be reached, respectively, at rosmundur.gudnason@statice.is and gudrun.jonsdottir@statice.is. This paper draws on Diewert (2003), Guðnason (2003a, 2003b, 2004a, 2004b, 2004c, 2005) and Guðnason and Jónsdóttir (2006). Erwin Diewert, Heiðrún Guðmundsdóttir, Örn Ingvarsson, Alice Nakamura, Mark Proud'homme, Mick Silver and the participants at the OECD-IMF Workshop on real estate price indexes the 6th-7th November 2006 and the 2006 Ottawa group meeting held in London, 14-16 May are thanked for helpful comments on the various earlier papers on which this chapter draws.

Guðnason, R. and G.R. Jónsdóttir (2011), "Owner Occupied Housing in the Icelandic CPI," chapter 9, pp. 147-150 in Diewert, W.E., B.M. Balk, D. Fixler, K.J. Fox and A.O. Nakamura (2011), *PRICE AND PRODUCTIVITY MEASUREMENT: Volume 1 -- Housing*. Trafford Press.

In Iceland, the approach of calculating housing cost as a simple user cost was adopted in November 1992.[2] To begin with, price measurements for housing covered only the capital city area. Since April 2000, however, they were extended to cover the whole country. The user cost method converts a part of the expenditure on a durable (such as a house) into a flow of services by taking into consideration the use of capital, the long term financial (opportunity) cost (interest), and the use of the durable (depreciation). With the full user cost approach, capital gains income is also subtracted.[3] This practice is natural in the case of firms as a part of measuring their profit, but there is disagreement regarding the appropriateness of doing this for households.

Conceptually, the Icelandic CPI measures price changes in household expenditures exclusive of changes in households' income. The stated aim is to measure changes in the price level of expenditures without regard for the amount of money needed or available to pay for the expenditures. Hence, capital gains are not taken into account. The real interest is taken to be the required return on (or opportunity cost of) capital tied up in the property or taken on credit. The long term real interest used in the calculation is intended to reflect a real return on the investment over the lifetime of the dwelling. In this respect, the real rate measures the capital gain. In the short run, the capital gain can be lower or higher than the rate of return, but it is approximated by the average long term real interest rate.

The fact that a part of the price of using capital is due to factors other than the service price for money makes the use of interest rates a quality adjustment issue. In order to determine the real interest rate, nominal interest rates must be adjusted for quality according to changes in inflation. Nominal interest rates reflect inflation, as well as risk and expectations; the higher the inflation, the higher the interest rates are.

When consumers buy property, they finance it with equity and mortgages and the average long term real interest rate in the model takes into account these two main types of financing. In the simple user cost model, the division between these two forms of finance is mainly based on information from the sales contracts used for house price measurement. As a result, the opportunity financial cost covering the lifetime of the durable is estimated by keeping the equity rate fixed but allowing the mortgage real interest share to vary. The required return on equity was determined in accordance with the long term rate of return that pension funds require. When this approach was adopted, this rate of return was 3 percent. That rate was adopted and retained.

Long term loans from the Housing Financing Fund were revamped in July 2004 and mortgage interest rates were lowered. Soon after that, commercial and savings banks greatly increased their housing loans at competitive interest rates. The initial fall in mortgage rates was included in the Icelandic CPI in July. However, as of August 2004 it was decided that the variable real mortgage rates, used in the calculation of the simple user cost of housing, should be calculated as a 60 month moving average. This decision was made in anticipation of frequent mortgage rate changes which might give rise to month-to-month volatility in the CPI.

---

[2] A similar user cost approach was adapted by the National Economic Institute just after 1980, when inflation was high in Iceland, to measure the profitability of domestic fishing and fish processing.

[3] Research into the use of the full user cost has been interpreted by some as showing that the results are likely to be very volatile. See Gillingham (1980 and 1983) and Garner and Verbrugge (2011). However, the interest rates used by these others are nominal, rather than real.

Subsequently, however, the feared volatility of real interest rates on housing credit did not materialize and the rates were stabilized at a substantially lower level than before. As of May 2005, Statistics Iceland decided to change the method of averaging real interest rates in the model for owner occupied housing in the CPI and a 60-month moving average was replaced by a 12 month moving average. This change led to a lowering of the Icelandic CPI. These procedures and rates are reconsidered regularly when the CPI is rebased in March each year.

The depreciation rate used in the user cost calculation was obtained mainly by considering the age of the housing stock. The value of the site and the building are not separated in the records on which the housing index is based. Thus, a mean depreciation is calculated for the building and site. The depreciation in the index is 1.25 percent of this real estate value.[4]

Given data for house prices, interest rates and depreciation, the formula for the annuity is:

$$(1) \qquad A_{HV} = P_H \left[\frac{r}{1 - (1+r)^{-N}} \right].$$

where A_{HV} is the annuity based on the house value, P_H is the present value of the house (collected in the HES), r is the real interest rate, and N is the lifetime of the durable (a depreciation rate of 1.25 per cent is used based on an assumed lifetime of 80 years with no scrap value at the end).[5] The house value, P_H, is price updated monthly with the house price index.

The average real interest rate, measured monthly, has hovered around 4 percent since 1992, the lowest rate being 3.6 percent in 2005 and the highest being 4.3 in 2008. When changes in real interest occur, however, they have a direct effect on the annual payment. Increases in the average real interest rate, in the instance of a long lifetime, increase the annuity (the imputed rent) by just about the same ratio.

The real interest rate also influences the value of the property used as the base for calculating the annuity, as lower interest rates normally lead to higher house prices. In calculating the present values of the sale contracts, the loans with fixed interest rates are discounted by a rate of return reflecting the change in the real interest rate. A rise in the real interest rate lowers the present value of a property. This fact is in accordance with the economic reality that a higher real interest rate leads to less demand and lower prices for housing.

---

[4] The 1.25 percent rate is stated to correspond roughly to a depreciation rate for structures of 1.5 percent with a lifetime of about 67 years.

[5] This user cost method is in some ways similar to Steiner (1961) suggestion in the Stigler report. In the Steiner user cost model the annuity method is used to measure depreciation and interest but real interest rates are not used.

References

Diewert, W.E. (2003), "The Treatment of Owner Occupied Housing and Other Durables in a Consumer Price Index" Discussion Paper 03-08, Department of Economics, University of British Columbia, Vancouver, Canada, available at http://www.econ.ubc.ca/discpapers/dp0308.pdf. This paper is forthcoming in W.E. Diewert, J. Greenless and C. Hulten (eds.), *Price Index Concepts and Measurement,* NBER Studies in Income and Wealth, forthcoming U. of Chicago Press.

Diewert, W.E. and Nakamura, A.O. (2011), "Accounting For Housing In A CPI," chapter 2, pp. 7-32 in Diewert, W.E., B.M. Balk, D. Fixler, K.J. Fox and A.O. Nakamura (2011), *PRICE AND PRODUCTIVITY MEASUREMENT: Volume 1 -- Housing.* Trafford Press..

Garner, T.I. and R. Verbrugge (2011), "The Puzzling Divergence of Rents and User Costs, 1980-2004: Summary and Extensions," chapter 8, pp. 125-146 in Diewert, W.E., B.M. Balk, D. Fixler, K.J. Fox and A.O. Nakamura (2011), *PRICE AND PRODUCTIVITY MEASUREMENT: Volume 1 -- Housing.* Trafford Press.

Gillingham, R. (1980), "Estimating the User Cost of Owner Occupied Housing," *Monthly Labour Review* 1980/February.

Gillingham, R. (1983), "Measuring the Cost of Shelter for Homeowners: Theoretical and Empirical Considerations," *Review of Economics and Statistics* XLV (2) 1983.

Guðnason, R. (2003a), "How Do We Measure Inflation? Some Measurement Problems," *International Working Group on Price Indices (Ottawa Group).* Published in the *Proceedings of the Seventh Meeting*, Paris, 27-29 May 2003, T. Lacroix (ed.), INSEE, Paris, France, November, 289-320.

Guðnason, R. (2003b), "Owner Occupied Housing: Market Price Approach to User Cost," invited paper at the Joint ECE/ILO Meeting on Consumer Price Indices, Geneva, 4-5 December 2003.

Guðnason, R. (2004a), "Simple User Cost and Rentals," paper presented at the Eighth meeting of the International Working Group on Price Indices (The Ottawa Group), Helsinki, Finland, 23-25 August.

Guðnason, R. (2004b), "How Do We Measure Inflation?" English translation of the title "Hvernig mælum við verðbólgu?" *Fjármálatíðindi (Economic Journal of the Icelandic Centralbank)* 1, 33-54.

Guðnason, R. (2004c), "Market Price Approach to Simple User Cost," *Statistical Journal of the United Nations* ECE 21, 147-155.

Guðnason, R. (2005), "Market Prices and User Cost," paper presented at the OECD seminar, Inflation Measures: Too High–Too Low–Internationally Comparable? Paris, 21-22 June.

Guðnason, R. and G.R. Jónsdóttir (2006), "House Price Index, Market Prices and Flow of Services Methods," OECD-IMF WORKSHOP, Real Estate Price Indexes, Paris, 6-7 November 2006. http://www.oecd.org/dataoecd/2/42/37583740.pdf

Steiner, P. (1961), "Consumer Durables in an Index of Consumer Prices," Staff Paper no. 6 in The Price Statistics of the Federal Government, New York: National Bureau of Economic Research, General series no. 73.

Chapter 10

DIFFERENT CONCEPTS FOR MEASURING OWNER OCCUPIED HOUSING COSTS IN A CPI: STATISTICS CANADA'S ANALYTICAL SERIES

Andrew Baldwin, Alice O. Nakamura and Marc Prud'homme[1]

1.   Introduction

The treatment of owner occupied housing (OOH) in a consumer price index (CPI) is conceptually difficult. The characteristics of a house, considered as a commodity, permit and encourage a variety of treatments. A house is a consumer asset, with a long useful life, which is generally purchased on credit, with active resale and rental markets in which households participate as both buyers and sellers. A consumer price index for OOH services may be built around the cost of using a home, the cash outlays on a home, its assumed rental value, or its purchase price. No one treatment is ideal for all uses. Different tradeoffs made among the differing needs for a measure of price level change, and nation specific data problems, have influenced national choices on the concept for OOH services in the CPI. There is considerable variety in how OOH services are defined in the official CPI statistics for different nations. This is in contrast with the treatment of OOH services costs in the system of national accounts (SNA), including for the calculation of gross domestic product (GDP); in that case, most countries, including Canada, use a rental equivalence approach.

The CPI is sensitive to the measurement of price change for OOH services. Shelter is one of the most important CPI components in terms of household expenditure shares, and a large share of the shelter expenditures are for OOH services.

Many consumer durables share some of the characteristics of owner occupied housing, but to lesser degrees. For example, motor vehicles like houses are purchased in large part on credit, but the amortization period is for no more than five years. In contrast, the amortization period for a mortgage loan can sometimes exceed 25 years. Also, expenditures on other durable goods comprise smaller proportions of household expenditures. Finally, few consumer durables

[1] Andrew Baldwin and Marc Prud'homme are with the Prices Division of Statistics Canada, and can be reached at Andy.Baldwin@statcan.ca and Marc.PrudHomme@statcan.ca, respectively. Alice Nakamura is with the University of Alberta School of Business and can be reached at alice.nakamura@ualberta.ca. This paper draws on Baldwin, Nakamura and Prud'homme (2006) and on previous work done over the years in this area by Andrew Baldwin and other staff members of Prices Division of Statistics Canada. The views in this paper are those of the authors and do not necessarily represent the opinions of the Prices Division or Statistics Canada.

Baldwin, A., A.O. Nakamura and M. Prud'homme (2011),
"Owner Occupied Housing in the CPI: The Statistics Canada Analytical Series," chapter 10, pp. 151-160 in
Diewert, W.E., B.M. Balk, D. Fixler, K.J. Fox and A.O. Nakamura (2011),
PRICE AND PRODUCTIVITY MEASUREMENT: Volume 1 -- Housing. Trafford Press.

have lower depreciation rates or longer expected lives than owner occupied dwellings.[2] Although it is usually understood that the alternative approaches to the treatment of OOH services in the CPI could be applied as well to some durable good, like motor vehicles, there is no other consumer durable for which a change from one approach to another would have such a large impact.

International comparisons of the inflationary performance of one country versus others are problematical when the countries have made different choices about how to measure OOH price level change. Faced with this challenge, the Fourteenth International Conference of Labour Statistics adopted a resolution that asked countries to provide, in addition to the All-items CPI, an index that excludes shelter. However, given the importance of shelter costs in household expenditures, it is not fully satisfactory to base international comparisons of inflation rates on an index of price change that *excludes* shelter.

An alternative approach that Canada has tried for dealing with this problem is to construct analytical CPI series for Canada using the main measurement concepts adopted by other nations, thereby facilitating bilateral comparisons of inflationary performance. The Prices Division of Statistics Canada in December 1985 began publishing analytical series as part of the Canadian CPI program.[3] DeVries and Baldwin (1985) explain that the Statistics Canada analytical CPI program initially focused on producing a single analytical Canadian CPI series comparable in methodology with the U.S. CPI for the years before and after 1983. The year 1983 was when the U.S. switched to the rental equivalence approach from the net purchase including interest approach (NP2).

In this report, the Statistics Canada analytical CPI series for dwelling services -- six series based on four main concepts of owner occupied accommodation -- are updated for the period from January 1996 to December 2005. One of the series adopts the concept of the *official CPI*. All-items level indexes embedding the various alternative homeownership series are also presented[4] so that the effects of the different OOH concepts on the overall CPI can be observed.

This study is a pilot project for the regular analytical series program. The estimates of comparative shelter costs in this paper are for one housing area: Ottawa. The data used were obtained from a third party and were, at the time of the study, only available for Ottawa.

One challenge for those outside of Statistics Canada who are interested in these analytical series is that the terminology that Statistics Canada uses, based on past practices in

---

[2] A World Bank study on Bosnia and Hercegovina that estimated depreciation rates for 23 different categories of durable goods found rates ranging from 8.9% to 1.8%; all exceeded the 1.5% depreciation rate assumed for OOH in the Canadian CPI. See State Agency for Statistics (BHAS) et al. (2002), p.16.

[3] Baldwin (1985) explains how the analytical concepts were expanded from two to six. The two money outlays concepts that were added build on the arguments presented in Turvey (1981). Turvey outlined both narrowly and broadly defined money outlays concepts for use as escalators. The United Kingdom, Ireland and Iceland adopted this approach. However, the United Kingdom has since added a depreciation component to its OOH index, so the U.K. CPI is now more comparable with the official Canadian CPI. Since the addition of the two money outlays series, there have been no changes except to discontinue the updating of the results for the NP2 series, since the United States is no longer using this. Two of the series, MO2 and NP3, were calculated for their theoretical interest and not because any official CPI was based on these concepts; in fact, the 1985 study likely contained the first empirical estimates ever based on these concepts.

[4] All of these higher-level aggregates differ only in their owned accommodation components; for all aggregates, all other components are based on the official concept.

Canada and other nations, differs from that used in influential recent reviews such as the OECD report by Christensen, Dupont and Schreyer (2005) which adopt the terminology used in the 2004 Consumer Price Index Manual published by the International Labour Office (ILO) on behalf of six international agencies (ILO et al. 2004), referred to hereafter as the 2004 International CPI Manual.[5] Thus in section 2 we briefly review the terminology of the 2004 International CPI Manual and how this relates to the Statistics Canada terminology for their analytical series. The concept used for owner occupied housing services in the official Canadian CPI is also outlined. These details demonstrate the maze of choices that statistical institutes face in specifying measures for the cost of housing services. The data used in this project and a small selection of empirical results are given in section 3. The selected results focus attention on consequences of some of the definitional choices.

2.   Conceptual Definitions

In chapter 23 of the 2004 International CPI Manual, four basic approaches for dealing with price measurement for durables are introduced: the (a) user cost, (b) rental equivalence, (c) payments, and (d) acquisitions approaches. These are described here.

2.1   Canada's Official Choice: a User Cost Concept

The basic idea of the Canadian official concept is to treat homeowners as landlords who rent dwellings to themselves.[6] Whatever a landlord could expense is included in the index, including depreciation, a notional item. Whatever cost items a landlord cannot expense for tax purposes are deemed out of scope. It incorporates six components: (1) mortgage interest costs, (2) property taxes, (3) homeowner's insurance premiums, (4) homeowner's repairs, (5) other homeownership costs including transaction charges (e.g., real estate commissions and legal fees), condominium charges and mortgage insurance, and (6) the replacement cost for that part of the stock assumed to be used up in the year in question.[7]

The official concept is referred to in Statistics Canada materials as a user cost measure of OOH services. However, the Statistics Canada usage of the term differs from the user cost

---

[5] The chapters of this manual are available at http://www.ilo.org/public/english/bureau/stat/guides/cpi/index.htm.

[6] The official CPI is a chain fixed basket index, which is now updated approximately every four years to reflect more recent expenditure patterns. During the estimation period of the analytical series it was twice updated, first, in April 1982, when it went from a 1974 to a 1978 basket, and then in January 1985, when it went from a 1978 to a 1982 basket. This updating of baskets has been associated with changes in group classification and methodology. Both are somewhat different for the 1982 basket as compared to earlier baskets (see Statistics Canada 1992, pp. 29-32, pp. 40 and 41). The analytical series based on the official concept therefore match the monthly movement of the corresponding official CPI series only from January 1985 forward, when they are all based on a 1982 basket. Also, the analytical series are all Laspeyres indexes with a 1982 base period, including the official concept series. To calculate the analytical series as chain indexes linked in the same way as the official CPI would be more difficult without necessarily improving the analytical usefulness of the series.

[7] On shelter in the Canadian CPI, see also Baldwin and Mansour (2003), Markle (1992), and Prud'homme (1995).

concept presented in the 2004 International CPI Manual. Key points of difference are that foregone interest on an owner's capital invested in their home is ignored on the basis that this is not an explicitly expensed cost, and accrued capital gains are ignored on the grounds that accrued capital gains are not generally treated by landlords as a negative expense.[8]

Some components of the official Statistics Canada concept are controversial because of measurement problems, such as depreciation. Because a landlord can expense the depreciation on a dwelling that he rents, the official measure includes a notional amount for "replacement cost" (or depreciation).[9] Each year, Statistics Canada carries out the Survey of Household Spending (formerly called the Family Expenditure Survey) to update the expenditure weights for most of the commodities in the CPI index basket. However, depreciation is not an out-of-pocket expense (or cash-flow), so its share in the basket must be imputed.

Between 1949 and 1997, the annual housing depreciation rate used for the Canadian CPI was 2%. Kostenbauer (2001) argued that there was evidence to suggest that a 2% depreciation rate is too high. As a consequence, the depreciation rate in the Canadian CPI was revised downward to 1.5%, effective January 1998.

The replacement cost incurred by homeowners is derived using average price data for residential properties obtained from the Survey of Household Spending and based on homeowner appraisals of the values of their properties at the end of the survey year. The average price data for residential properties are multiplied by the "house-to-property ratio," estimated by Statistics Canada, to obtain estimates of the average price of residential houses (exclusive of land). Then the estimated average price of residential houses is multiplied by the assumed depreciation rate to obtain an estimate of the replacement cost. The national replacement cost index that is produced by Statistics Canada is a weighted aggregate of individual area indexes. The weights reflect relative shares of the total value of the national owner occupied housing stock, compiled from the Survey of Household Spending. The replacement cost index is updated every month from the index movements of the New Housing Price Index (NHPI) exclusive of land.[10]

The mortgage interest component of the official concept is also controversial. It is intended to estimate price induced changes in the amount of mortgage interest owed by the target population on outstanding mortgages. The Statistics Canada practice is to hold the volume of mortgage loans, by age of mortgage, constant so that interest owed depends only on house prices and interest rates; not on the changes in lump sum payments or changes in the loan-to-value ratios or amortization periods of the outstanding loans. The house price attached to an outstanding loan dates from the month of purchase. The interest rate dates from the month that

---

[8] Finland, Iceland, Sweden and the United Kingdom have also adopted simplified user cost concepts (see Christensen, Dupont and Schreyer 2005). See also Diewert and Nakamura (2007) in this volume.

[9] Depreciation is the only component in the CPI that is not a cash flow.

[10] Other concerns have also been raised about the replacement cost component of the official concept. The price component that pertains most directly to the replacement cost for the owned housing component is for new dwellings, but new dwellings are seldom sold without lots. Thus, dwelling price estimates necessarily depend on the estimates of builders as to what their houses would sell for without their serviced lots. This estimate is likely to be more approximate if a builder has held onto a lot quite a while before building on it, and if the market for residential land is volatile. There is reason to believe that the dwelling price series fails to entirely remove the impact of changes in land prices, and hence that what is calculated is something between an index of dwelling prices and an index for dwelling and lot together.

the loan was last renegotiated, or the month of initiation. Thus, the interest owed on the stock of mortgages in the current month is a function of current and lagged house prices and interest rates, mixed according to the proportion of new and existing mortgages.[11]

2.2 The Rental Equivalence Concept

An index based on the rental equivalence concept measures changes in the cost of consuming the dwelling services of a fixed stock of owner occupied housing by imputing rents based on observations for the market rents for tenant occupied dwellings.

2.3 The Money Outlays (or Payments) Concept

The payments approach, which Statistics Canada terms the *money outlays approach*, deals with the cash flow costs of home ownership, including mortgage payments.[12] An index based on this concept measures the price induced changes in the consumption related cash outlays on owner occupied homes. Imputed costs are excluded by definition, as are investment related outlays. Most of the components for the official Statistics Canada concept represent cash disbursements, and are in scope under a money outlays concept; this includes repairs, property taxes, insurance premiums and mortgage interest. The important omission from the preceding list is the replacement cost of depreciation, which is included with the official approach, but excluded as an imputed item for the money outlays/payments concept.

In the empirical portion of this study, two variants of this concept are used, one including and one excluding net equity payments (MO1 and MO2, respectively). Net equity payments consist of down payments on owner occupied homes, plus the principal portion of loan repayments when those houses are purchased on credit, less sales of owner occupied homes.

2.4 The Net Purchase (or Acquisitions) Concept

With the acquisitions approach, which Statistics Canada terms the *net purchase approach*, the entire cost of a product is charged to the period of purchase, just as with products that are not durable.[13] A series based on the net purchase concept measures changes in current transaction prices for owned accommodation. Net purchases of owner occupied dwellings consist of all purchases of new as well as existing owner occupied dwellings by the household sector less sales of such dwellings; that is, purchases of new dwellings by the household sector plus net household sector purchases of existing dwellings from sellers outside the household sector.

---

[11] See Statistics Canada (1992, pp. 113-117).

[12] Ireland uses the payments approach.

[13] Australia and New Zealand use net acquisitions concepts.

When net purchases of pre-existing dwellings are unimportant, an index based on this concept will closely approximate price movements for new homes.

In the empirical portion of this study, the net purchase series for owned accommodation (labelled NP1) includes a home purchase component whose weight is based on net purchases but excludes mortgage interest.[14] This variant is consistent with the treatment of consumer durables in the official CPI, being based entirely on actual (i.e., not hypothetical) prices. For owned housing, the CPI is based on the actual prices for dwelling and lot together.[15]

The scope of the net purchase approach can be extended to include mortgage interest payments. This concept was previously used for a (now discontinued) Statistics Canada analytical net purchase series labelled NP2. From 1953 to 1984, the homeownership component of the U.S. CPI for urban wage earners and clerical employees was based on net purchases including mortgage interest. Under this concept, mortgage interest comprises those negotiated interest payments that are likely to be made.[16] Under this variant, the net purchase weight could vary greatly for a given volume of home purchases depending on the degree of credit financing.[17]

Blinder (1980) argues that the weight attached to a home purchase should be the same whether or not it is purchased on credit.[18] A net purchase approach series including interest was inspired by Blinder's article, and was calculated for the first time as an analytical series in 1985 (NP3). This net purchase concept provides a measure of the change in current consumer prices that takes account of changes in interest rates, but without exaggerating their impact.

3. Hedonics

If older houses are of inferior quality, they will depreciate faster, independent of other effects. To control for the complexities of a heterogeneous housing stock, Kostenbauer (2001) and others including Diewert (2003) have recommended the use of hedonic methods.

A house is the sum of its physical parts such as the building materials used and the method of heating, as well as of its "basic attributes" including the age of the house, the size,

---

[14] This approach is recommended by some for judging the effectiveness of monetary policy in meeting its price stability targets. It measures the change in current transaction prices but does not reflect interest rate hikes that might be a concomitant of a tight monetary policy intended to reduce the inflation rate.

[15] A replacement cost index for homes is necessarily based on an index for dwellings. The term "hypothetical" applies because this index must be derived from a question about what the dwelling or serviced lot would sell for separately, though they are sold as a package.

[16] The "likely to be made" qualification is necessary because so many mortgages are terminated before the end of their original amortization period due to renegotiations of the mortgage or the sale of the home.

[17] If a member of the target population buys a home for $100,000 using cash, that purchase will increase the home purchase weight by $100,000. If the same home is purchased with a $75,000 mortgage loan at 13% interest, the interest over the first 10 years of a 20-year amortization period would be about $87,000, which is almost twice the weight in the owned accommodation index compared with the first purchase, though the purchase price is the same.

[18] A net purchase series based on down payments and discounted mortgage payments is similar to the outlays series on an acquisition basis proposed by Turvey (1981), but he considers allowing changes in terms of credit, including the loan-to-value-ratio, to be reflected in his proposed index.

type of roofing, and so on. Even a highly simplified hedonic approach to housing may go a long ways toward managing the heterogeneity problem. As Kostenbauer (2001) notes, the steps are: (a) identify the basic attributes, (b) specify the regression equation relating house prices to the attributes, and (c) estimate the parameters. If the regression is specified in a semi-logarithmic form then the effect of each attribute on the house value is given as a percentage mark-up.[19]

The interpretation of basic cross section hedonic regressions is as follows. Assume that a sample includes a house constructed in 1981 and another in 1982. The price of the two houses differs because (i) the 1981 house is one year older than the 1982 house and (ii) the 1982 house may have different attributes. If the regression successfully controls for differences in basic attributes, the coefficient corresponding to "age of the house" is the estimated premium of a 1982 house over a 1981 house. This is an approach that Statistics Canada is now developing.

4.   Selected Empirical Results for a Pilot Update

The data for this pilot update of the Statistics Canada analytical CPI series are for resale houses in the Ottawa area over the period of 1996 to 2005. The data were obtained from the Multiple Listing Service (MLS) that is managed by the Ottawa Real Estate Board. Information on a large number of dwelling characteristics is included.

The distribution of expenditures over the various components of the OOH services costs is shown in tables 1 and 2. The expenditure share values differ considerably depending on the treatment of OOH services adopted, as would be expected.

Table 3 shows the growth rates over the 1996 to 2005 period obtained using the various measures and the implications at the Shelter and the All-items levels of aggregation for the CPI. The range of differences once the various measures are aggregated to the All-items level can also be seen in this table.[20] Note the slightly less than six percentage point difference between the growth rate in the CPI with the MO1 versus the NP1 approach (21.4% vs. 27% at the All-items level). On a monthly basis the differences are 0.16% vs. 0.20%.

---

[19] Thus, the presence of a sunroom will have a greater impact on the price of a more expensive house.

[20] The analytical series for All-items (or housing or shelter) incorporating a given homeownership concept is estimated by taking a weighted average of the series for All-items excluding owned accommodation based on the official concept and the series for owned accommodation based on the given homeownership concept. The expenditure weight for the All-items excluding owned accommodation series is always the same but the weight of the owned accommodation series depends on the given homeownership concept, so that the percentage weight of the All-items excluding owned accommodation series changes.

Table 1. Distribution of Expenditures for Owned Accommodation for Ottawa, by Homeownership Concept, Based on 2001 Expenditures (%)

Title	Official concept	Rental equivalence concept	Money outlays (payments) concept		Net purchase (acquisitions) concept	
			Without equity payments (MO1)	With equity payments (MO2)	Based on purchases (NP1)	Based on down payments and discounted mortgage payments (NP3)
Maintenance and repairs	8.6	3.9	10.4	7.5	8.0	8.0
Condominium charges	0.5		0.6	0.4	0.5	0.5
Property taxes (including special charges)	20.7		24.9	18.1	19.3	19.1
Insurance premiums	3.4	1.1	4.1	3.0	3.1	3.1
Mortgage insurance	0.8		1.0	0.7		0.7
Mortgage interest cost	44.1		53.2	38.7		
Replacement cost	17.1					
Real estate commissions	2.4		2.9	2.1	2.2	2.2
Legal fees	0.8		1.0	0.7	0.8	0.8
Other shelter services	1.6		2.0	1.4	1.5	1.5
Equivalent rent		95.0				
Down payment						21.2
Principal fraction of mortgage payments				27.4		
Home purchase					64.6	
Discounted mortgage Payments						42.9
Owned accommodation	100.0	100.0	100.0	100.0	100.0	100.0

Note: Basket shares shown in this table may not exactly sum to 100 due to rounding.

Table 2. Owned Accommodation's Relative Share, by Homeownership Concept, in 2001 Household Expenditures (%)

Title	The official concept	Rental equivalent concept	Money outlays (payments) concept		Net purchase (acquisitions) concept	
			Without equity payments (MO1)	With equity payments (MO2)	Based on purchases (NP1)	Based on down payments and discounted mortgage payments (NP3)
Shelter	62.0	63.8	57.5	65.1	63.7	63.8
All-items	17.3	18.4	14.8	19.3	18.3	18.4

Table 3. Growth Rates, January 1996 to December 2005 (%)

	Owned accommodation	Shelter	All-items
Official	20.5	23.4	23.6
RE	17.4	21.3	22.1
MO1	12.5	18.8	21.4
MO2	18.5	21.7	22.2
NP1	44.7	38.8	27.0
NP2	32.5	31.1	24.9

References

Baldwin, A. (1985), "Analytical Consumer Price Index Series for Owned Accommodation," Supplement to Catalogue 62-010 (July to September 1985 issue of *Consumer Prices and Price Indexes*), Statistics Canada.

Baldwin, A. and E. Mansour (2003), "Different Perspectives on the Rate of Inflation, 1982-2000: The Impact of Homeownership Costs Treatment of Owner Occupied Accommodation," Cat. No. 62F0014MIE, No. 16.

Baldwin, A., M. Prud'homme and A.O. Nakamura (2006), "An Empirical Analysis of the Different Concepts for Owned Accommodation in the Canadian CPI: the Case of Ottawa, 1996-2005," OECD-IMF Workshop, Real Estate Price Indexes, Paris, 6-7 November. http://www.oecd.org/dataoecd/2/43/37583728.pdf

Blinder, A.S. (1980), "The Consumer Price Index and the Measurement of Recent Inflation", in A.S. Blinder, J.E. Triplett, E. Denison and J. Pechman (eds.), *Brookings Papers on Economic Activity* 2, Brookings Institute.

Christensen, A.-K., J. Dupont and P. Schreyer (2005), "International Comparability of the Consumer Price Index: Owner-Occupied Housing," presented at the OECD Seminar, "Inflation Measures: Too High -- Too Low -- Internationally Comparable? Paris 21-22 June.

Devries, P. and A. Baldwin (1985), "Impact of Different Homeownership Methodologies on Consumer Price Index Behaviour between Canada and the United States," *Canadian Statistical Review* (April), vi-xv.

Diewert, W.E. (1974), "Intertemporal Consumer Theory and the Demand for Durables," *Econometrica* 53, 497–516.

Diewert, W.E. (2003), "The Treatment of Owner Occupied Housing and Other Durables in a Consumer Price Index" Discussion Paper 03-08, Department of Economics, University of British Columbia, Vancouver, Canada, available at http://www.econ.ubc.ca/discpapers/dp0308.pdf. Forthcoming in W.E. Diewert, J. Greenless and C. Hulten (eds.), *Price Index Concepts and Measurement,* NBER Studies in Income and Wealth, University of Chicago Press.

Diewert, W.E. and A.O. Nakamura (2007), "Accounting for Housing in a CPI," chapter 2, pp. 7-32 in Diewert, W.E., B.M. Balk, D. Fixler, K.J. Fox and A.O. Nakamura (2009), *PRICE AND PRODUCTIVITY MEASUREMENT: Volume 1 -- Housing.* Trafford Press.

Andrew Baldwin, Alice O. Nakamura and Marc Prud'homme

International Labour Office (ILO), International Monetary Fund, Organisation for Economic Co-operation and Development, Eurostat, United Nations, and The World Bank (2004), *Consumer Price Index Manual: Theory and Practice*. http://www.ilo.org/public/english/bureau/stat/guides/cpi/index.htm

Kostenbauer, K. (2001), "Housing Depreciation in the Canadian CPI," Prices Division, Statistics Canada, Catalogue No. 62F0014MIE, Series No. 15; www.statcan.ca:80/english/IPS/Data/62F0014MIB.htm November.

Markle, T. (1992), "Alternative Concepts of Homeownership in the Consumer Price Index (CPI)". Statistics Canada: Cat.No.62-001, *The Consumer Price Index,* September, 42-53.

Prud'homme, M. (1995), "Alternative Concepts of Homeownership for the CPI: 1992 to 1994", Statistics Canada Cat. No.62-001-XPB, *The Consumer Price Index*, October, i-x.

State Agency for Statistics (BHAS), Republika Srpska Institute of Statistics, Federation of BiH Institute of Statistics, World Bank (2002), "Welfare in Bosnia and Herzegovina, 2001: Measurement and Findings," December. http://www.worldbank.org/html/prdph/lsms/country/bih/docs/BiH_ANNX_poverty10a_updated.pdf

Statistics Canada (1992), *The Consumer Price Index Reference Paper Based on 1992 Expenditures*, Cat.No.62-553.

Turvey, R. (1981), "Durable Goods, Dwellings and Credit in Consumer Price Indices," *ILO Bulletin of Labor Statistics* 1, xxi-xxv.